Organic Garden

Vegetables

by George F. Van Patten

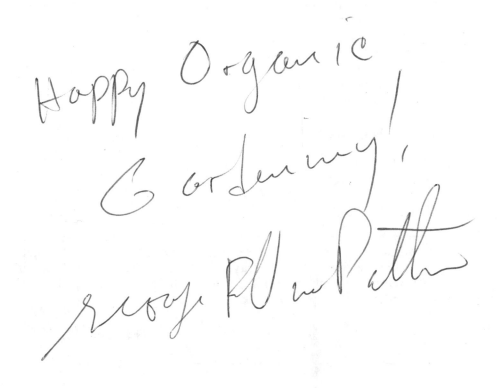

Happy Organic
Gardening!

George Van Patten

Published and distributed by Van Patten Publishing, Portland, Oregon.

Artwork: Estella Van Patten
    Growing Edge Magazine
    George F. Van Patten
    Patricia Field

Book Design: G. F. Van Patten
Cover Design: Anna Asquith
    Barbara Neidig
Cover Photo: Joan Pavia
Back Cover Photos: Larry Turner
Copy Editors: Bruce Taylor
    Brenda Y. Rogers
Technical Editor: Vern Nelson
Kitchen Editor: Jill Miller
Typesetting: Qume CrystalPrint

Copyright 1991, George F. Van Patten
First Printing

9 8 7 6 5 4 3 2 1

I would like to express my sincere thanks to all of the wonderful gardeners that helped to make this book a reality. Many individuals contributed information and drawings. Thank you all for your help in making *Organic Garden Vegetables* the best possible book.

Table of contents

Seeds and Planting 4

Seedlings: Buying & Growing 5

Soil 6

Garden Beds 8

No-till Gardens 10

Compost 11

Fertilizers 14

Green Manures 16

Crop Rotation 18

Watering 18

Vegetables 22

Seed Suppliers 143

Index 144

Seeds

Careful seed selection can make the difference between a successful garden and complete failure. Some seed varieties are better adapted to growing in certain conditions than others. For example, the early-maturing, cold-tolerant, Oregon Spring tomato grows in cool weather, setting flowers and fruit well before the larger beefsteak varieties. If you live in a cool region, with a short growing season, choosing Oregon Spring rather than a late-maturing beefsteak will make a fruitful harvest almost certain. Or if you love broccoli but live in a warm climate, planting heat-tolerant Premium Crop rather than Green Valiant will keep broccoli on your table much longer.

Many of the seed varieties available today were developed for modern agriculture. They were bred for qualities such as long shelf life, uniformity, disease resistance, and the ability to withstand mechanical harvesting with little damage; taste is usually last on the list. Eating vine-ripened, carefully selected varieties that taste superior, rather than tough vegetables that were developed for mechanized handling, makes gardening much more rewarding.

Open-pollinated seeds, also referred to as heirloom seed varieties, are the products of different parent plants, selected at random by nature. Seeds produced from different parent plants through random cross-pollination are known as open-pollinated, or heirloom varieties. You can produce these seeds yourself, and save them to plant the following year; they will produce plants very similar to their parents. Some open-pollinated seeds are very popular today, such as the Kentucky Wonder pole bean. But since the advent of hybrids, many varieties have become scarce; some have become extinct. Several groups have been organized to preserve the heirloom varieties. *The Seed Savers Exchange, RR 3, Box 239, Decorah, IA 52101* is the the biggest.

Hybrid or F_1 hybrid seed has revolutionized modern agriculture and gardening. Hybrid seed is produced by crossing two different true breeding parent plants with desirable characteristics. The F_1 hybrid offspring has *hybrid vigor*, the ability to grow stronger and faster than the original parents. The greater the vigor, the more environmental obstacles it can overcome to produce a better plant. Hybrids are uniform in shape, size and conformity. Even though the seeds are often more expensive, they are an excellent value. Carefully selecting hybrid seed for such qualities as taste, disease and pest resistance, cold and heat tolerance or whatever conditions prevail in your climate will help make your garden a success.

Today a few hybrid seeds replace thousands of open pollinated varieties. Some may become extinct. Growing just a few varieties makes it easy for an entire crop to be wiped out by insects or disease.

When selecting seed, you may notice some of them carry the label "All American Selection" or "AAS Winner". Seed varieties that were chosen as All American Selection winners have demonstrated superior growth and flavor in a wide variety of climates across America. Buying AAS varieties is a safe bet.

Some seed is treated with a fungicide to prevent damping-off, a disease that causes seedlings to rot at the soil line. Typically, the fungicide is colored and the some seed companies state in their catalog or on the seed packet that it is treated. Some seed is only available with a coating of fungicide. Most this seed is treated with the fungicide Captan which is red. At least one major seed producer is using naturally occurring diatomaceous earth to protect seed from the damping-off fungus.

If you have a large garden or can take care of seed for several years to keep it viable, purchasing it in larger portions is most economical. Most of the cost of retail seed is in the packaging. You can buy one gram of tomato seed for $1.05, for example, rather than 1/4 gram at $0.90. You decide which is best for you.

Planting

The key factors in successful germination of vegetable seeds are the soil's moisture and temperature. Seeds require consistent moisture and a specific temperature range to germinate. When at or near the optimum temperature, germination is certain and rapid. If above or below this range or if moisture is inconsistent, seeds will not germinate and may rot.

When germinating seeds, keep an eye on the moisture content and the temperature of the soil. It is easy to overwater seeds before they sprout. Remember, they have no roots and need very little water, just enough to keep the soil surface moist. Compacted soil with a crusty surface is almost impossible for most seeds to penetrate. Placing a piece of newspaper, burlap, a thin layer of peat moss, or fine mulch over the seed bed helps retain moisture evenly and keeps soil from forming a crust. Remember to remove the paper or burlap as soon as the seed pops through the soil.

Outdoor soil temperature should be at least 60_0 (15° C) or warmer for warm season summer vegetables to sprout. The soil can be warmed by building a raised bed (page 8) and sprouting plants under a cold frame (page 51). The cold frame or cloche protects seedlings from pelting rain and harsh wind, as well as helps to warm the air and the soil.

Seedlings

Transplanted seedlings get an extra 3- to 4-month head start on direct-seeded crops, and they mature earlier. A healthy seedling is predictable and virtually guarantees uniformity in plantings, while direct-seeding often results in lower germination. A healthy seedling is predictable and virtually guarantees uniform plantings.

Tomato, cucumber, pepper, lettuce and squash seedlings are some of the most common to buy and usually quite economical. Also, you can purchase seedling starts of several different varieties, rather than buying numerous packets of seed that may take you several years to use.

Hardening-off: Seedlings grown indoors or at a nursery have not been exposed to the harsh elements outdoors. They must be hardened-off, that is, gradually introduced to their new outdoor environment. If tender seedlings are set out in the hot sun or cold of night, they may suffer shock and become stunted. To harden-off seedlings, place them outdoors in a shady location or under a cold frame for a day or two, and bring them indoors at night. Next, place them in the sunshine for a couple of hours and leave them in the shade the rest of the day. Increase the amount of sunshine gradually over the course of a week. Some vegetables, such as brassicas, are more cold tolerant than others. Check specific vegetable listings to see which can be set out early or late.

Buying Seedlings

Purchasing vegetable starts at a retail nursery takes skill. Seedlings always sell well on the first sunny day in early to mid spring. If the weather does not cooperate, the seedlings are held and become potbound. As a result, the little plants may stay at the nursery for a month or two before being sold.

Always buy seedlings that are kept in the shade or in a shade house. Do not buy seedlings that are kept in a sunny location. The small amount of soil heats up, "cooking" the roots, and stunting growth. The temperature is more constant in a shade house, which protects the tender plants from climate extremes.

The root system is the most important part of the seedling to examine. If the roots have not filled the pot, the soil will crumble away. If the plants are potbound, the roots will be matted up on the bottom, encircling the small containers.

The best seedlings to transplant have a root system that holds the soil together and have just begun to wrap around the small container.

If only rootbound plants are available, soak the soil with water before planting. Carefully tear off the matted roots, then gently separate the remaining roots so that they will better penetrate the soil better.

You may prefer to buy seedlings with root systems that are not fully developed and hold them at home in a partially shady location to harden-off for a week or two before transplanting. This way you can watch their progress as they gradually get used to their new environment.

Pull plants apart gently when transplanting from flats. Take care not to squeeze the soil, which compacts roots and crushes tender root hairs.

Vegetable seedlings are raised for the convenience of the wholesale grower, who wants to produce a five-to six-week-old plant that looks good at the nursery. These plants are not always the best garden performers in your area. In Portland, Oregon for example, California Wonder bell pepper seedlings are a big seller. They grow well in a greenhouse, but when moved to the garden, they grow *very* slowly until the hot weather arrives. Always keep in mind that when soaked by hot or cold temperatures, small transplants seldom fully recover. It is a harsh shock for these little plants when they are moved from a warm shade house or greenhouse to cool soil and nighttime temperatures. Help them survive by carefully and gradually introducing them to their new environment.

Growing Seedlings

Raising your own seedlings is more difficult than germinating seed in the garden, but provides the option of picking the varieties that perform the best in your climate. If grown properly, they produce transplants that are far superior to those found at a nursery.

Start seed indoors in shallow nursery flats, egg cartons, peat pellets, cell blocks or any small containers. Use bagged potting soil or fine sifted organic soil from your garden. Seedlings can also be grown in a cold or hot frame. The seedlings have a small, shallow root system and must be watered regularly, especially in a heated home.

After sowing seed, place the container in a sunny, south-facing window. If there is not enough light shining through the window and the seedlings have lanky, spindly growth, set them under a fluorescent light.

A cold frame is a perfect place to transfer one- or two-week-old brassicas in cold weather and less hardy seedlings when the weather warms. The cold frame stays 10 to 15° warmer than the daytime temperature and 5 to 10 degrees warmer at night.

Numerous fluorescent growlights are available that cost from $3 to $18. They are also a good heat source. Leave the lamp on for 16 to 20 hours per day and keep it within 2-4 inches of the seedlings for maximum growth.

Fertilize the little seedlings with fish emulsion or any soluble, complete mix. Be sparing with the fertilizer, applying it quarter strength because the little plants have a small root system and can not absorb much fertilizer.

Kelp meal is an excellent compost starter.

Soil

Air, water, minerals, and organic matter are the most important nonliving elements of soil. Pores in soil are conduits for air and water. Plenty of space must be available in soil for air and water to move in and out. Minerals used in gardening must first be altered by a slightly acidic water solution, bacteria, and other soil life, and incorporated into humus before plants can use it.

Humus, organic matter, humus, is the binding fiber. It is as important to the soil as dietary fiber is to the human body. Humus keeps the soil loose and spongy, and holds nutrients in an available form for roots to absorb.

Organic matter fuels the soil's bacteria. Heat, air and water are also needed for these bacteria to act, and all are promoted by good soil structure and texture. When the soil warms in the spring, the bacteria increase in population and activity. It is through their activity that nutrients become available to plants.

To get the feel of your soil's texture, scoop up a handful of moist soil and rub it through your fingers. Clay soil feels and looks slippery. Sandy soil feels and looks gritty. Silty loam, which is in between clay and sand, almost feels greasy but less slippery than clay. The majority of soils are a combination of clay, sand and loam.

Clay Soils

Clay, adobe, or heavy soil consists of fine to medium flat mineral particles packed tightly together. About 100 particles of fine clay soil would fit into this period (.). Clay soil is very dense and weighs much more than sandy or loamy soils. This soil holds water well, but leaves little room for air, and inhibits root growth. The finer the mineral particles, the heavier the clay and the slower the drainage.

Heavy clay soils are difficult to work when wet, sticking to tools and clumping into rock-hard clods when dry. Heavily compacted clay soil, or hardpan, is common around new building and heavy traffic sites.

Clay soils hold fertilizers well but tend to be acidic and mineral poor in rainy climates. Organic matter, compost, leaf mold, and lime, blended with clay, add minerals and make millions of tiny air pockets, improving drainage and root growth. Perfecting the structure of heavy clay soil may take three years or more of adding compost.

Root growth is restricted in clay soils and they produce poor root crops, but acid-loving plants flourish in moist, acidic clay soils. To improve fine clay soils add 20 to 50 percent compost to the top 12 inches of soil or 30 to 50 pounds of gypsum per 1,000 square feet. Contrary to popular belief, adding small amounts of sand to clay soil does not promote better drainage; it binds with clay to form a cement-like product.

Sandy Soils

Small, medium, and large mineral particles in sand allow excellent root penetration and air space. Light, sandy soils are generally mineral rich and easy to till even when saturated with water. Sandy soils warm quickly in the spring and produce early root crops and heat loving melons. Sandy soils do not hold fertilizers well - particularly when overwatered.

Compost, blended with sandy soil, binds the large mineral particles together so that they hold water and fertilizer better. The compost is soon "eaten" by bacteria and earthworms. Organic matter in hot climates is consumed rapidly. The more often the soil is cultivated, the more organic matter that is used or oxidized.

Mulch, spread on top of sandy soil, keeps it cooler and reduces evaporation. Winter cover crops or green manures are essential to hold moisture, prevent runoff, and retain life in the soil. Compost and cover crops are some of the best fertilizers to use with sandy soils.

Loam Soils

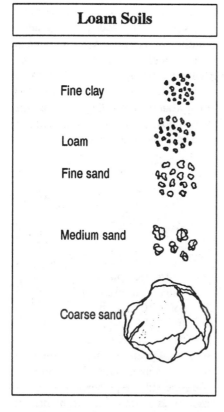

Fine clay

Loam

Fine sand

Medium sand

Coarse sand

Dark, rich loam soils are ideal for gardening. They are easy to work and hold air and nutrients well.

Coarse loam contains large soil particles which hold air and allow root growth, plus enough clay to retain moisture. Fine loamy soils contain more clay and silt with less sand. Loam soils are very fertile and most common in some old river or lake beds.

Everything from artichokes to zucchinis will grow with ease in fertile, loamy soil. A layer of organic mulch spread over the surface will increase water retention, keep the surface cool, and support soil life.

Wet Soils

More rainfall is received by wet soils each year than can evaporate, and they contain high levels of organic matter. Wet soils tend to be less fertile because the rain leaches (washes) out many of the nutrients. Wet soils are usually acidic. Add lime to decrease acidic qualities of this soil. It is difficult to over-lime a wet soil. Lime has a neutral pH of 7. As the soil pH rises toward 7, it becomes increasingly difficult to change.

Dry Soils

Dry soils receive less annual rainfall than can evaporate, and have low levels of organic matter. They are unleached and more fertile because they hold more minerals or nutrients, but salt buildup can be a problem. Typically, dry soils contain high levels of alkaline salts. To lower the alkalinity of these soils, till in compost, and sulfur, build a raised bed containing lots of organic matter on top of the soil, or leach out excess salts by watering *very* heavily. See "Lowering the pH" below.

Soil usually falls in two or three of the above categories. Few soils are all clay or 100 percent sand. They are combinations of the two.

The consistency of topsoil changes from one location to the other. Soil on one side of your yard may have different qualities than soil just a few feet away.

Check with your local nursery for more specific details about the soil in your area.

PH and Liming

PH is a scale from 1 to 14 that measures acid-to-alkaline balance. One is the most acidic, 7 is neutral, and 14 is most alkaline. Clay soils are usually acidic and many sandy soils are alkaline. Most plants will grow best in a slightly acidic soil with a pH between 6 and 7. Within this range, roots can absorb and process available nutrients. If the pH is too low (acidic) the nutrients are bound by acid salts and the roots are unable to absorb them. An alkaline soil, with a high pH, will cause toxic salt buildup, limiting water and nutrient intake by roots.

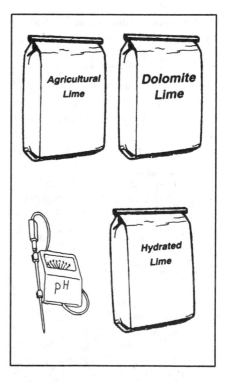

There are several ways to measure pH. A pH soil test kit, litmus paper, or electronic pH tester (which is easiest to use) may be found at most nurseries. When testing pH, take two or three soil samples and follow the manufacturer's instructions carefully.

If your soil has a pH above 7 or below 6, it is easy to change. Adding lime to acidic clay soil will bring the pH up, lessening acidity. But adding too much lime will make some nutrients unavailable, or even burn plant roots. Therefore, it is best to add lime over the course of several years if you need to raise the pH more than one point. After adding lime, it will take up to six months for it to alter the pH completely.

Soil application rates for lime.

35 lbs/1000 square feet of very sandy soil

50 lbs/1000 square feet of sandy soil

70 lbs/1000 square feet of loam

80 lbs/1000 square feet of heavy clay soil

Types of Lime

Agricultural or ground limestone (calcium carbonate) is one of the most common forms of lime and an excellent choice. It is slow acting and will remain in the soil for several years.

Dolomite lime (calcium magnesium carbonate) combines calcium with magnesium to formulate an excellent pH-altering substance, and adds two much-used nutrients as well. Always buy slow-acting dolomite in the finest form available so it begins acting after application. Even the finest grade will remain in the soil for up to five years.

Ground oyster shells contain calcium carbonate and small amounts of phosphorus. These shells are commonly available at feed stores. They are used as chicken grit to supply calcium. Oyster shells are very slow acting, and will help to regulate the pH for years.

Hydrated lime (calcium hydroxide) is quick acting and caustic to plants and microorganisms. Use only in small amounts, if at all.

Quicklime (calcium oxide), manufactured by searing or burning limestone, is fast acting, but caustic and may burn or kill plant and soil microorganisms.

Wood ashes are a source of lime as well as potassium (potash), and many ashes contain magnesium. Hardwood ashes are about twice as alkaline as softwood ashes. The main drawback to wood ashes is that they leach out of the soil rapidly.

For best results, apply lime at least a month before planting in the spring, and preferably the fall before. Do not apply lime to a freshly manured soil or it will combine to form ammonia gas, which will release valuable nitrogen into the air.

Lowering the pH in alkaline soils is less common. Most often the best way to lower an alkaline soil is to add liberal amounts of compost, acidic peat, or manures. If the soil has a pH over 8, build a raised bed on top of the soil at least six inches high, so that the alkaline salts and water stay below the level of most feeder roots. If you can see white alkaline salts on the surface of the soil, water *very* heavily to leach the alkaline salts down deeper into the soil. This practice may have to be repeated every spring if the alkaline salts reappear.

Sulfur is the most common element used to acidify the soil; however if added in large quantities, it is toxic to plants. Check with your local nursery or county extension service for more specific guidelines on lowering the pH of alkaline soil if large amounts of compost and small amounts of sulfur do not do the trick.

Garden Beds

The first planting in garden beds can be made as soon as the ground is able to be worked in spring. Raised beds, whether double dug or not, dry out the soonest and can be worked first. Sunken beds, used to combat the sweltering heat of the desert, are ready when the weather warms. The old-fashioned flat row gardens are the last to become ready. The more compost added to any bed, the sooner it can be worked and planted. No-till garden beds are just what their name implies. They do not need to be tilled and are ready to plant as soon as the weather warms.

Raised Beds

Raised beds provide improved drainage, heat up earlier in the spring and stay warmer longer in the fall. In raised beds, you can plant vegetables two to four weeks earlier in the spring and harvest two to four weeks longer in the fall, than you can growing in traditional flat rows. Raised bed planting can also be much more intensive, with plants spaced close together. When intensively planted, vegetables shade out weeds, lowering maintenance.

Raised beds can be made of mounded soil with sloped earthen sides or be framed with cedar or pressure-treated planks. The best preservatives to use on the wood are Cuprinol 10 or products that contain copper naphthenate. Either chemical treatment preserves wood for up to 4 years. Be sure to use rust-proof galvanized nails or lag bolts to fasten the sides together. Once made, raised beds seldom need to be deeply worked as long as you add organic matter to the surface annually.

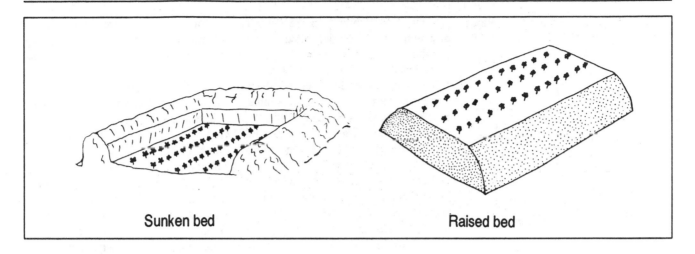

Sunken bed   Raised bed

To build a raised bed: decide on a location. Orient the bed to receive maximum sunlight. The ends should face east and west; the long sides should face north and south. Mark the dimensions with stakes and twine. Cultivate or double dig the soil.

An alternative method is to cover ground weeds with a layer of newspaper at least 12 pages thick. Next, lay down a 1- or 2-foot layer of leaf mold or compost as a base on top of the newspapers. Then shovel out a pathway on each side of the 3- to 5-foot-wide raised bed. Make the bed no wider than it is comfortable to reach half way across. A 4- or 5-foot-wide bed is ideal. Pile the soil from the pathways on top of the compost to form the raised bed that is from 6 to 24 inches high. Six inches is the minimum of height necessary to reap all of the benefits of a raised bed.

Raised beds of made of mounded earth are easier to hoe and rototill than those framed with rigid sides. They are also easier to relocate, and clods may be readily raked off the sides or ends.

If your soil is heavy clay, with poor drainage, loosen the clay soil with a pick and shovel or broadfork and add a layer of gypsum to help break it up before covering the bed with newspaper and compost.

Double Digging

The French began double digging as an intensive form of agriculture to serve the Paris market around the turn of this century. It was later expounded upon by many authors, including John Jeavons in his book *How to Grow More Vegetables*, Ten Speed Press, 1982. The basic theory is simple: roots grow deeply into the soil. Cultivate the soil to a depth of two feet or more below a raised bed and plants grow stronger and healthier. Plants can also be spaced much closer together to dramatically increase yield per square foot.

Intensive raised bed, double-dug gardens and dense planting techniques yield a higher overall yield per square foot than conventional gardens, but fruits are smaller and sometimes deformed. Gardeners who plant intensively cull out the small, weak crops and eat them while waiting for the balance of the crops to mature.

Broadfork

Sunken Beds

Desert climates with sandy soil that heats up quickly and drains well, Present conditions opposite to those that make a raised bed so productive.

So it makes sense to reverse the raised bed, making it into a sunken bed that stays cooler and functions as a catch basin for water.

To make a sunken bed, simply shovel out a 4-foot-wide trench up to a foot deep, pitching the soil onto the pathways.

Use mulch, soaker hoses and drip irrigation to conserve water just as you would in a raised bed. You will find that these beds stay about 10° cooler than flat beds and retain water much better.

Flat Beds

Traditional flat-bed gardens are still popular among many gardeners. The crops are planted in rows spaced from 6 to 24 inches apart.

While flat beds are relatively easy to maintain, they lack the benefits of improved drainage and warmer soil.

No-Till Gardens

There are two basic types of no-till gardens: those with the mulch/compost on top of the soil and the type with compost placed below the soil.

The first type of no-till garden is for gardeners that don't like to work. The principle is simple: rather than toiling at cultivating the soil, create fertile soil like Mother Nature does by adding layers of fertilizer and compost to the soil's surface. The nutrients in the compost continue to leach downward, creating rich topsoil. The roots and the earthworms do the cultivation work; all you do is watch the garden grow.

Deep roots break up the subsoil and pump minerals deposited in the subsoil to the surface. When the plant is finished producing, the roots are left in the soil to decompose, which further aerates the soil and adds more nutrients. Earthworms and other subsoil life forms always have plenty of food from the decaying vegetation. Earthworms are most active during the cool months of fall and winter, and reproduce mostly in the spring. *If they do not have food and cover to keep the ground from freezing in the winter, they perish.*

The life-giving mulch also prevents rapid temperature fluctuations. The sun can bake the surface of bare soil, increasing the temperature significantly. The surface temperature of soil protected with mulch in a no-till garden stays about the same as deeper levels. This temperature buffering protects fragile surface feeder roots. To achieve warmer temperatures required to germinate seed in cool spring weather, just spread the protective mulch aside so the sun can warm the soil. After the seedlings grow a few inches tall, brush the mulch back around them.

Moisture evaporation is slowed dramatically by a protective layer of mulch on the surface. Water soon evaporates from barren soil, but is retained much longer when a heavy layer of mulch/compost prevents escape.

Sprinklers and rain pelt the soil's surface with droplets of water. This constant pounding creates a crusty surface layer on bare soil which promotes runoff, keeping water from penetrating. In a no-till garden, you can water with a heavy stream flowing from the garden hose with little or no runoff. The layers of mulch readily absorb the water, letting it seep slowly downward, completely penetrating the soil.

Weeds are smothered by successive layers of mulch and only an occasional weed may need to be pulled. Once underway, few weeds get a chance to sprout, since the soil is not cultivated, no weed seeds are brought to the surface.

Insects and diseases are kept in check by natural predators that find favorable conditions for life in a surface-mulched garden. Of course the gardener helps by practicing crop rotation and planting disease- and pest- resistant varieties. For more information on no-till gardening see: *"The Ruth Stout No-Work Garden Book,"* Rodale Press, 1971.

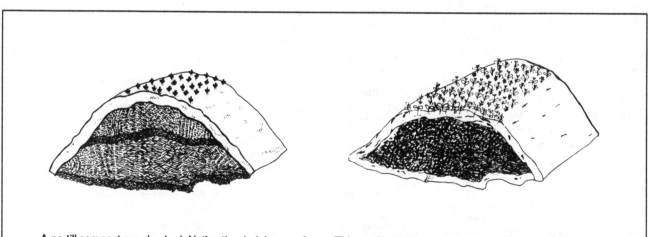

A no-till compost growing bed. Notice the dark layers of wood chips on the bottom and in the middle of the pile. The chips help aerate the pile.

This no-till compost growing bed is made from leaves and grass clippings. It does not have a layer of wood chips for aeration.

The second type of no-till garden takes more work, but is extra productive, especially in cold weather. It is similar to a hot bed, which is made by digging a hole several feet square and a foot or two deep and filling it with cooking compost. The decomposing compost serves as a heat source for a garden bed above. Unlike a hot bed, this no-till method requires less maintenance.

To make this no-till garden, pile up organic matter, as you would to make a compost pile, 3- to 4-feet high and 4- to 5-feet wide to form a raised bed. The top of the bed is 2 or 3 feet wide, sloping down to a 4- to 5-foot base. The fresh compost can easily be piled on a grassy or weedy ground; the thick layer of fresh organic matter smothers weeds.

Dig a path 2- to 4-inches deep and 2 feet wide along both sides of the row of raw compost. Pitch the soil from the path on top of the raised bed of compost. Weeds must be removed from this soil. When the raw compost is covered with 2 to 4 inches of fine soil, plant it with seed or seedlings.

As the compost decomposes, heat and nutrients are released to warm and fertilize the young plants. By the time the roots penetrate deep into the compost below, it will have cooled enough to form a perfect environment.

Compost

Composting is easy, rewarding and profitable. The basics are simple: collect organic matter, pile it up and let it rot. In fact, smart gardeners plant on top of compost piles. See "No-Till Gardens" page 10. All you do is keep microorganisms and bacteria in the pile well supplied with the proper proportions of air, food and water.

The relationship between the amount of carbon and nitrogen found in all compost material is called the carbon/nitrogen (C/N) ratio. The best compost materials have a C/N ratio of 1/30, expressed simply as 30. For example, barnyard manure has a C/N ratio of 15, and sawdust about 400. Manure composts rapidly, while sawdust may take two years or more to decompose. The higher the number, the higher the carbon content. The closer to 30 the C/N ratio, the faster the compost will heat and break down. Look for green organic materials with a high nitrogen content such as grass clippings or leaves to ensure the fastest composting. With the proper materials supplying adequate organic nitrogen, a compost pile can be started any time of the year, even in the middle of winter.

There are two basic types of compost piles - hot and cold.

Hot compost piles are fueled by adequate nitrogen-rich organic matter, air and moisture that are always available for microorganisms to turn the compost into humus. A *critical mass of at least 3 feet by 3 feet* allows the compost pile the insulation and volume to "cook" rapidly. Decomposition is so fast that finished compost is ready in 2-4 weeks.

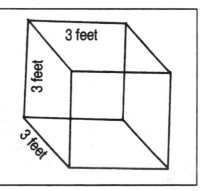

Cold compost piles lack adequate amounts of air, moisture, nitrogen-rich material or the critical mass of 3 feet square. Decomposition is slow but steady, taking a year or longer.

Sheet composting is a form of cold composting that is very easy. To sheet compost, spread organic matter out in a "sheet" or layer 6- to 12-inches thick and leave it to decompose. The organic matter can be tilled under before or after it has fully decomposed.

Air

A layer of wood chips or dry brush below the pile helps air to circulate up under the heap, where it is most needed. A 2- to 4-inch layer of dry organic matter sandwiched between green matter every 12 inches supplies sufficient aeration. Very diverse sizes and textures of the organic matter also creates a perfect air environment. For the lowest work level, the pile needn't be turned. Enough air for decomposition is supplied when the organic matter is of various sizes and textures. The outer layer of debris on the pile forms a seal around the pile. Any disagreeable odors are kept inside the heap while it is decomposing.

When air is inadequate, decomposition slows and the pile starts to smell. Turning the pile is more work but aerates the heap faster, helps curtail unpleasant odors and speeds decomposition.

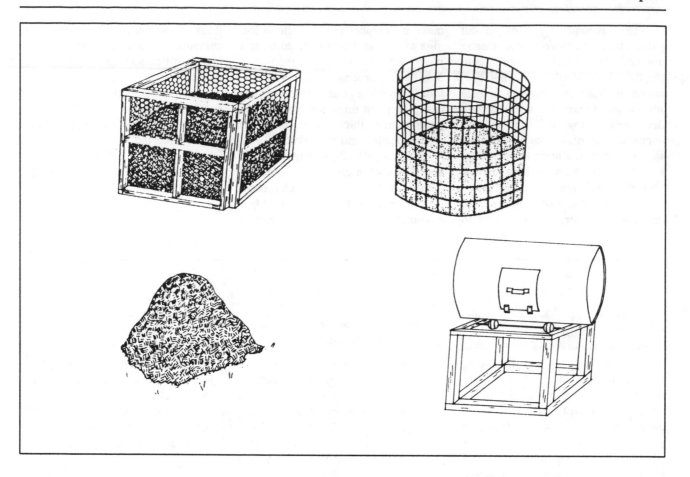

A length of 4-inch perforated drain pipe, a tube of wire mesh, bundled cornstalks or bamboo inserted down into the center of the compost pile forms a ventilating stack, which will help aerate the pile.

Heat

Heat speeds decomposition. The temperature in the center of the compost heap should be at least 55º (13º C). Decomposition alsfdo takes place at lower temperatures, but is slower. Temperatures from 140 to 160º (60-71º C)kill almost all plant diseases, harmful insects, weed seeds and roots. A "hot" compost pile will generate temperatures of up to 170º (77º C) for up to a week or more. Check the temperature of the compost pile by inserting a thin metal into the center of the pile for a few minutes. If the rod is warm when removed, it's probably hot enough. An inexpensive soil or food thermometer will give an exact reading at different locations of the pile.

Moisture

The moisture content of a compost pile should be between 40 and 60 percent. Moisture level is easy to check: the pile will have the consistency of a wrung-out sponge, or "glisten" with wetness.

Steam rises from the pile as heat builds. So much water is used that the center of the pile may become dry. Insert a probe into the pile to test for heat and moisture. Ideally, the probe should come out warm, moist and with no foul odors. Add water to the pile if there are any dry pockets.

A crispy pile that is full of ants is too dry. The surface layer can be dry, but the inside of the pile should be evenly moist.

Too much moisture causes poor air circulation and is signaled by a dank smell, slimy compost and excessive flies. Turn the pile and add dry matter to aerate. A plastic cover or layer of soil will also keep it from smelling and deflects excess rainwater.

Add water while building the heap to ensure even moisture distribution throughout the pile.

Finished Compost

Finished compost, humus, is rich, dark and crumbly with a sweet, earthy smell. Humus can be applied to all crops, any time of the year, as a soil amendment or as a mulch/fertilizer sidedressing. Don't worry about overdoing it! Compost made in a "hot" pile is ready in about 2-4 weeks, once it cools to around 80º (27º C), Cold compost may take up to a year before it's finished.

Even though finished compost is "stable" and will not break down rapidly, it keeps better when covered to prevent leaching out of nutrients. Use the finished compost within six months or many of the beneficial qualities will be lost.

Location

Build compost piles on a level ground surface with good drainage. Cultivate the soil below to break it up, so it will absorb nutrients and provide a safe haven for earthworms when the pile gets too hot. Easy vehicle access is important if you expect to have grass clippings and other chopped green matter delivered by landscapers or neighbors.

A compost pile should be convenient to use for both you and your neighbors. Locate it close enough to the house so that tossing kitchen scraps is easy. Collect the kitchen scraps in a gallon plastic container with a lid that seals. Throw the kitchen scraps into the center of the pile so they do not attract scavengers.

The heap can be unsightly, and occasionally smell, if not properly maintained. Locate it out of view, and where a good breeze is common.

Do not move the compost pile from place to place. The soil below builds up a population of beneficial bacteria and microbes that will migrate into the pile. Decomposition progresses faster when these microbes and bacteria are readily available.

Good Compost Material

Note: All organic matter decomposes faster when bruised and chopped into small pieces.

Plant residues: Any and all trimmings and thinnings from your organic garden. The greater the variety of organic matter the better. Diverse compost materials maintain

good air circulation and keep matting to a minimum. Throw in everything!

> **Grass clippings are probably the best all-round compost material. They contain plenty of nitrogen and compost *very* quickly. Fresh composting grass clippings often reach temperatures in excess of 150° (66° C)! Many of your neighbors will be happy to dump their chemical free grass clippings on your compost pile.**

Kitchen waste: Coffee grounds, egg shells, oyster and crustacean shells, vegetable scraps, sour milk, anything organic. Fish and meat scraps should be avoided because they attract scavengers.

Leaves break down faster if they are green and chopped. Autumn leaves decompose much more slowly. City maintenance crews pick up leaves each fall. Call your local city maintenance to get the specifics to get a load of leaves delivered to your house. Add lime to counteract acidity.

Conifer foliage: Pine, fir and cedar needles break down fairly slowly. They make a good layer for aeration.

Weeds are okay if the pile gets hot enough in the center to cook the roots and seeds to a nonviable state. But avoid adding perennial weeds with strong, sprouting underground root systems to cold piles.

Fair Compost Materials

Ash: Wood and paper ashes add potassium (potash) but leach out quickly and provide few long-term benefits.

Lime (dolomite): - An *occasional* dusting "sweetens" and stabilizes the pH. Microbes work the best in a pH that is just below the neutral 7.

Greensand and granite dust add potassium.

Paper: Shredded newspaper and recycled paper break down a little faster than new, unshreadded paper. Do not use slick, wax or ink-colored paper; the inks may contain heavy metals.

Peat moss adds no nutrition and tends to form dry pockets.

Rock phosphate and bone meal add phosphorus.

Sawdust robs the compost pile of nitrogen, which aids decomposition. Weathered sawdust, like weathered straw, decomposes faster than fresh.

Sod and soil add weight.

Wood chips, hedge clippings and small branches should be cut into smaller pieces or run through a chipper if possible. Add in small amounts for aeration. Wood chips are broken down by a slow acting fungus, and takes longer than other, faster decomposing ingredients.

Do Not Compost These Materials

Charcoal briquettes do not break down. Furnace coal contains excessive amounts of sulfur and iron.

Chemical fertilizers are not good compost activators because they do not contain any proteins for the microbes to eat, and they may kill beneficial organisms.

Insecticides, herbicides, rodenticides, if concentrated, may kill any life in the heap. But grass clippings treated with herbicides, such as Weed 'n Feed, create no problems in *hot, active* piles.

Cooked kitchen scraps putrefy and attract scavengers.

Diseased plants with such afflictions as club root, dry rot, leaf spot or blight should be avoided. Potato stems and leaves are notorious carriers of blight. Burn or pitch infected material into the landfill .

Dung: Human, cat, dog or any meat-eating animal's feces transmit parasites harmful to humans.

High-cholesterol greases and fats break down slowly and attract scavengers.

Metal: Aluminum, plastic, greasy, painted metals and materials that are not biodegradable.

Mud, sand and gravel have no nutrient or bacterial value and add weight.

Perennial weeds: crabgrass, dandelions, etc. that sprout from roots. But they are okay to add if the compost pile is hot enough to "cook" them to death.

Quicklime (calcium oxide) destroys humus.

Sludge, Milorganite and other fertilizers derived from sewage waste may contain diseases.

Soapy dishwater could contain sulfates, but biodegradable soaps, such as Ivory, cause no harm.

Soil does not enhance compost and slows aeration.

Compost Activators

Compost activators provide protein and bacteria. The right bacteria usually exists in a "cooking" compost pile and is unnecessary to add.

New compost piles: To speed biodegradation in new piles, borrow a couple of handfuls of compost from the center of a neighbor's pile to spread on your pile. Several commercial compost activators are also on the market.

Natural activators include alfalfa meal, blood meal, bone meal, compost, cottonseed meal, fish meal, fish waste, seaweed, hoof meal, horn meal, manure, raw meat scraps, and rich organic soil. Sprinkle them over the compost pile and cover with more layers of compost.

Kelp meal is an excellent compost starter.

Fertilizers

There are over 15 different elements called nutrients that are essential for plant life. Carbon, hydrogen and oxygen are absorbed from the air and water. The rest of the nutrients are absorbed mainly from the soil. The primary, or macro-nutrients, nitrogen (N), phosphorus (P) and potassium (K), are the elements a plant uses the most. Almost all fertilizers show the N-P-K percentages in big numbers on the front of the package. Secondary nutrients include calcium and magnesium and are also used in fairly large quantities. The remaining nutrients, called trace elements, are necessary in minute amounts. A *compete* fertilizer contains all of the primary and secondary nutrients, plus a complete range of necessary trace elements.

Nitrogen (N) is mainly responsible for leaf and stem growth, and for overall size and vigor. It is most active in young buds, shoots and leaves. Nitrogen is water soluble and quickly washed or leached from the soil. Consequently, nitrogen is required often and in relatively large doses.

Nitrogen deficiency causes older leaves turn yellow, and sometimes drop. Growth is stunted; leaves are smaller; fewer flowers and fruit develop.

Excess nitrogen causes plants to grow too fast. Stems become spindly and the leaves lush green. But the plant tissue is soft, weak and more susceptible to damage from insects, disease, drought, heat wilt, and cold.

Phosphorus (P) is associated with overall vigor, flower, and seed production. Highest levels are required during germination, seedling and flower growth. Decomposing organic matter, the effects of changing heat and moisture on the soil release phosphorus and other elements into the soil.

A lack of phosphorus is easily confused with a nitrogen deficiency because both have many of the same symptoms. However, phosphorus-deficient plants have dull green leaves, and often the stems will turn shades of purple. Overall growth is slow, maturity is delayed, flower and fruit development is retarded. Acid soils may need more phosphorus, because less is able to be "fixed" by the roots. It is uncommon for phosphorus to leach out of the soil.

Excess phosphorus is unlikely.

Potassium (K) or the compound potash (K_2O) increases foliage chlorophyll and helps plants make better use of light and air. It encourages strong root growth and is associated with disease resistance and water intake.

A lack of potassium makes plants grow slowly and is not easy to detect. Many times leaves have mottled yellow stems and fringes; older leaves may appear scorched on the edges; new growth may die back. Do not confuse these symptoms with salt or fertilizer burn, which causes burned leaf tips that may curl under.

Excess potassium is very unlikely. About one percent of the potassium in the soil is available to plants. Insoluble potassium is found in organic matter and minerals. It moves within the soil slowly, by the weather heating, cooling, raining and blowing, which releases it into solution, making it available to roots.

Magnesium (Mg) is found as a central atom in every chlorophyll molecule and is essential to the absorption of light energy. Magnesium aids in the utilization of nutrients. It also neutralizes soil acids and toxic compounds produced by plants.

Calcium (Ca) is fundamental to cell manufacture and growth. Plants must have some calcium at the growing tip of each root. The easiest way to supply the secondary nutrients magnesium and calcium is to add dolomite lime to the soil every few years.

Trace elements are essential to chlorophyll formation and must be present in minute amounts, but little is known about the exact amounts that are needed. They function mainly as catalysts to plant processes and nutrient utilization. Trace elements include iron (Fe), sulfur (S), manganese (Mn), boron (B), molybdenum (Mo), zinc (Zn), and copper (Cu). Trace elements are usually abundant in most soils. However, extreme acidity or alkalinity may lock them up, making them unavailable to plants. Liberal applications of compost or liquid seaweed will remedy this problem.

Symptoms of **secondary and trace element deficiencies** for specific plants are found their individual listings.

Organic Fertilizers

Organic fertilizers, unlike chemical fertilizers, continually build the soil, promote better texture and structure as well as nourish soil life. The addition of organic fertilizers over a long period enhances the soil instead of contributing to its sterility, as chemicals do.

Note: This list shows only average nutrient yields. The actual yields will vary with the source.

Tea: Organic fertilizer tea concoctions may contain just about any soluble organic nutrient diluted in water. Fish emulsion and liquid seaweed are readily available commercial organic teas. Soluble fertilizers, including worm castings, manures and guanos, make excellent U-mix organic teas.

The nutrient(s) are mixed with water, left to sit for a few days, and then applied. A dilute tea may be applied as often as each watering. Make sure you stir the tea before applying.

Four basic fertilizer mixes.

2-4-3

1 part bone meal
3 parts chopped alfalfa hay
2 parts greensand

3-3-4

3 parts fine granite dust
1 part blood meal
1 part bone meal
5 parts seaweed meal

4-5-4

2 parts blood meal
1 part soft phosphate
4 parts hardwood ashes

4-6-4

2 parts cottonseed meal
1 part soft phosphate
1 part fine granite dust

Applying Fertilizer

Cultivate in well-rotted manures and fertilizer meals when preparing beds in the fall or spring. When sowing seed, or transplanting seedlings, dig the hole several inches deeper than necessary, add a handful of a complete fertilizer mix, then cover it with soil before inserting the seed or transplant. Do not side dress seeds or new transplants with fertilizer on the roots will tend to stay on the surface or grow upward toward the fertilizer. If growth slows later in the season, apply a side dressing or liquid fertilizer. Regular applications of soluble teas will keep vegetables growing at peak performance. Foliar feeding, spraying dilute soluble fertilizer directly on leaves, makes nutrients immediately available. A high-nitrogen soluble fertilizer such as fish emulsion will green-up a tired garden. A dilute liquid seaweed application will solve most trace element deficiency problems. Use a siphon mixer or small spray bottle to apply soluble teas.

Basic fertilizer rules to follow:

1. Feed with a complete N-P-K fertilizer when planting.
2. Apply a high-nitrogen supplemental fertilizer to leaf crops every 2-4 weeks.
3. Apply a high-phosphorus fertilizer monthly to boost flower and fruit development.
4. Apply a biweekly liquid fertilizer to container plants.

Green Manures

Green manures (cover crops) planted on barren soil will attract earthworms by providing food, moisture and cover. Cover crops slow erosion, add and retain nutrients and moisture, slow weed development, and improve overall soil structure. The longer your garden beds are covered with vegetation, the less the nutrient loss. In fact, most nutrients in the soil are lost during the winter through leaching, when there are no crops to retain them. Having one crop immediately follow another will not only keep your garden smaller, it will use less fertilizer, lime and compost. It will also require less weeding and overall work.

Green manure crops are cut down and tilled under, or simply covered with a heavy layer of mulch, the following spring. For complete cover crop culture instructions, see: *The Organic Garden Book: Basics*, Van Patten Publishing, 1991.

Green manure crops fit into two categories: legumes that "fix" nitrogen, and nonlegumes.

Nitrogen-fixing Legumes

Nitrogen is "fixed" or converted by many leguminous plants, including peas and beans. Legumes gather nitrogen from the air and "fix" it through the bacteria-containing nodules on their roots.

An inoculant bacteria (*rhizobium*) colonizes the root nodules of leguminous plants so that nitrogen fixing can take place. Numerous strains of this bacteria live in the soil, but to ensure its presence, *it should be added to the soil when sowing the legume for the first time.* Purchase the inexpensive inoculant along with the nitrogen-fixing cover crop seeds at the nursery. Normally the dry, powdered inoculant is mixed with moist seeds when they are planted, or dissolved in water and applied directly to the soil. Most packets contain several different rhizobium bacterium that will inoculate a variety of plants.

For subsequent crops to take full advantage of the nitrogen fixed in the soil, the beans must be grown as a cover crop and tilled under *before they bloom.* A common misconception is that nitrogen fixed by legumes stays in the soil after harvest. The legumes use all the nitrogen they produce to grow. To deposit the nitrogen in the soil, the legumes must be tilled under before they use all of the nitrogen. Grow beans as a cover crop, and till them under before flowers set to get full benefit of the nitrogen.

Alfalfa or Lucerne is a very deep-rooted perennial that grows to three feet tall. It provides much green matter and fixes a good supply of nitrogen, some calcium, magnesium and potassium in the soil.

Soybeans thrive in all but the most alkaline soil and withstand drought.

Fava beans grow five to seven feet tall and will winter-over in many climates. See page 31 for more details.

Velvet beans produce long vines and grow well in poor, sandy soils. They make a good cover crop in the South.

Black medic grows vigorously in neutral, well-limed, reasonably fertile soil.

Alsike clover flourishes in fertile soil and grows well in wet, alkaline ground.

Alyce clover is a favorite in warm climates. It grows best in sandy or clay loams with good drainage.

Crimson clover will grow in most any soil. it Grows well in mild Northern climates southward.

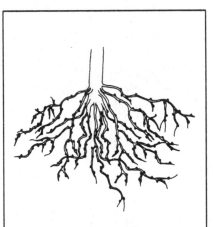

Nitrogen-fixing nodes on the roots of a legume.

Dutch White clover has pretty flowers and is a good winter cover crop in cool, moist climates.

Persian clover is grown in the warm southern and mild Pacific regions. It prefers moist clay soils.

Red clover is a low-growing crop with an extensive root system. It grows well in all climates.

Sweet clover will grow in any climate when planted in fairly well-limed soil. A fast, low-growing annual.

Cowpeas are grown throughout America in all soils. its strong roots readily penetrate hardpan.

Field peas, including **Austrian Field peas** grow best in well-drained soils, but will tolerate most other soils.

Lupines are tall and extremely deep-rooted, flowering perennials. They add much nitrogen and phosphates to soil.

Vetch is available in many varieties that grow well in both warm and cool regions.

Nonlegume Cover Crops

Nonlegume cover crops are mostly fast-growing grasses. They are valued for their ability to protect the soil, and fro the organic matter and nutrients they provide when they are cultivated under at the start of the normal growing season.

Barley needs rich, loamy soil and is a poor performer in acid or sandy soils.

Buckwheat is a large and vigorous plant with a huge root system that grows best during warm weather.

Field bromegrass grows in many soils and makes an excellent winter cover crop.

Millet is an excellent choice for poor soils in arid South and Southwest climates.

Mustard is a very fast growing, short, shallow rooted plant, and produces lots of (edible) green matter.

Oats grow in cool, moist climates on just about any soil in the United States.

Rye, ryegrass and Italian ryegrass are fast-growing, produce an extensive root system, abundant bulky green matter and tolerate most soils.

Sudangrass tolerates all but the wettest soil. A good choice for rapid organic matter production.

Weeds are fast-growing and many make excellent cover crops.

Wheat grows best in fertile, slightly acidic soil. Different varieties grow well in summer and winter.

Crop Rotation

Crop rotation is simple and easy. The basic rule of crop rotation is to grow unrelated crops on the same soil, and wait at least three years before replanting members of the same family.

Different crops have different nutrient needs, and do not share diseases or attract the same species of insects. Rotating crops improves soil texture and weeds do not get a chance to find a comfortable home.

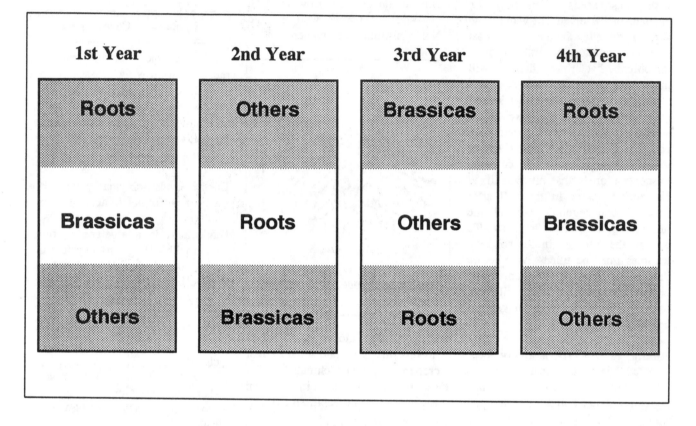

When the same crop grows year after year in the same soil, many nutrients are used up and others become bound in an insoluble form in the soil. This causes nutrient depletion and imbalance, and after several years it becomes impossible to grow any crop in that location. Repeating the same crop allows associated insects, which have wintered over in the soil, to resume activity with each planting, and thrive to epidemic proportions.

The crop rotation schedule outlined below divides vegetables into four categories: roots, brassicas, others, and perennials. The perennials, such as asparagus and rhubarb, are grown in the same bed for many years and do not participate in the rotation scheme. Root crops require little nitrogen and should follow brassicas, which are some of the heaviest feeders and insect-prone vegetables. Finally all others are grouped into a single category. To carry out this plan, follow the diagram. If this 3-year plan is too much trouble, simply alternating root crops with above-ground crops will help garden fertility, disease and insect control immensely.

Watering

Water application depends on the soil, climate, time of the year, and the plants being grown.

Each type of soil - clay, sand, and loam - has its own water-holding capacity. Clay soil holds about twice as much water as sand and must be watered about half as often. Water applied to the soil's surface must wet the top layer to full capacity before passing through to the next layer.

The texture of the soil is vital to water absorption. Humus-filled soil will absorb water three to five times faster than clay soil. The humus also helps prevent clay soil from cracking, and holds moisture in sandy soils. Water should soak into the soil quickly to prevent evaporation and runoff. The humus functions like a water bank for roots; water is deposited and held when plentiful, and withdrawn as when needed.

Tailor watering to the age of your crop. Be careful when planting seed or seedlings in

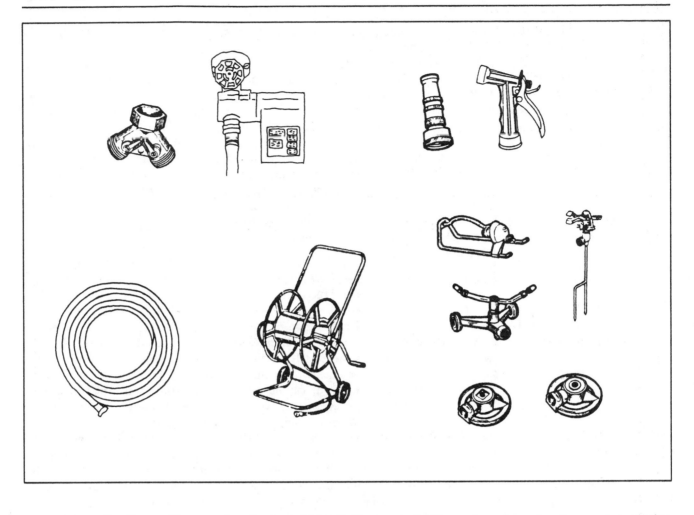

summer heat. Small seedlings need frequent surface watering because the small root systems have not yet developed. They will need more water and shading until established during hot weather. Older, more mature plants benefit from more infrequent, deep watering.

Wind dries soil rapidly. It also causes plants to use much more water. A mulch on the surface of the soil will slow evaporation substantially.

A couple of basic rules of thumb about watering mature plants include: water deeply and infrequently to promote deep root development. Most mature plants require 1-2 inches of water per week to sustain healthy growth. For example, a 100-square-foot bed will use from 10 to 25 gallons of water per day or about 1 3/4 inches of water per week. A 5/8- to 3/4-inch watering hose will deliver about one inch of water over a 5,000-square-foot area in 4 to 5 hours.

Water late in the day in dry climates to decrease moisture loss from evaporation. However, do not water just before sundown; to help prevent fungus water should evaporate from the foliage and soil surfaces before nightfall. Morning watering regimens are best in wet climates where mold and fungus are more prevalent.

Hoses that are the most durable and easy to handle are made from rubber, but they are also the most expensive. The best value are hoses with reinforced vinyl exteriors and rubber interiors, which cost about half as much as all-rubber hoses. The standard hose sizes include 1/2-, 5/8- and 3/4-inch-diameter. The 5/8-inch diameter hose is considered the best value. It is lightweight and carries adequate water for most gardening needs.

All-brass fittings are superior to plastic that will easily crack or scar when dropped or dragged across concrete or asphalt.

Sprinklers

Overhead sprinkling is the easiest way to apply water, but it is probably the worst for most vegetables. Besides losing over half of the water to evaporation, it wets foliage, which leads to fungus, insect attack, and disease.

Sprinklers that throw small, light droplets are best for unmulched vegetable beds. Large water droplets constantly bombard the surface of the bare soil. This pounding compacts the soil quickly, forming a concrete-like crust that slows water absorption, and is difficult for seedlings to penetrate.

Sprinklers that apply "city water," or well water that is full of chlorine and other salts tend to promote salt buildup on leaves and in the root zones.

Typically, a sprinkler will wet the ground to a depth of a foot or more each hour. Most sprinklers throw a circular pattern of water; but gardens are more often square or rectangular. Oscillating sprinklers are more expensive, but throw a square or rectangular pattern and may offer the best overall value.

Hand Watering

Hand watering is time consuming if you plan to apply enough for deep penetration, but it gives you a chance to inspect the garden and blast undesirable insects from plants. Increase pressure to form a jet of water by closing the end of the hose off with your thumb. When you are not blasting insects, the hose can run at full pressure, soaking the mulch-covered soil faster.

Watering cans are great for watering seedlings and individual plants or to apply liquid fertilizers. Well balanced plastic, or rust-proof metals. Cans that do not splash ar the best for hand watering.

Brass, twist-type nozzles, emit a fine spray that graduates to a heavy stream of water, and are more versatile than pistol-grip nozzles.

A water wand is one of the best choices for hand watering. When equipped with a pressure-breaking head, it slows water velocity and assists penetration.

Flood Irrigation

Flood, or basin irrigation, is one of the oldest irrigation methods in the world. Flooding leaches salt buildup and carries away nutrients. Flooding also compacts soil, and can uproot young plants. It uses water very inefficiently. Water flows a maximum of nine inches laterally through soil. If roots are located a foot away from a flood irrigation ditch, they do not receive water. The land that is being flooded must have a very slight incline to carry the water

evenly to all portions of the ditch. If the incline is too great, the plants on the uphill end will receive less water than the plants further downhill. Flood irrigation also leaves the soil muddy for days after application. When the soil finally dries out, an impenetrable surface crust generally forms. Flood irrigation is relatively efficient only when used around the base of trees and shrubs.

Drip Irrigation

Drip irrigation cuts water use by 30 to 50 percent. Water is applied in droplets or fine sprays through a network of low-pressure tubing over a long period of time. The water soaks into each plant's root zone slowly. Evaporation from sprays, runoff, and puddling are eliminated. Only a fraction of the soil surface gets wet, which makes it difficult for weeds to get started.

Water applied slowly will penetrate up to one foot within 15 minutes. Some drippers can be regulated to run very fast or closed down to run slower.

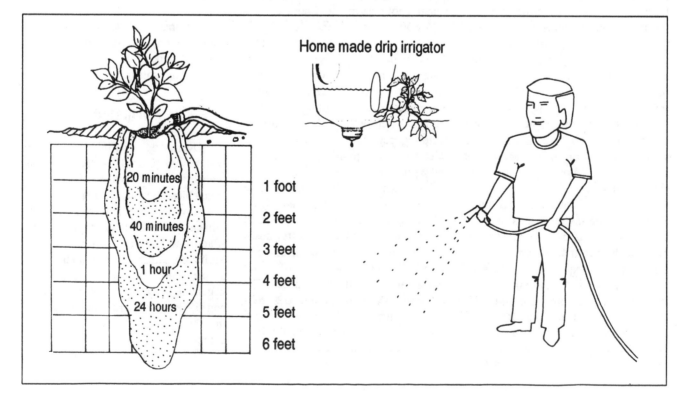

Home made drip irrigator

In cold climates, drip systems must be removed to protect them from becoming brittle after prolonged freezes.

You may control drip systems with manual shut-off, or automatic valves. Antisyphon valves are required by many health codes to prevent water from mixing with the house water system.

A "Y" valve fitted at the faucet makes it possible to run two drip lines independently.

Soakers and Leaky Pipe

Leaky pipe is made from recycled tires. It applies water fairly evenly from one end to the other. The pipe will rupture if used with high pressure. Turn the water down to a trickle or install a pressure\flow reducer to prevent excess pressure. The break can be mended by wrapping a dry pipe tightly with electricians or duct tape.

Lace the pipe between vegetables on top of the mulch, or if possible, install enough leaky pipe to cover each bed and lay it under the mulch for maximum efficiency. Take care when cultivating; do not puncture the hidden leaky pipe.

Soaker hoses made from vinyl polyester, polyethylene and rubber are resistant to rot and fungal attack.

Canvas soaker hoses are susceptible to rot, mold and mildew; daily draining will protect them from these afflictions. if your water is full of salts, soaker hoses may become clogged from salt buildup. To flush, turn the hose on full blast for a few seconds. Be careful when running water at full flow in inexpensive vinyl hoses. They tend to split under the increased pressure.

Homemade slow-watering devices include pitchers, inverted bottles, and plastic containers.

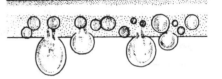

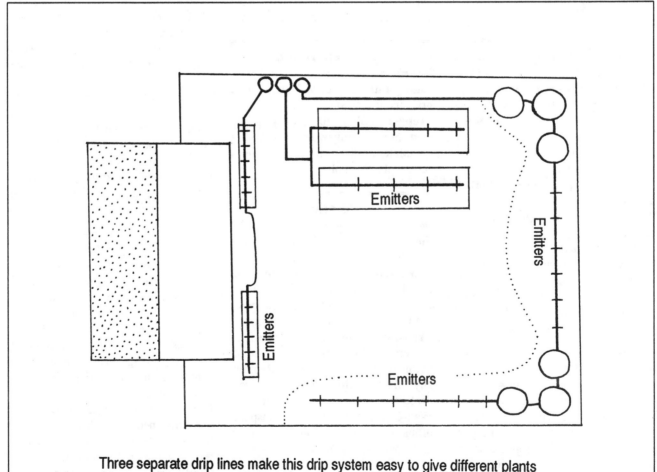

Three separate drip lines make this drip system easy to give different plants the exact amount of water they need.

Artichoke, Globe (Cynara scolymus)

This large herbaceous perennial thistle, native to the Mediterranean, grows three to five feet tall and spreads about the same distance. The dramatic, arching, silvery leaves contrast well against green foliage. The massive flowers are a showy lavender and quite fragrant. Dried flowers are beautiful. Use in flower beds or vegetable gardens. Do not allow the flower heads to bloom if you plan to eat them. Globe artichokes are somewhat demanding in care. They require loose, well-drained soil and regular feeding to produce rapid growth which yields the most tender artichokes. A heavy mulch in mild winter climates will protect them from frost. In cold climates with at least 100 frost-free days, production is not as high and artichokes are grown as annuals or overwintered indoors.

Basic Facts

Germination temperature: Minimum: 50° (10° C). Optimum: 70°. (21° C) Maximum: 90° (32° C).

Offshoot or division propagation: Separate rooted offshoots with spade annually. Transplant on 2- to 4-foot centers.

Productive life: 3-5 years - also grown as an annual

Annual yield per mature plant: 6-12 heads.

Time between planting and harvesting: 1 1/2 years.

Cultivation difficulty: Fussy, heavy feeder, good drainage, winter cold protection required.

Save seed from the best tasting, most robust plants. Let heads bloom and pick the "hairy" seeds out as they dry.

Climate

Zones 8-9, artichokes grow as a perennial. In less temperate climates, grow as an annual. Lift, bring the entire plant indoors during the winter and keep it moist if temperatures dip below 15°. Produces best in a cool, moist summer and mild winter. Needs full sun in mild climates. Give partial shade in hot climates to slow leaf dieback and keep heads from premature opening and getting tough.

Soil Preparation

Light, humus-rich soil with good drainage is a must.

Prepare soil in fall or early spring. Add 50% compost/manure and a complete fertilizer mix to each 1-foot square planting hole.

Planting

Sow seed indoors in containers a month before the last frost.

Sow outdoor seed after last frost 1/2 to 1 inch deep, 1 inch apart. Thin to 6-inch centers. Transplant and space 2-4 feet apart the following spring.

Transplant divisions (side shoots) or nursery seedlings from one month before, or after the last frost. Remove any old or withered outer leaves. Protect from frost with a cloche or Wall-O-Water. Divide and transplant offshoots annually to renew crop and ensure annual harvest.

Crop Care

Water regularly until established. Water deeply after established.

Mulch heavily after soil warms. Mulch conserves water and cools soil. **Weed** regularly, apply liquid seaweed or fish emulsion every 2-4 weeks during summer. Deep water thoroughly during dry spells.

After first frost, cut leaves and cover with 2-3 feet of mulch (oak leaves are the best) to protect from cold. Remove mulch the following spring, after the last frost.

Remove plants that are over 5 years old; they become disease prone and produce poorly.

Harvesting

Produces flower heads in the spring in mild southern climates, and during summer to fall further north.

The first year, remove heads and compost them before they develop.

The following year, harvest the central or main heads first. The heads should be plump and swollen (2-6 inches across) with the scales green and unopened. Cut 2-3 inches below the head. Harvest smaller heads as they develop until first frost.

Feed after first harvest with a manure side dressing or tea. Do not stimulate new growth before winter. Do not feed 30 to 60 days before freezing weather.

In the Kitchen

Fresh: Prepare by washing the unopened flower head in a bowl of water. Trim 1/4 of the prickly leaf tips off with scissors and remove the tough outer layer of leaves. Dip the base in lemon juice to preserve color. Steam for 45 minutes or boil for 30 minutes - until the leaves separate and can be removed with a slight tug. Pressure cook at 15 lbs., large: 15 minutes, small: 8 minutes. Add garlic, celery and vegetable oil to the cooking water to enhance flavor. Serve hot or cold with a butter, vinaigrette or mayonnaise sauce.

Storage: Place whole heads with a 2-inch stem in a plastic bag. They will keep in the refrigerator for 15-30 days.

Freezing: Wash and blanch 8-10 minutes in boiling water, dry and wrap securely in freezer paper or pop into a plastic freezer bag.
High in Ca, Fe and potassium

Varieties

GREEN GLOBE is the most popular and about the only one available. It yields large, sweet green heads on a sturdy plant. Available (Bu, Le, Me, Ni, Pa, Ric)

GLOBE IMPROVED has all the qualities of Green Globe, but seems to produce a little better. Available (Bg, Pi)

VIOLELLO is more hardy than green globe but not quite as flavorful. Available (Cg)

Problems

Fungus, gray mold (*botrytis*), called petal blight, can be serious, but is uncommon. Motley brown spots creep together quickly on head and foliage. Remove and destroy affected plants.

Aphids may attack succulent young heads. Spray with a jet of water or insecticidal soap.

Slugs and snails can be bothersome during damp spring weather. Hand-pick, dust with diatomaceous earth, install a slug fence or invite them to a slug and snail hotel.

Asparagus (*Asparagus officinalis*)

You can enjoy garden-fresh "spears" of this ancient herbaceous perennial in all but the very coldest of climates. The fleshy, octapuslike roots sprout shoots that grow into delicate fernlike foliage. Male plants produce foliage and females yield insignificant, small flowers that set pea-sized red berries by mid summer. Commercial asparagus crops are grown in *very well-drained soil that stays dry in winter*. Fast-growing shoots or "spears" pop through the soil after winter dormancy for a delightful early spring harvest that lasts 6-8 weeks. A second, smaller harvest in the fall is also possible by cutting all the fernlike foliage back to the ground about midsummer. Large-diameter, fast-growing shoots are the most tender.

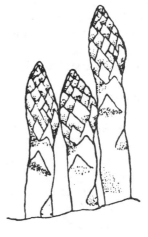

Basic Facts

Germination temperature: Minimum: 50° (10° C), Optimum: 75° (24° C), Maximum: 95° (35° C).

Transplant 1- or 2-year-old root crowns.

Productive life: 10-30 years or longer.

Annual yield per mature plant: 15-25 spears.

Time between planting 1-year-old root and harvesting: 1-3 years.

Cultivation difficulty: Quite fussy, must have excellent soil preparation, *very* good drainage, regular feeding and hand weeding.

Seed saving: Collect small red berries from female plants. Let them dry slowly in a paper sack. Plant the following spring.

Climate

Zones 4-10 including Hawaii, but grows best when cold weather forces dormancy in winter.

The ideal location is along a sunny south wall. Asparagus is an early spring crop; the warmer weather it receives, the more tender the harvest.

Soil Preparation

Grows in the same plot for 10-30 years or longer, and excellent soil preparation is essential.

Must have *very good, deep drainage,* regardless of soil type. In the fall or very early spring, dig a trench at least 1 foot deep and 1 foot wide, removing *all* perennial weed roots. Pile the soil neatly alongside the trench and mix with an equal amount of compost. Loosen the soil about a foot deeper in the bottom of the trench.

Cover the bottom of the trench with a 3- to 4-inch layer of a 50% mix of compost and manure. Lime acidic soils to neutralize the pH. Add 5 pounds of rock phosphate per 100 square feet of trench. Blend the amendments and fertilizer together with a spading fork.

Planting

Sowing seed: Sow 1-inch deep in wide beds or rows. Thin to 4- to 6-inch centers when 3-6 inches tall. Seeds are tough. Germination is hastened by soaking seeds overnight in water.

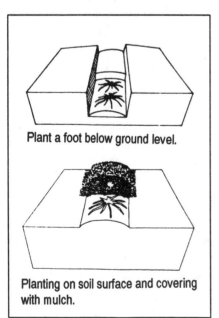

Plant a foot below ground level.

Planting on soil surface and covering with mulch.

When the soil can be worked in the spring, spread the 1- or 2-year-old root crowns out and place one root per foot, crown up, in the bottom of the amended trench. Cover the roots with one inch of the soil/compost mix, that was piled alongside the trench. As the crowns sprout, gradually cover them with the soil/compost mix leaving the growing tip visible. Bear in mind that older crowns are more temperamental and difficult to start.

An alternate planting method simply incorporates 50% well-rotted compost/manure in the top foot of soil. The crowns are set on the surface of the compost and covered with 6-12 inches of compost/manure to form a raised bed.

Note: Deeply planted asparagus yields about two weeks later and fewer stalks are produced than shallow-planted roots, but they are larger and more succulent.

Plant about 40 roots per person. When a large garden is planted, you can eat asparagus *all* season.

Crop Care

Weed Regularly: Asparagus is a poor competitor with weeds. Transplant or compost asparagus seedling "weeds" so they do not compete with larger roots.

Water regularly until established. Water deeply during dry summer weather. Water regularly during harvest. Plump spears are the most tender, while pencil-thin shoots are tough and fibrous.

After spring harvest, add a 1-inch or more layer of compost or manure and a gallon of complete organic fertilizer.

Tuck the bed in for the winter by covering with a 2- to 12-inch layer of compost in the late fall. Cut frost-browned stems a few inches above ground from midwinter to the following spring.

Harvesting

The first and second years of seed growth, do not harvest the first spears that appear. Let them continue to grow into fernlike bushes.

The year after planting root stock, harvest 1/3 of the spears that appear by cutting near the soil line with a sharp knife or asparagus fork. Cutting below the soil line may injure roots or sprouting shoots. You may also snap spears off with a quick flick of the wrist.

After the second year of rootstock growth, harvest spears when they are 4-5 inches tall. Cut daily if possible. Do not let spears grow too tall or they will become tough and fibrous.

For a fall harvest, cut back all of the fernlike foliage to the ground a month or two after the main spring harvest. A second, smaller crop of succulent spears will sprout for an autumn harvest.

An alternative method is to plant twice as much asparagus as normal. Harvest half of the bed until the "normal" end of the season then let the plants grow to fern. You then cut the ferns from the unharvested half of the garden. Cutting the ferns induces roots to send up new shoots that are eaten the rest of the summer!

In the Kitchen

Fresh: Cut or snap off the tough bottom where the spears break easily. Save the trimmings for soup. Cut spears into bite-size pieces or bundle 6-8 lengths per serving together with a string. Set, tops up, in a tall pan, containing 1/2 cup of boiling water and cover. Use a steamer to cook smaller pieces. Cook 5-8 minutes or until tender. Drain, using a colander, and serve with a butter or white sauce.

Storage: Set in the refrigerator in a canning jar half full of water. Cover the top with a plastic bag. Use within 3 days.

Freezing: Blanch whole stems, 1 minutes in boiling water, or 4 minutes steamed. Package in a plastic bag and freeze.

Food value: A good source of B vitamins, calcium, iron and vitamin C.

Varieties

JERSEY GIANT is a new, all male variety developed at Rutgers University that puts all of its energy into producing large succulent spears rather than berries. Matures mid- to late spring. Exceptionally high yield. Available (Bu, Ju, Le, Pa, Pi, Th)

MARY WASHINGTON is a good producer and readily available during the spring in root crowns at nurseries and from mail-order companies. Fairly rust resistant and yields well. Available (Au, Bea, Bu, Fa, Fi, Gc, Ju, Hi, Le, Ma, Mc, Me, Mi, Ra, Sc, Sw, Th).

ROBERTS yields well and is resistant to rust. Available (Fi).

WALTHAM produces very well and the buds stay tight longer, which extends the harvest. Fairly rust resistant and tender. Available (Fi).

Problems

Asparagus beetles and their young grubs (larvae) are a most serious threat. They eat stems and strip leaves. The 1/4-inch-long metallic black beetle has easy-to-identify orange squares on wing covers. Fall cleanup removes hibernating adults. Chalcid wasps, a natural enemy, controls small numbers of beetles. Hand-pick visible beetles. Spray pyrethrum on infestations.

Slugs and snails attack succulent spears when they emerge. Look for their silvery mucus trails. Control mollusks with a dusting of diatomaceous earth, dolomite lime, or slug hotels.

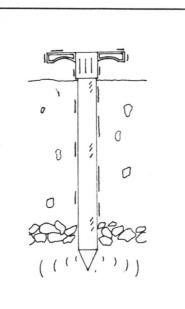

Gophers are herbivorous and find fleshy roots a real treat. If gophers are a problem in your area, line planting holes with poultry wire. Vibrating, noise-making devices set in the ground have been reported successful by some and unsuccessful by many more frustrated gardeners, at keeping gophers out of the garden. Traps are effective, but require skill to operate effectively. Plant euphorbia, nicknamed the "gopher plant" because it tends to deter the rodent.

Rust first appears as reddish-brown pustules on summer foliage, that burst to release a fine rusty powder (spores).
Control: Remove and "hot" compost or destroy infected foliage.
Prevention: Spores need moisture to germinate. Avoid rust by planting in sunny spots with a minimum of dew.

Leggy, thin spears can be caused by harvesting too heavy or too late (past June) the previous year. Other possibilities include harvesting too soon after planting, or failure to fertilize.

Loose stems: Wind can rock and loosen stems. The space alongside stems is subject to fungal attack. Construct a windbreak and tamp soil around the bases of stems.

Mushy black spears are caused by frost. Remove frost-killed shoots. If frost is expected after spears emerge, cover with a protective mulch or lightweight plastic.

Roots that fail to sprout spears were probably damaged by a moisture-related disease. Make sure your planting patch is well drained. (see: "Soil Preparation").

The average garden contains approximately 6, 000 slugs! These members of the mollusk family consist of 90% moisture. Snails are very similar to slugs except snails have a outer protective shell that lets them live in more arid climates. They hibernate in the winter, emerging in the spring to eat all the succulent new growing shoots.

Beans

The most difficult aspect of bean cultivation is deciding which kind to grow. The choices are almost limitless. Bush and pole pod varieties can be green, blue, purple or yellow. They taste best when eaten garden-fresh, pod and all. The seeds of pinto, fava and Lima beans are normally shelled from the pod and eaten fresh, or they may be stored for over a year when dried. The edible seeds and pods are only part of the benefit beans can offer the garden. Beans are legumes that add nitrogen and improve soil structure. Nitrogen from the air is "fixed" on root nodules with the help of beneficial *rhizobia* bacteria. The bacteria usually exists in the soil, but may not be plentiful in earth that has suffered the wrath of synthetic chemicals. For highest yields and nitrogen fixing, *inoculate bean seeds with the bacteria*, purchased at the nursery, before sowing. A fraction of this nitrogen is stored in the roots that are left in the soil after the beans have been harvested.

For subsequent crops to take full advantage of the nitrogen fixed in the soil, the beans must be grown as a cover crop and tilled under *before they bloom*. A common misconception is that nitrogen fixed by legumes stays in the soil after harvest. The legumes use all the nitrogen they produce to grow. To deposit the nitrogen in the soil, the legumes must be tilled under before they use all of the nitrogen. Grow beans as a cover crop, and till them under before flowers set to get full benefit of the nitrogen.

Bush Beans (*Phaseolus vulgaris* var. *humilis*)

Bush or snap beans grow into 1- to 2-foot-tall bushes that mature quickly, Some varieties yield up to five pickings over a six-week period. They like warm soil (above 60º (16º C)), with good drainage, and disdain heavy clay. Small white, purple or red flowers bloom shortly before small succulent pods set. Start the season with fast-growing bush beans and finish the fall with later maturing pole beans. Bush bean pods are available in green, yellow and purple. The flavorful yellow wax varieties are easy to spot when harvesting. Purple varieties are also easy to see and turn a vibrant green when cooked.

Basic Facts

Germination time: 7-14 days.
Germination temperature: Minimum: 60º (61º C), Optimum: 80º (27º C), Maximum: 95º (35º C).
Approximate seeds per ounce: 30-60.

Seed required to sow 10-foot row: 3/4 ounce.
Yield per 10-foot row: 6-10 pounds.
Seed required to sow 1 X 4-foot raised bed: 1/2 ounce.
Yield per 1 X 4-foot raised bed: 8-12 pounds.
Life expectancy of stored seed: 2 years.

Estimated time between sowing and first picking: 8-10 weeks.
Intercrop: Corn, flowers, potatoes.
Effort to cultivate: Easy.
Seed saving: Let pods dry on bushes, then shell. Place seeds in a cool, dry location with air circulation to continue drying. Cross-pollination is unlikely.

Climate

Zones 3-11. Need full sun and warm weather (60-95° (16-35° C)). The soil must be 60° (16° C) for seeds to germinate. Choose a location that is sheltered from the wind.

Soil Preparation

Prefers free-draining soil with a nearly neutral pH (6.3-6.8). Add lime if soil is too acidic.
Cultivate soil in the spring incorporating a liberal amount of compost and manure. Apply low-nitrogen complete fertilizer before planting.

Planting

To sprout seeds before sowing, soak in a glass of water for 2-4 hours. Pour the water out of the glass and rinse the seeds once or twice a day with water to retain moisture. In 2-3 days, a shoot will sprout. The bean sprout is very fragile at this point. Carefully remove and sow seed by placing it on its side in the planting hole.

Sow inoculated seed (see "Beans" page 26) 2-4 weeks after the last frost when the ground has warmed to 60° (16° C). Purple varieties tolerate somewhat colder soil than green beans, and can be sown a month earlier if grown under row covers. If cold weather stunts seedlings, sow another crop to ensure an abundant harvest.
Sow seed 1- to 1 1/2-inches deep on 4- to 6-inch centers in wide raised beds, or sow seed 1 inch apart in rows spaced at 12-18 inches.
Succession crops: Sow seeds every 2-4 weeks through midsummer for a continual harvest.
Plant 10-20 plants for each person.

Crop Care

Protect tender seedlings from slugs, snails and Mexican bean beetles.
Hand-pick weeds until beans grow tall enough to shade weeds. Bush varieties need less mulch because they form a "living mulch" that shades the ground.
Mulch to control weeds and conserve water after the ground warms to 70° (21° C).
Regular watering throughout cropping is essential to ensure pod development.
Fertilize with a low-nitrogen complete tea mix after the first picking and weekly thereafter to encourage more pods to set.

Harvesting

Start picking when succulent pods are about 4 inches long. Ripe pods snap easily when bent. Make sure to harvest before the seeds within the pod bulge, becoming tough and stringy. Pick regularly to prevent pods from maturing and to prolong the harvest. Hold the stems as you pick the pods to keep from loosening or uprooting bushes. A pair of scissors or small pruners may make harvesting easier.
If picked regularly, harvesting will continue over a month.
Avoid picking when foliage is wet; it tends to spread disease.

In the Kitchen

Fresh: Hybrid varieties seldom need "strings" removed, especially if pods are picked while young and tender. Slice or snip off tough ends and remove "strings" from older tough pods. Slice pods on an angle into uniform 1/2-inch pieces. Immature, succulent pods can be cooked whole after tips are removed. Steam for 8-10 minutes or boil 6-8 minutes - until tender. Or pressure cook at 15 lbs. for 3 minutes. Save (freeze) nutrient-rich boiled water for soup, stews or sauce stock. Cook partially covered to preserve color; cover completely to preserve nutrients. Or stir fry in vegetable oil until tender. Eat with butter or use in a salad.
Storage: Place whole pods in a plastic bag. They will keep in the refrigerator for about 5 days.
Freezing: Blanch in boiling water for 2 1/2 minutes or steam for 3 minutes, dry, seal in a plastic bag and freeze.

Varieties

Green Varieties

Blue Lake (55 days) types produce many pencil-pods on compact bushes. A good choice for eating fresh or freezing. Resistant to mosaic virus. Available (Fi, Gc, Ha, Le, Me, Ni, Pa).
Jumbo (55 days) is a cross between the Italian Romano and the Kentucky Wonder. The extra-long, dark green pods are packed with tender beany flavor. The plants bear very heavily. Available (Fi, Ha, Jo, Ni, Pa, Pi).

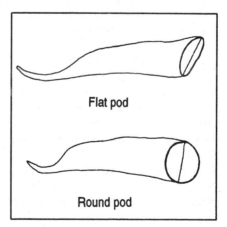

Flat pod

Round pod

VERNANDON "HARICOT VERTS" are light fine French "filet" beans. The long, slender, round, pencil pod shape makes them perfect to eat whole. The taste is sensational. Heavy bearing plants are resistant to anthracnose and bean virus. Available (She).

BUSH ROMANO (60 days) is a flavorful gourmet Italian bean. Inch-wide flat pods are tender and meaty. Good yield and sweet eating. Available (Cg, Le, She, St).

TENDERCROP (53 days) is especially appealing to organic gardeners. It is resistant to mosaic, mottle virus and powdery mildew. Good producer of round pencil-pods. Available (Fi, Ha, Me, Ni, Pa)

TOPCROP (53 days) developed by the USDA, is early and a heavy producer. The meaty round pods are a good choice to eat fresh or freeze. Available (Bu, Fa, Fi, Hi, Ju, Ma, Me, Pa).

Colored Varieties

KINGHORN WAX (57 days) has stringless yellow waxy pods with creamy yellow flesh. Sets pods in abundant clusters that are convenient to pick. Available (Ma, Ma)

ROC D' OR (57 days) is a French yellow wax with slender, long round pods and a delicate, light buttery flavor. Steam 3- to 4-inch pods whole. Resistant to anthracnose and bean viruses. Available (Bu, Gc, Jo, She, St).

PENCIL POD BLACK WAX (55 days) is an old-time variety with yellow waxy pods and dark seeds. Flavorful and heavy bearing. Plump round pods are good fresh or frozen. Available (Gc, Me, So).

ROYAL BURGUNDY (51 days) has a deep purple pod that turns green when cooked. Easy to see and a little more tolerant to cold. Available (Cg, Ma, She, Te).

Pole Beans (*Phaseolus vulgaris*)

Pole snap beans have the richest flavor. Their tendrils cling to a supporting trellis as they climb rapidly to over 8 feet. They yield heavily if *picked clean* regularly from midsummer until the weather cools in the fall. Pole beans are a good choice for containers, or where space is limited. The long vines yield twice as much as bush beans, but start producing about two weeks later. Growing to near eye level, they are easy to harvest, remain clean and are less prone to insect attacks. Like their bush cousins, pole beans like well-drained warm soil and hate heavy clay. The white, purple or red flowers continue to bloom and set pods soon after the flowers fold. A trellis can be made by lashing three, 8-foot poles together to form a wigwam, by stretching twine between two wires (twine rots and can go into the compost pile), or by securing poultry wire along the ground and tacking the top to a fence.

Basic Facts

Germination time: 7-14 days.
Germination temperature: Minimum: 60° (16° C), Optimum: 80° (27° C), Maximum: 95° (35° C).
Approximate seeds per ounce: 30-60.
Seed required to sow 10-foot row: 3/4-1 ounce.
Yield per 10-foot row: 10-12 pounds.
Life expectancy of stored seed: 2 years.

Estimated time between sowing and first picking: 10-12 weeks.
Intercrop: Brassicas, corn, leaf crops, flowers and potatoes.
Effort to cultivate: Fairly easy, requires a trellis.
Seed saving: Let dry on vines and shell. Cross-pollination is very unlikely.

Climate

Zones 3-11. Need full sun and warm weather (60-95° (16-35° C)). Soil must warm to at least 60° (16° C) before seeds will germinate. Choose a location that is sheltered from the wind.

Soil Preparation

Prefers free-draining soil with a neutral pH. Add lime if soil is acidic. **Cultivate soil** the previous fall or in the spring, incorporating a liberal amount of compost and manure. Apply a low-nitrogen complete fertilizer before planting.

Planting

To sprout seeds before planting, soak in a glass of water for 2-4 hours.

Pour the water out of the glass and rinse the seeds once or twice a day with water to retain moisture. In 2-3 days a shoot will sprout. The bean sprout is very fragile at this point. Carefully remove and sow seed by placing it on its side in the planting hole.

Sow inoculated seed (see "Beans" page 26) 2-4 weeks after last frost when the ground has warmed to 60° (16° C). Purple varieties tolerate cooler soil than green beans and can be sown a month earlier in raised beds if grown under row covers. Also see "No-till Gardens", page 10.

Sow seed 1- to 1 1/2-inches deep, 6-8 inches apart, in rows spaced at 24 inches. Thin to one plant per 4-6 inches.

Crop Care

Protect tender seedlings from slugs, snails and Mexican bean beetles.

Mulch after the ground warms to control weeds and conserve moisture.

Regular watering throughout cropping is essential to ensure strong pod development. Mulch heavily to conserve water and stabilize temperature after the ground has warmed.

Fertilize with a low-nitrogen tea after the first picking, and weekly thereafter, to encourage more pods to set.

Harvesting

Start picking when young pods are 4-6 inches long. Make sure to harvest before the beans within the pod bulge and become tough. *Pick vines clean* regularly to prevent pods from maturing, and to prolong the harvest. Hold the stems as you pick the pods to prevent vine damage.

If picked regularly, harvesting will continue until the weather cools in the fall.

Avoid picking when foliage is wet; it tends to spread disease.

In the Kitchen

Fresh: Prepare and cook the same as bush beans, page 27.
Storage: The same as bush beans, page 27.
Freezing: The same as bush beans, page 27.

Varieties

Green Varieties

BLUE LAKE (70 days) varieties have stringless, straight, brittle, long, round pods that are a favorite to eat fresh, or for canning and freezing. Excellent flavor, tender and meaty. Available (Bg, Bu, Fi, Gc, Gs, Ju, Ma, Pa, St).

KENTUCKY WONDER (70 days) varieties are old-time favorites that produce well, and are long on flavor. Long, straight pods are a silvery green. White-seeded varieties mature earlier, and the strings develop slower than later maturing brown-seeded varieties. Available (Bu, Fa, Fi, Gc, Gs, Ha, Jo, Ma, Me, Ni, Pa, So, Te).

ROMANO (70 days) varieties consistently yield large, flat, tender green pods over a long season. Gourmet flavor is superb, fresh or frozen. Available (Bu, Fa, Fi, Gs, Le, Ni, Pa, Pi, Sc, Th))

SELMA STAR (60 days) produces long, straight, stringless pods that are tender and delicious. A good warm climate choice to eat fresh, frozen or canned. Available (Pa)

Colored Varieties

KENTUCKY WONDER WAX (74 days) offers a prolific yield of plump, straight round golden yellow pods. Mild and buttery taste. Grows well in cooler climates. Available (Te).

VIOLET PODDED STRINGLESS (70 days) sprouts and grows well in cool soil. Sets abundant pods with excellent flavor, even after pods become long. Available (Te).

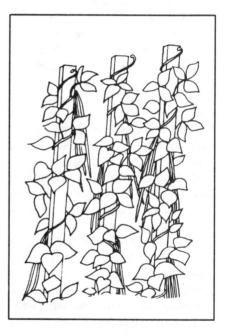

ASPARAGUS, or YARD-LONG BEANS, (*Vigna uniquiculata sesquipedalis*) (75-95 days) are not true beans, but are members of the pea family. Depending on variety, pods can grow from 2- to 4-feet long, Harvest when 12- to 18-inches long to ensure tenderness. These long beans thrive in hot weather and are drought tolerant. The taste is sweet and similar to beans. Kids love them. Available (Le, Ric, Sc, So).

Runner Beans *(Phaseolus coccineus)*

European runner beans belong to a separate cool weather species of beans. They produce fuzzy, long, flat, sweet pods during cool summer weather. The flavor is too beany for most people to eat fresh, but they are delicious when cooked. Runner beans are more demanding to cultivate than other beans, but *very* heavy bearing. They stop setting flowers if just a few pods are left to mature or if the temperature rises above 85° (29° C). The flowers are some of the most spectacular available and many gardeners plant them solely for their captivating blossoms. High productivity is achieved in warmer climates by planting in partial shade, or interplanting with corn. Runner beans form a dense screen of foliage that also makes an excellent wigwam for children.

Basic Facts

Germination time: 7-14 days.
Germination temperature: Minimum: 50° (10° C), Optimum: 70° (21° C), Maximum: 85° (29° C).
Approximate seeds per ounce: 30.
Seed required to sow 10-foot row: 1 ounce.
Yield per 10-foot row: 25 pounds.
Life expectancy of stored seed: 2 years.
Estimated time between sowing and first picking: 12-14 weeks.
Intercrop: Corn, leaf crops, brassicas, flowers and potatoes.
Effort to cultivate: Fussy, require good soil preparation, a trellis, and regular picking.
Seed saving: Seeds tend to cross-pollinate; grow only one variety and let seeds dry in pods.

Climate

Zones 3-11. Needs full sun in mild climates. Produces best in partial shade in warmer regions. Runner beans *stop producing when the temperature climbs beyond 85° (29° C) and if pods are allowed to mature.* When the temperature drops below 85° (29° C) pods start producing again.

Soil Preparation

Must have free-draining soil with a neutral pH. Add lime in late winter if soil is acidic.
Cultivate soil in fall, incorporating a liberal amount of compost and manure. Apply complete low-nitrogen fertilizer before planting.

Planting

To sprout seeds before planting, soak in a glass of water for 2-4 hours. Pour the water out of the glass, and rinse the seeds once or twice a day with water to retain moisture. In 2-3 days a shoot will sprout. The bean sprout is very fragile at this point. Carefully remove and sow seed by placing it on its side in the planting hole.

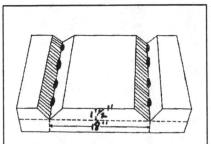

Planting depth of runner beans.

Sow inoculated seed (see "Beans" page 26) of green varieties after the last frost. Sow a month earlier if grown under row covers, or if grass clippings are used to make a "hot" no-till raised bed (page 10).
Sow seed 1 1/2 to 2 inches deep, 4 inches apart in rows spaced at 18 inches. Sow a few extra seeds at the end of rows to transplant and fill gaps.
In cold climates, start seeds indoors 4-6 weeks before the last average frost. Set seedlings in cold frame to harden-off before transplanting.

Crop Care

Protect tender seedlings from slugs, snails and Mexican bean beetles.
Mulch to smother weeds, conserve moisture, and keep the ground cool.
Regular watering throughout cropping is essential to ensure pod development.
Fertilize with a low-nitrogen tea after the first picking, and weekly thereafter to encourage pods to set.

Harvesting

Start picking when young pods are 4-6 inches long. Make sure to harvest before the beans within the pod bulge and become tough.

Pick regularly for a heavy two-month harvest. Pick daily if necessary, to prevent pods from maturing and prolong the harvest. *If just a few pods ripen, flowering stops forever.* Hold the stems as you pick the pods to prevent damage to vines.

Once seeds swell in larger pods, shell for cooking seeds.

In the Kitchen

Fresh: Prepare and cook pods the same as bush beans, page 27. Prepare and cook shelled runner beans the same as shelled beans, page 32.

Storage: Store pods the same as bush beans, page 27. Dry seeds the same as dry beans, page 33.

Freezing: The same as bush beans, page 27.

Varieties

RED KNIGHT (70 days) is a red-flowering, stringless variety developed by the British. Hummingbirds love the choice crimson flowers. Vines grow to 10 feet, producing a long harvest of meaty, flavorful pods. Available (She).

SCARLET EMPEROR (75-85 days) produces spectacular flowers and tender, sweet, beany pods. The seeds are slower to develop than Scarlet runners, and can mature a little longer before picking. The pods are huge. Available (Bg).

SCARLET RUNNER (72 days) varieties were developed by Europeans for cool, mild climates. Stunning scarlet flowers bloom on vines before producing long, plump, juicy pods. Pick while very young, before pods get tough. Available (Gc, Gs, Pi, Sc).

WHITE KNIGHT (73 days) runner beans are vigorous climbers that produce lovely cascading white blossoms. Yields a heavy crop of completely stringless, thick, tender, green beans. Very sweet flavor. Available (She).

Shelling and Dry Beans (*Phaseolus vulgaris*)

The beans in this group are similar to bush beans but their seeds develop more rapidly. The pod or shell is normally shucked and the large beans are eaten fresh, or dried for winter dishes. Some varieties of shelling beans are very tasty when immature and eaten in the pod. Most varieties prefer warm, well-drained soil, but others thrive in somewhat cooler ground. Hot summers and autumn weather with little dew or rain is necessary for seeds to mature and dry. Flowers set just before pods appear and range in color from black on white to scarlet.

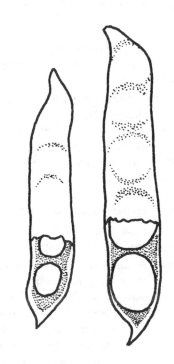

Broad or fava beans (*Vicia faba*) are also included in this category because they are normally shelled and eaten fresh or dried. The only native Mediterranean bean, favas have large seeds and grow in broad, flat pods up to 18 inches long. They are flavorful in immature pods, fresh shelled, or dried and stored. Some varieties are cold tolerant to 15° or less, plus they fix large amounts of nitrogen in the soil (see "Beans" page 26). They prefer a long cool winter or spring to mature pods. Hot weather causes blossoms to drop.

Note: A few people, usually of Mediterranean heritage, have a genetic enzyme deficiency that causes a severe or fatal reaction to fava beans and pollen.

Basic Facts

Germination time: 7-14 days.
Germination temperature (fava): Minimum: 50° (10° C), Optimum: 70° (21° C), Maximum: 85° (29° C), (others): Minimum: 60° (16° C), Optimum: 80° (26° C), Maximum: 95° (35° C).
Approximate seeds per ounce: (fava) 15, (others) 20-30.
Seed required to sow 10-foot row: 1-2 ounces.
Yield per 10-foot row: 20 pounds.
Life expectancy of stored seed: 2-3 years.
Estimated time between sowing and first picking: (Spring sowing) 10-14 weeks, (favas sown in autumn) 25 weeks.
Intercrop: Crops that require shade in hot weather and flowers. Potatoes.
Effort to cultivate: Easy, pole varieties require a trellis.
Seed saving: Let pods dry on plants, shell and lay out on a screen to let dry completely before storing.

Climate

Zones 3-10. Need full sun. Shelling beans need a long, hot summer days and a dry fall. Fava beans need cool weather, below 85°. If rain prevent the beans from drying on the plant, harvest entire plants and let them dry under cover.

Soil Preparation

Prefer free-draining soil but will grow in most soils. Add lime to neutralize pH if soil is acidic.
For spring sowing: Cultivate soil in the spring or the previous fall, incorporating a liberal amount of compost and manure. Apply a low-nitrogen complete fertilizer before planting.
For autumn sowing: Prepare ground in September, incorporating plenty of compost and manure. Apply a low-nitrogen complete fertilizer when preparing soil.

Planting

To sprout seed before planting, soak in a glass of water for 2-4 hours. Pour the water out of the glass, and rinse the seeds once or twice a day with water to retain moisture. In 2-3 days a shoot will sprout. The bean sprout is very fragile at this point. Carefully remove and sow seed by placing it on its side in the planting hole.
In spring, inoculate seed and sow broad bean varieties one month after the last average frost. Sow more tender seed after the last frost, when the ground has warmed to 60° (16° C). Seeds can be sown a month earlier if grown under row covers.

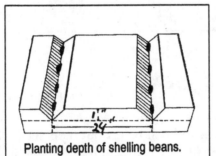

Planting depth of shelling beans.

Sow 1-inch deep on 8-12-inch centers in wide beds, or sow seed 4 inches apart in rows spaced at 18-24 inches.
To overwinter a crop, sow frost resistant broad (fava) beans from mid-September through October. Sow broad bean seed 1 1/2 inches deep 4-5 inches apart; rows are 2-3 feet apart.

Crop Care

Protect tender seedlings from slugs, snails and Mexican Bean beetles. Hand-pick or carefully hoe weeds until beans grow to 6 inches.
Watering is necessary to establish seedlings and during dry weather, especially after pods set.
Mulch to conserve water, stifle weeds, and stabilize soil temperature.

Fertilize with a low-nitrogen tea or a blend of chicken manure and seaweed once or twice during the growing season.
An earlier harvest is ensured by pinching off the top inch of bush after the first pods have set.

Harvesting

For pod beans, harvest immature pods when they are 2-3 inches long. Pick before the seeds within the pod bulge and pods become tough.
For fresh shell beans, harvest pods after seeds are fully formed but still soft. Shell the pods and eat tender beans fresh or steamed.
For dry beans, let the pods dry on plants in arid climates. Snip plant off at soil level when 90 percent of the leaves have yellowed and dropped. Complete drying in the shade under cover. In moist climates, hang plants upside down under cover to dry.
Shell dry pods individually or thrash by holding plants upside down inside a barrel and bang them back and forth until the seeds fall. Thrashing is also accomplished by laying out a large canvas on which dried bushes are set. Flail plants with a broom. Separate lighter leaves, pods and stems from heavier bean seeds by hand.

In the Kitchen

Fresh: Shelled beans are packed with protein and great taste. Cooking shelled beans in butter or olive oil releases the fat-soluble vitamins, which makes them available to the body. They make an excellent dish when combined with meats, onions, cheese and other vegetables. Cook fresh shelled seeds by steaming 6-10 minutes, or boil 6 minutes - until tender. Save (freeze) nutrient-rich broth for soup, stew or sauce stock. Or prepare and cook the pods same as bush beans, page 27.

Dry: Wash dry beans before soaking. Soak in 3-4 times the volume of water as beans. Remove any floating, discolored or moldy beans. Strain out the soaking water; replace with fresh water. Boil beans until tender. You may want to add onion and garlic while cooking to impart their flavor in the beans. Beans can be baked, pureed, fried and combined with many other ingredients as the base of numerous recipes. One favorite is *huevos refritos* (refried beans) made by heating cooked beans in a skillet with butter and mashed into a thick paste.

Storage: Store pods the same as bush beans, page 27.

Freezing: Treat pods the same as bush beans, page 27. Shuck seeds from pod, blanch for 2-3 minutes, dry, seal in a plastic bag and freeze.

Dry shelled bean seeds slowly in the oven at 110º (43º C) for 3-4 hours or set on a screen in the sun for 2-3 days until completely dry. Store dried beans in a jar. Open the jar every few days to stir the beans. The beans take a couple weeks longer to dry completely. Once you are sure the beans are dry, secure the lid tightly.

Varieties

Shelling Varieties

LIMA beans (*P. lunatus*): (65-90 days) Bush varieties require 85 frost-free days. Sprawling bushes yield a short-lived harvest that is about half the volume of pole types. Pole varieties require a minimum of 130 frost-free days to mature, but they bear until frost. Neither bush nor pole types will set pods in cooler climates. Produces flat green pods containing 3-4 tasty white, tan or green seeds. Eat fresh, or dry for later use. Available (Bu, Fi, Ma, Ni, Pa, Pl, St).

RED KIDNEY BUSH (70 days) varieties are a late-maturing bean that can be shelled and eaten fresh, or dried for winter use. This old-fashioned favorite is sweeter than most, and a good producer. Available (Bu, Fa, Fi, Gc, Le, Ma, Me, Ni, Pa, Te).

SOLDIER (68 days) beans have a white, kidney-shaped seed. The eye has a maroon figure of a soldier. Drought tolerant and adapted to cool climates. An excellent baker. Available (Gc, Jo, Sc, Te)

SPECKLED BAY (Taylor's Horticultural) (68 days) yields creamy colored seeds with "freckles," similar to those are pintos. Excellent fresh shelled or dry. Grows well in cool climates. Available (Ma, Me, Te).

Broad (Fava) Bean Varieties

APROVECHO SELECT FAVA produces weighty large flavorful greenish-brown seeds on bushes that grow up to 5 feet in good soil. Fresh or dry, it's the best tasting fava on the market. Available (Abu).

WINDSOR (75 days) varieties produce broad, short green pods with 3-5 large white, tan or green seeds. Very flavorful fresh shelled, but not as good when dried and cooked. Sturdy bushes can grow to 4 feet. Available (Bg, Gc, Gs, Hi).

Problems

Beans and peas, both legumes, are afflicted by several bacterial and viral diseases. These maladies are most common during periods of warm temperatures, high humidity, and abundant rainfall. Avoid working with these legumes when foliage is wet; diseases are transported in water. Shelling beans that mature on the vine are more susceptible to disease than pod beans which are harvested sooner. Make sure soil is well drained. Do not grow beans or peas on the same ground more than two years in a row, preferably one year, without growing other crops in rotation. Rotating crops discourages disease, lowers insect populations and rejuvenates soil. Fall cleanup helps prevent insects and diseases from overwintering.

1. Bean and pea aphids: The black bean aphids are easy to spot, and usually attack tender, new growth just before blooming. Green pea aphids are a little more difficult to see and less common. During hot, damp weather, they multiply rapidly.

Control: Squish between fingers and blast off with a jet of water at 4-7 day intervals; spray with insecticidal soap or pyrethrum.

Prevention: Encourage or release predators: lacewings, hoverflies and ladybugs.

2. Bean and pea thrips are minute black- or yellow-winged insects. They feed on the surface of leaves and pods, leaving silvery patches. Yield is reduced and pods distorted.

Control: Spray with a jet of water or insecticidal soap. Release lacewings.

Prevention: Remove weeds. Encourage or release lacewings, which are thrip predators. Fall cleanup.

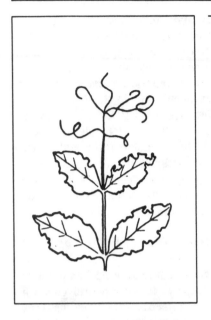

BEANS	SYMPTOM	PROVABLE CAUSES
Seed & Seedlings	missing	4, 24, 30
	poor gemination	17, 24, 30
	holes in seeds	3, 5
	wilt	10, 30
Stems	external brown streaks	8
	internal brown streaks	13
	wilted	10, 13
	aphid infestation	1
	cut off at soil line	4
Leaves	yellowing	7, 13, 16
	distorted	13, 16
	notched	3, 27, 28
	holes	6
	white patches	12
	aphid infestation	1
	spots, brown	8, 11
	spots, cottony	12, 14, 15
	spots, yellow	8
	wilted	10
Flowers	missing	18
	flowers but no pods	19
	notched	3
Pods	missing	19
	distorted	1, 2, 12
	spots, dry texture	8, 12
	spots, wet & greasy	9
	spots, cottony	12, 14, 15
	spots, silvery	2
	tunneled	5, 23

3. Bean weevils are 1/8-inch long, with lengthwise alternating brown and yellow stripes. Chunky **pea weevils** are smaller with intermittent white and dark markings eon a brown body. They chew U-shaped notches in leaf fringes and flowers. Both lay eggs, which hatch into white grubs that bore into seeds. Look for their entrance holes in pods. These pests are prolific in hot weather.
Control: Remove and destroy affected pods. Dust with rotenone. Heat bean and peas used for seed to 135º (57º C) for four hours.
Prevention: Fall cleanup and soil tillage.

4. Cutworms are fat, 1/2- to 1 1/2-inch-long, smooth-skinned gray to brown (some have stripes or spots) larvae of night-flying moths. They attack numerous vegetable stems near the ground and can sever the stem of seedlings. See page 54 for a drawing of a cutworm.
Control: Promptly hand-pick from the soil near damaged plants. Sprinkle cornmeal around base of plants or apply *Bacillus thuringiensis*.
Prevention: Encircle plants with a stiff 3-inch-wide barrier of cardboard or plastic anchored an inch deep in the soil. Birds, firefly larvae,

braconid wasps, Nc nematodes, tachinid flies, moles and toads are predators.

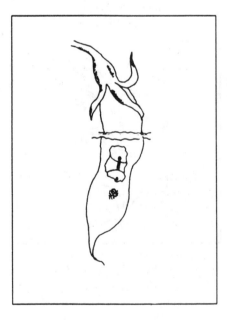

5. Borers are wormy caterpillars that can be white, green or reddish, and grow to an inch long. They tunnel into pods, eating one seed after another.
Control: Hand-pick from leaves and pods. Apply *Bacillus thuringiensis* if infested.
Prevention: Fall cleanup, crop rotation. Plant early in the season before borers are rampant.

6. Mexican bean beetles and their larvae have voracious appetites for pods, stems and leaves which they skeletonize. Adults, about 1/3-inch long with 16 spots on a coppery brown domed body, are often mistaken for ladybug beetles. Larvae are 1/3-inch long with rows of dark spines on their back. Most common in the South and from the Midwest east.

Control: Hand-pick, apply ryana or as a last resort rotenone.

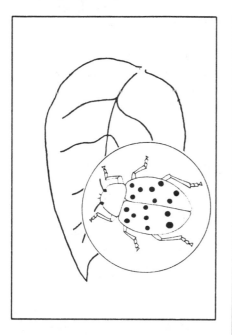

Prevention: Release predatory wasp *Pedibis foveolatus*, use floating row covers to exclude the beetles.

7. Whitefringed beetles are 1/2-inch long with a short, sturdy snout, and brown-gray body. The adult is much less of a pest than the larvae which is chunky, up to 1/2-inch long, light yellow, and legless. Favoring legumes, they feed on roots, turning plants yellow; finally they wilt and die. A major pest in the South.
Control: Apply rotenone.
Prevention: Remove weeds and debris. Fall cleanup; turn soil under. Do not plant peas and beans together. Fertilize regularly.

8. Anthracnose causes slightly sunken irregular brown spots on pods, leaves, and stems. As disease progresses, spots turn pink; if not treated, plants die.
Control: Remove and destroy *all* affected plants.
Prevention: Apply a garlic and water spray. Avoid handling wet foliage; rotate crops. Use seed grown in western states where the disease is virtually nonexistent. Do not plant discolored seed, or seed from discolored pods.

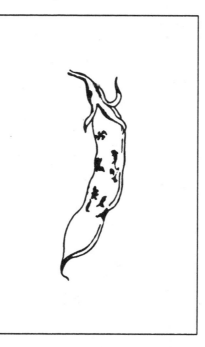

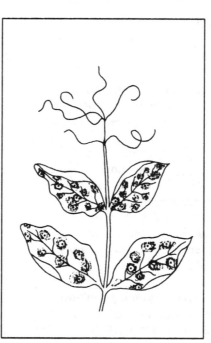

9. Bacterial blight causes brown, greaselike spots on leaves and pods. One species, halo blight, is recognized by a yellow "halo" that forms around brown spots. Affected areas later turn yellow or brown as they dry. If disease is contracted early in the growing season, death may result.

Control: None.
Prevention: Avoid handling wet foliage; rotate crops. Use seed grown in western states where the disease is virtually nonexistent. Do not plant discolored seed, or seed from discolored pods.

10. Bacterial wilt usually infects and kills bean seedlings; if attacked when larger, death may not occur. Leaves wilt and the young plant soon dies from this seed- and soil-borne disease.
Control: None
Prevention: Fall cleanup to prevent overwintering. Avoid handling wet foliage; rotate crops. Use seed grown in western states where the disease is virtually nonexistent. Do not plant discolored seed, or seed from discolored pods.

11. Bean rust looks like rust; many small reddish orange pustules can be seen on foliage. The pustules burst to send a multitude of spores out to colonize more foliage. Badly infected leaves turn yellow, dry, and die.
Control: Harvest pods when ripe. Remove foliage and "hot" compost, or discard. Remove affected stakes. Disinfect stakes with lime sulfur spray or dust.
Prevention: Purchase rust-resistant varieties. Fall cleanup, three-year crop rotation. Plant upwind from infected fields. Spray with a mild lime sulfur solution when first signs appear.

12. Downy mildew is most common on Lima beans in the Middle and North Atlantic states but can affect other legumes. Causes white cottony blotches on pods. Motley white to yellowish spots may occur on peas. Most common during wet weather with cool nights and warm days.
Control: Destroy *all* affected plants.
Prevention: Plant resistant varieties; rotate crops in three-year or longer cycles.

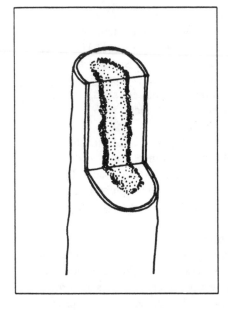

13. Fusarium wilt causes stunted growth, yellowing, rolled leaves and a meager harvest. Identify by splitting open infected stem; brown, rusty streaks run vertically through stem, but no discolored spots or streaks appear externally. Roots gradually turn dark when attacked by this soil-borne disease.
Control: Remove and destroy *all* affected plants.
Prevention: Grow wilt-resistant varieties; rotate crops.

14. Gray mold (*Botrytis*) appears on beans and occasionally on peas, especially in damp weather. A velvety gray, hairlike mold grows in and on pods and foliage.
Control: Remove and destroy *all* infected foliage.
Prevention: Allow better air circulation; rotate crops.

15. Powdery mildew is a white, dustlike powdery mold that appears on both sides of pea leaves late in growth. Growth is stunted a little; if severe, death occurs. Pick all pods as they ripen.

Control: After harvest, till all vines under soil or hot compost.

Prevention: Avoid overhead sprinkling. Allow good air circulation.

16. Mosaic viruses, carried in the sap, are transported from plant to plant by aphid vectors. Leaves may yellow, or develop mottled lime and dark green spots; edges curl downward and growth is stunted. Affected seedlings dwarf severely and produce few pods.
Control: Infected plants can't be saved. Remove and destroy.
Prevention: Sow disease-free certified seed.

17. Seeds do not germinate. The most probable cause is that (bean) seeds were sown before the soil was warm enough and they rotted in cold, wet soil. Other causes could be old, inviable seed excessive moisture, or dry soil. Sprout seed by soaking

in water (see "Planting" page 27). Keep soil warm, evenly moist, and apply *rhizobia* bacteria inoculant when planting.

18. No flowers on bushes and vines is uncommon. It is usually caused by too much nitrogen in the soil, or by birds eating flowers. Use a low-nitrogen fertilizer, and cover with plastic netting to exclude birds.

19. No pods can be caused by birds eating flowers or large bumblebees knocking them off. Cool temperatures during flowering can discourage pollinating insects. Hot, dry weather may inhibit pod formation. Keep roots moist and cool with mulch and regular watering.

20. Small or "C" shaped beans means the plants have suffered from water stress.
Control: Water plants regularly. Once small beans set, they stay small after suffering drought.
Prevention: Keep well watered, especially after flowers set.

Other pests that attack beans are:

21. Beet leafhopper (whitefly): page 39
22. Cabbage fly root maggots: page 53.
23. Corn earworm: page 70
24. Garden springtail: page 106
25. Potato leafhopper (bean jassid): page 120
26. Seedcorn maggot: page 71
27. Spider mite: page 137
28. Cucumber beetle: page 76
29. Tarnished plant bug: page 65
30. Wireworms: page 61
31. Damping-off: page 61

Do you have some good recipes that you would like to share with us? We would like to know about them. Maybe we'll add them to our next book.

Write down your recipes and mail them to Van Paten Publishing 4204 S.E. Ogden St., Portland, OR 97206. If we use your information, we'll note your name in the book and send you a free copy of the book your information was used in.

Beet *(Beta vulgaris)*

Beets are native to the Mediterranean region, and are a good winter crop in mild climates. This biennial, grown as an annual, is a good spring, summer, and fall crop in most other climates. They develop best during warm sunny days and cool nights. Plant bolt-resistant varieties for summer harvests in hot climates. Broadcast seeds in thick patches every 2-4 weeks for a constant supply. Four or five plants grow from each seed, and the seedlings require thinning. However, the globe variety Monopoly is a monogerm, only producing one beet per seed. Thin young beets, and eat the succulent tops or transplant when seedlings are 1 or 2 inches tall. Harvest beet roots when they are the most tender, about half the size found in supermarkets. White or golden globe varieties do not bleed when sliced, and roots and greens together taste milder than red beets. The key to a sweet-tasting beet is even soil moisture and rapid growth.

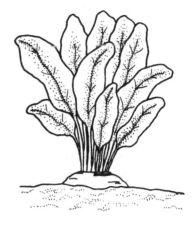

Basic Facts

Germination time: 10-14 days.
Germination temperature: Minimum: 40° (5° C), Optimum: 75° (24° C), Maximum: 95° (35° C).
Approximate seeds per ounce: 1400.
Seed required to sow 1 X 4-foot raised bed on 2-inch centers: 1/8 ounce.
Yield per 1 X 4-foot bed: 10-20 pounds.
Seed required to sow 10-foot row: 1/8 ounce.
Yield from a 10-foot row: 10-15 pounds.
Life expectancy of stored seed: 4 years.
Estimated time between sowing and first picking: 8-11 weeks.
Intercrop: Brassicas, leaf crops, onion family, flowers.
Effort to cultivate: Easy, and beets hold in the garden very well.
Seed saving: Crosses readily with other beets, and chard. Biennial seeds are produced the second year. When sown early in the spring, hot summer weather forces premature seed formation in the summer. Grow only one variety per year to save seed.

Climate

Zones 2-11. Grow year round in zones 9-11. Needs full sun, but tolerates partial shade. Beets prefer mild weather. Temperatures above 80° (26° C) can make roots tough and lower sugar content.

Soil Preparation

Ideal soil is a slightly alkaline loam (with a pH up to 8.0), but small globe varieties will grow in most fertile, well-drained soils with a pH above 6.0. Lime acid soils to raise the pH. If you have heavy clay soil, plant shallow-rooted globe varieties.
Lightly cultivate the soil in the spring adding a complete fertilizer. Do not add much nitrogen-rich compost and manure before planting, or "hairy" roots will result.
Rake seed bed smooth. Seeds sprout poorly through crusted soil.

Planting

A germination inhibitor is contained within the seed's tough hull. Soak seed in water for 2-4 hours before planting, to dissolve the inhibitor and soften the seed. Or scarify seed by shaking in a bag with gravel, brushing with sandpaper or a file before sowing.

Sow first seed after the last frost of spring. Plant 1/2-inch deep on 1- to 2-inch centers in raised wide beds or 1-2 inches apart in rows spaced at 12 inches. Make sure seeds come in firm contact with soil and are kept evenly moist. Sow 4 weeks earlier under a cold frame or plastic tunnel.

After sprouting, carefully transplant 1-inch-tall beets into bare spots or thin and compost. Keep soil moist until established.

Sow succession crops at 2-4 week intervals. Plant in partial shade during midsummer to avoid heat, and to increase germination rate.

Crop Care

Weed by hand around tender young beets, and hoe lightly if possible after leaves are 4-6 inches tall.

Apply mulch to check weed growth, cool soil and retain moisture. Add more mulch as needed.

Keep soil moist. Allowing soil to dry will cause white rings to form (zoning), but affects flavor very little. Moist conditions after soil dries could cause splitting.

Harvesting

Start harvesting beets when they start to crowd one another. The leaves and bulbs are tender when immature. Golf ball-sized roots 1 1/2-2 inches across are the sweetest. Soil should be somewhat moist to remove roots easily. If necessary, insert a small fork or trowel alongside deeper growing roots and gently unearth with an upward motion of the digging tool.

Harvest larger beets as needed, to eat fresh. Roots hold in the soil well, but develop a tough skin that must be peeled. Cut tops 2 inches above roots or keep tops intact until slicing to cook or roots bleed. Tender roots that have not suffered water stress have no white rings when sliced open.

Store beets in the soil, mulching the surface with oak leaves or conifer needles to keep soil from freezing. Larger beets develop a tough skin, but keep well if not allowed to freeze.

Lift roots grown for storage by October, after they have matured fully, but before a hard freeze. Lift longer varieties with a fork; take care not to bruise roots. Cut off the tops, leaving an inch of stem on the root to prevent bleeding.

In the Kitchen

Fresh: beet greens (leaves) are sweet, tender, more nutritious than spinach and very rich in iron and minerals. Use the leaf, cutting away the fibrous, tough stem. Steam 5-8 minutes or boil 4-6 minutes - until tender.

Steam sliced roots 8-12 minutes or boil 6-8 minutes - until tender. Or simmer garden-fresh onion, mustard and horseradish with whole "baby" or chopped beets in water until tender. Peel skin on larger roots before slicing or dicing if it is tough. White and golden varieties are mild in flavor, and do not bleed when cooked with other ingredients.

For less bleeding of medium and larger beets, wash and boil until tender whole beets. Add just enough water to cover the beets. Drain and cool long enough to handle beets. Skins slip off easily. Compost skins, slice, butter, and serve.

Storage: Store washed beets in plastic bag in the refrigerator for up to two weeks.

Lightly brush away the soil before storing; consume or compost damaged beets. Cut the tops off 2 inches above roots and pack in layers of dry peat or cool sand in a box and store in a cool basement or shed. The temperature should stay between 33-45° (1-7° C) for longest storage. They will keep for up to 6 months.

Freezing: Blanch (boil) greens and sliced beets 2 1/2 minutes or steam 3 minutes, dry, bag and freeze.

Pickling: Early Globe and Forono are the best varieties to pickle.

Varieties

Globe Varieties

Globe beets are by far the most popular for home gardeners. Both greens and roots are superb when garden-fresh. Globe varieties mature fast, reaching 2-4 inches across, and can be planted every 2-4 weeks for fresh produce from spring until the first hard frost of autumn.

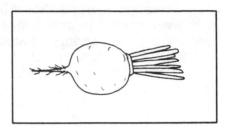

ALBINA VEREDUNA (Snowwhite) (60 days) is pure white flesh and thick skin, which makes it perfect for storing. A mild, sweet, rich flavor that may surpass red beets. Curled and wavy tops are delicate, tasty greens. Available (Cg, Te, Th).

DETROIT (50 days) varieties are a rich red and prized for their fast, compact growth; very sweet flavor and ease of cultivation. DETROIT LITTLE BALL is an excellent choice for early or late sowing and produces excellent *baby* beets for pickling. DETROIT DARK RED has sweet tops and roots. An all-round good performer in all climates. DETROIT SUPREME, an AAS winner, boasts a uniform shape and is an excellent choice for an end-of-season harvest. Available (Bu, Fa, Fi, Gc, Gs, Ha, Le, Ma, Pa, Pi, She, St, Te).

EARLY WONDER (50-55 days) types have excellent tops for steamed greens and produce tender, fine-grained roots. One of the most popular and probably the best all-round choice. Available (Bu, Cg, Fa, Fi, Hi, Ma, Me, Pi, Pl, Te).

GOLDEN beets (76 days) are a beautiful golden orange throughout. The flesh is tender, sweet, and mild tasting whether it's young or fully mature. Tops are delicious steamed. Does not "bleed" in soups, salads, or stir-fry. Sow thicker than red varieties; goldens have a lower germination rate. Available (Cg, Fi, Gc, Hi, Ma, Ni, Pi, She, So).

MONOPOLY (55 days) developed by the Dutch, sprouts only one plant per seed. All other beet "seeds" contain clusters of 4 or 5 sprouts. This breakthrough saves thinning. Leafy tops, sweet flavor, long-keeping and speedy growth make this a fine choice for any need. Available (Th, She)

Cylindrical Varieties

Although cylindrical beets are available in fewer varieties, uniformity makes them a prime choice for decorating salads, and for preserving. They grow up to 8 inches long and about 2 inches wide.

CYLANDRA (58 days) has an oval shape, with deep red flesh. It's very popular for its long keeping ability and fast, consistent growth. Available Bu, Fa, Fi, Gc, Ha, Ju, Ma, Pa, Pi, Th).

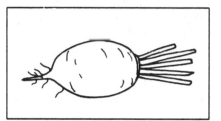

FORONO (70 days), a high yielder, is super sweet, with ruby-red flesh. Excellent fresh or preserved in canning jars. The tops make very tasty greens. Available (Te).

Conical or Tapered Varieties

This group takes longer to mature. The larger roots and greens are normally harvested at the end of the growing season, and stored for later use in the winter.

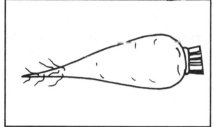

LUTZ GREEN LEAF (Winter Keeper) (60 days) has glossy green tops and white stems. The leaves are the most succulent and flavorful of all beet greens. Large, dark, red, fleshy root is very sweet. Available (Bu, Gc, Gs, Hi, Le, Ni, Pa, Pi, Te, So).

Problems

Beets are remarkably easy to grow and are normally trouble free. The leaves may discolor and have unsightly irregular spots from their extreme sensitivity to trace element deficiencies (boron). Even though the leaves demonstrate mineral deficiencies, roots are seldom affected. After beets hold in the garden a few weeks, the skin becomes tough. This skin helps deter pests and disease. Peel the skin off before preparing.

BEETS	SYMPTOM	PROVABLE CAUSES
Seedlings	eaten	13, 14
	falling over	14
Leaves	holes, chewed	3, 8, 9, 10, 11, 13
	swollen veins, cupped	1
	rolled leaves	2
	spots	5
Plants	premature seeds form	7
Roots	small & tough	Lack water or fertilizer
	large & tough skin	belated harvesting
	tunneled	4
	rotten	4
	hairy & poorly formed	7
	split	15

1. Beet leafhopper, called whitefly in the West, transports the viral curly top disease (see "Melons" page 100) to beets and numerous other flowers and vegetables. The insect is 1/8-inch long with a green to yellow wedge-shaped body and wings. Common west from Missouri, it infests crops from May through June, spreading curly top disease. This lone vector carries the disease that causes bulging veins in rolled or cupped leaves that become brittle. Stunted growth and death are common in the advanced stages of curly top.

Control: Remove and "hot" compost affected plants.

Prevention: Plant resistant varieties. Spray leafhoppers with insecticidal soap. Introduce lacewing larvae that feed on beet leafhopper nymphs. Remove weeds. Fall cleanup.

2. Beet webworms are found in all 50 states, and are most destructive in the West. They can be yellow, green or black, with a black

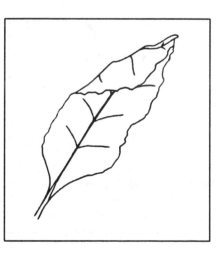

stripe down the back and various dark spots. The pests fold themselves into an envelope of leaves after feeding on foliage.

Control: Hand-pick and smash; spray with sabadilla or pyrethrum.

Prevention: Keep a wary eye peeled for the pest and control at first sight.

3. Black blister beetles, also known as old-fashioned potato bugs, or Yankee bugs, grow to 3/4-inch long with a dark, slender, winged body. They normally feed on foliage in swarms that attack numerous plants.

Control: Hand-pick, but use gloves, they discharge a *skin blistering* fluid. Spray with sabadilla.

Prevention: Luck!

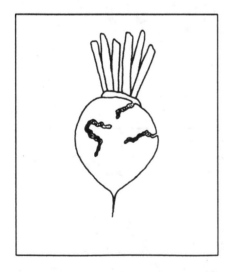

4. Carrot weevils produce dingy white, legless 1/3-inch-long grubs that tunnel into root crops, causing stunted top growth and rotten roots. The dark, copper colored, 1/4-inch

beetle winters over in weeds or debris around the garden, depositing grubs in the soil about May.

Control: Cultivate soil to expose grubs to elements. Apply rotenone on infestations.

Prevention: Cover plantings of root crops with spun fiber row covers to exclude beetles. Fall cleanup and soil tillage. Crop rotation with non root crops.

5. Root knot nematodes are minute wormlike pests that burrow into roots, causing and internal as well as damage. Fungus (rot) may start to grow in the damaged areas.

Control: Remove and eat roots, trimming off damaged areas. Sprinkle diatomaceous earth around roots.

Prevention: Rotate beets with alfalfa, corn or soybeans which do not attract nematodes.

6. Leaf spot, a soil-borne fungal disease, causes small brown spots on leaves and stems. Heavily infected foliage dries out and dies. The fungus overwinters in soil on infected plant tissue.

Control: Remove and destroy plants.

Prevention: Deep tillage, fall cleanup, and 3-year crop rotation.

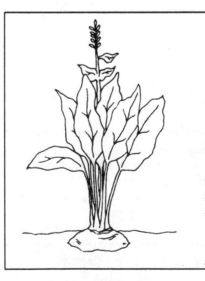

7. Bolting, running to seed prematurely, is usually caused by dry soil, or a lack of humus in the soil. It

also occurs if seeds are sown too early, experiencing hot weather after a cold snap, or if seedlings are overcrowded.

Control: Keep soil evenly moist, and mulch.

Prevention: Grow bolt-resistant varieties, such as Bolthardy, available (She).

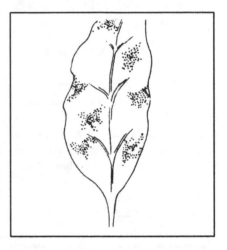

8. Boron deficiency is quite common in beets. Irregular spots form on leaves, that later dry and die back. The roots are not affected and remain good to eat.

Control: None

Prevention: Add kelp meal along with supplemental feeding and when preparing the soil.

9. Poorly formed or "hairy" roots are the result of adding too much fresh, rich manure or compost shortly before planting, or growing in rocky or heavy clay soil.

Prevention: Cultivate soil and prepare a fine seed bed. Add well-rotted organic matter and manure the year prior to planting.

Other pests that attack beets are:

10. Flea beetle: page 54
11. Garden springtail: page 106
12. Leafminers: page 128
13. Slugs & snails: page 55
14. Damping-off: page 61
15. Water stress: page 62, number 15.

Brassica Family

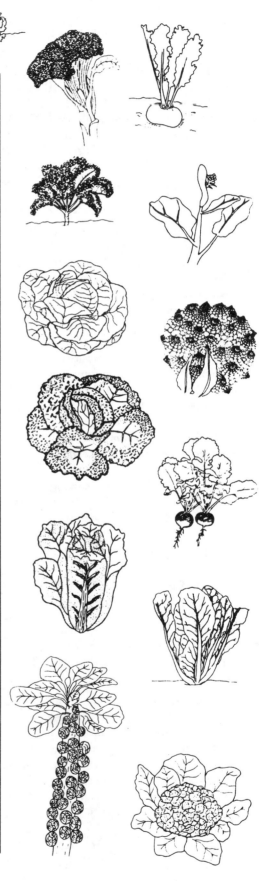

The brassica family includes broccoli, Brussels sprouts, cabbage, Chinese cabbage, bok choi, pak choi, cabbage, cauliflower, collards, kale, kohlrabi, mustard, radish, endive (rocket, roquette, rugola or arugula), rutabaga, and turnip. Some members of this family are very frost tolerant, and all are dependable producers during cool, damp weather. Growing brassicas during long, hot summers takes careful variety selection, regular watering, mulch, and a little shade. Also called cole crops (cole is the Old English word for cabbage), this family has one common trait: the genetic potential to thicken various parts. Radishes, rutabagas and turnips produce thickened roots; Brussels sprouts, cabbage and endive have swollen leaf heads; broccoli and cauliflower yield immature swollen flowering branches; the stem of kohlrabi is swollen. The rest, collards, kale and mustard, have somewhat swollen leaves.

Brassicas are heavy feeders. They require large amounts of nitrogen, potassium and calcium, but relatively little phosphorus. Liming the soil with dolomite neutralizes the pH. It also adds necessary calcium; a calcium deficiency stunts growth and causes leaf fringes and internal darkening in cabbage and Brussels sprout heads.

Most brassicas adjust well to transplanting, but contrary to popular belief, transplanting is not necessary for broccoli, cabbages, cauliflowers and Brussels sprouts to set heads. With favorable weather, direct-seeded brassicas can be harvested only one or two weeks later than 6-week-old seedlings planted at the same time.

Brassicas are quite cold-hardy. Some of the late and overwintering varieties are extremely cold-hardy, able to withstand temperatures well below 15°. Young plants are not as cold tolerant as older ones. Sugars, along with other substances, dissolve within cells to form a substance similar to antifreeze. That is why Brussels sprouts and several varieties of cabbage taste sweeter after being nipped by frost. Gradually increasing cold weather also causes brassicas to pump water out of cells; when a hard freeze strikes, there is not enough water to expand and rupture cells, preventing damage. However, if weather freezes suddenly, frost damage will occur.

All but Chinese cabbage and radishes are biennials grown as annuals; therefore, most seed saving requires two years. Saving seed requires extra garden space and extra care because many brassicas will cross-pollinate one another. For this reason, most gardeners prefer to buy seed.

Broccoli (*Brassica oleracea*, Italica Group))

Broccoli is extremely nutritious, and if harvested regularly, many varieties will bear for over a month. This brassica produces best in cool climates. In hot weather, broccoli can bolt suddenly and be plagued with insect attacks. If seedlings are subjected to a sudden cold snap, the florets may "button" - form tiny, premature heads. The unopened flower shoots and stems (spears) are eaten in most varieties. If the buds pass their prime, somewhat bitter tasting yellow flowers sprout. Plant early or late in the season to avoid bolting and insect infestations. Chinese broccoli (broccoli raab) produces short, edible leafy tops with a mustardlike flavor. Broccoli grows well in containers. The silvery gray foliage is nice to look at, but difficult to keep looking nice.

Basic Facts

Germination time: 7-12 days.
Germination temperature: Minimum: 40° (5° C), Optimum: 80° (27° C), Maximum: 100° (38° C).
Approximate seeds per ounce: 8000.
Yield per plant: 1-2 pounds.
Life expectancy of stored seed: 4 years.
Estimated time between sowing and first picking: 9-12 weeks (summer and fall varieties) (overwintering) 30-45 weeks.
Intercrop: Flowers, most other vegetables, except brassicas.
Effort to cultivate: Easier than most brassicas if insects are kept under control.
Seed saving: Difficult; many brassicas readily cross and as a biennial, it must be grown for two years.

Climate

Annual in all zones. Grows best in cool weather (60-65° (16-18° C)). Needs full sun, tolerates some shade in warm weather. Temperatures below 50° (10° C) and above 80° (27° C) cause smaller heads to form. Broccoli likes sun but dislikes heat. Short-season types tolerate slightly below freezing temperatures, while overwintering varieties are quite cold hardy.

Soil Preparation

Must have nutrient-rich soil that drains well. This heavy feeder produces small, tough heads in poor soils. Add dolomite lime, which adds two important nutrients, calcium and magnesium, if the pH is below 6.5. Lower pH if over 7.5.
Prepare soil the previous fall or early spring adding a complete fertilizer, and kelp. Add lots of nitrogen-rich compost and manure for optimum growth.
Rake seed bed smooth, removing surface debris.

Planting

Do not plant broccoli where other brassicas grew the previous two years. See "Crop Rotation" page 18.
For an early crop, sow seed 1/2-inch deep in flats or small pots indoors, or in a cold frame 6-8 weeks *before* the last frost date. Harden-off seedlings in a cold frame or by setting outside for a few hours daily. Transplant when 3-6 inches tall on 12-inch centers after last frost. Set seedlings an inch or more deeper than they were in the seed bed. Pack soil *firmly* around roots before watering in.
Sow seed 1/2-inch deep directly into beds after last frost. Space seed on 1-inch centers in wide raised beds and thin to 12 inches apart when seedlings are 6 inches tall.

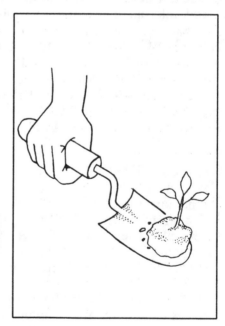

Direct seed overwintering varieties on 1 1/2-foot centers from July in the north to September in southern states. Heads must mature before frost.
Water seeds and seedlings regularly until established.

Cover seedlings with floating row cover to keep flea beetles and cabbage root maggots out. Apply a dusting of diatomaceous earth, sawdust or a mix of lime and wood ashes to discourage root maggots.

Plant 4-6 plants per person.

Crop Care

Weed seedlings by hand and hoe lightly if space allows. Early crops may need protection from birds.

Apply mulch after seedlings are 6 inches tall to check weed growth, cool soil, and retain moisture. Add more mulch as necessary.

Water regularly. Broccoli roots are shallow, and dry out easily. Wilting from water stress will stunt head formation and may cause bolting. Mulch helps retain moisture.

Watch closely for pests, and treat problems promptly. Pack soil around base of plant if it is loosened by wind.

Do not stimulate tender new growth on overwintering varieties by fertilizing late in the fall. The succulent growth is very susceptible to frost damage.

Fertilize every 2-4 weeks with manure tea or fish emulsion. Strong vegetative growth is essential for large heads to form later. Lack of food causes small or "button" heads.

Harvesting

Broccoli raab is ready to harvest first, and continues to produce for several months. The flavor is tangy, like broccoli with a hint of mustard. Harvest stems when they set small, unopened florets. Cut the 4- to 6-inch main stem first and harvest lower shoots and leaves regularly.

Harvest flower shoots (heads or spears) using a sharp knife or pruners when well formed but before they open. When flowering, the spears can become bitter and woody.

To harvest many small lateral florets, first cut the central spear high up on the stem when it is about 2 inches across. Harvest smaller side shoots and leaves regularly as they ripen. Do not strip all shoots until the last harvest.

Harvest nutrient-packed leaves to eat in salads or steam with greens. Spears are normally 4-6 inches long and harvest should continue for 5-6 weeks.

If heads flower, production will soon stop.

In the Kitchen

Note: The vitamin content of leaves is much higher than stalks or flower heads. Trim leaves and steam with other greens or add to fresh salads. The entire plant is rich in vitamins A and C, with some B vitamins, calcium and iron.

Fresh: Soak insect-infested tops in warm water for 15 minutes and flush with water. Cook young succulent broccoli in whole spears, splitting the bottom of the stock to ensure even cooking, or cut spears into bite-size pieces. Set, tops up, in a tall pan, containing 1/2 cup of boiling water, and cover. Use a steamer to cook smaller pieces. Steam 8-10 minutes, or until tender. Drain and serve with a butter or a white sauce.

Storage: Broccoli keeps for 3-4 days in a plastic bag in the refrigerator

Freezing: Steam blanch for 3-5 minutes, or boil blanch for 2-3 minutes, dry, place in a plastic bag, and freeze.

Varieties

Green Sprouting or Calabrese Varieties

GREEN COMET (58 days), the only broccoli to win an AAS gold metal, yields a 1-pound main head, and numerous side shoots after 2-3 months of growth. Cold tolerant, with uniform, tight, sweet heads. Available (Bu, Fi, Ha, Ju, Le, Ma, Pa, Pi, Sha, She, Te).

GREEN VALIANT (66 days) is slower growing but produces a huge, well-formed head, followed by a succession of large side shoots. Thin skinned, sweet and tender. Available (Jo, St).

PREMIUM CROP (60 days). This AAS winner, developed in Japan, matures quickly and tolerates warm weather. The single large head has a fine flavor and is good fresh or frozen. Available (Bu, Fa, Fi, Gc, Ha, Ju, Le, Ma, Pa, Th, Sha).

SHOGUN (75 days), developed for early fall planting and spring harvest is cold tolerant, but seeds won't germinate in cold weather. Produces a large flavorful head followed by smaller side shoots. Available (She, Te).

UMPQUA (80 days) is an exceptional open pollinated variety developed by Tim Peters from Territorial Seed Company. UMPQUA produces one large, dark green head with several small buds. Excellent flavor and grows very well in the cool, moist climate of the Maritime Northwest. Available (Te).

WALTHAM 29 (74 days) produces well in most regions of America, and makes an excellent winter crop in Southern California. Plant in the summer for a fall harvest of succulent 9-inch heads with few side shoots. Available (Gc, Gs, Le, Ma, Me).

Colored Varieties

PURPLE SPROUTING (220 days), hardy to 10° or less, is easier to grow than green sprouting varieties. Plant in early August or September for a Feburary-March harvest. Large yield of small, sweet heads. Available (Bg, Cg, Te).

WHITE SPROUTING (250 days) is planted in late summer to harvest after Purple Sprouting has finished the following spring. Containing some cauliflower genes, mild-flavored heads are creamy white. Available (Bg, Cg, Te, Th)

Specialty Varieties

ROMANESCO (80-100 days) broccoli from Italy yields one large bright chartreuse head containing small, conch-shell-shaped florets. Plant this long-season heirloom variety in early summer for a delicate, sweet, flavorful fall harvest. Available (Bg, Bu, Cg, Fi, Gs, Jo, She, Th)

BROCCOLI RAAB (Chinese broccoli) (60 days) soon yields numerous small florets and leaves. Harvest 4- to 6-inch tops throughout the growing season. The broccoli flavor with tangy mustard pungency is delightful. Available (Bu, Ha, Jo, Ni, Th).

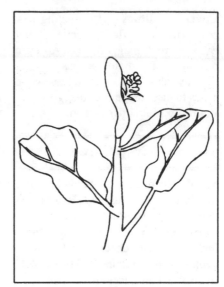

Brussels Sprouts (*Brassica oleracea*, Gemmifera Group)

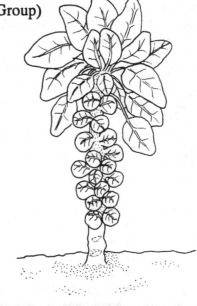

Brussels sprouts have an excellent, sweet flavor when grown, harvested, and cooked properly. Enjoy a long harvest from August through March by planting early and late varieties. The fresh, firm, tightly packed heads are sweeter and more tender after being nipped by frost. This brassica requires regular feeding and watering for strong growth through the summer. Use a low-nitrogen complete fertilizer mix. Too much nitrogen causes loose sprouts and lanky stems, which are less cold tolerant. The tips of stems are pinched off by commercial growers 3-5 weeks before harvesting so sprouts will fill the stem simultaneously. Some gardeners remove healthy lower leaves as they harvest sprouts so more light will help swell sprouts, while others retain leaves to help shed rain from sprouts.

Basic Facts

Germination time: 7-12 days.
Germination temperature: Minimum: 40° (5° C), Optimum: 80° (27° C), Maximum: 90° (32° C).
Approximate seeds per ounce: 8000.
Yield per plant: 50-100 sprouts.
Life expectancy of stored seed: 4 years.

Estimated time between sowing and first picking: 12-15 weeks (early varieties), 15-18 weeks (late varieties).
Intercrop: Flowers, most other vegetables, except brassicas.
Effort to cultivate: Fairly easy if you follow basic brassica growing rules and keep abreast of pests.
Seed saving: Difficult, many brassicas readily cross and as a biennial, it must be grown for two years.

Climate

Annual in all zones. Grows best in cool weather (60-65° (16-18° C)). Needs full sun, but tolerates some shade in warm weather. Brussels sprouts like sun but loathe heat. Growth is curtailed when temperatures climb beyond 85° (29° C). Short-season types tolerate freezing temperatures, while long-season varieties are quite cold hardy.

Soil Preparation

Must have nutrient-rich soil, but tolerates well-drained heavy clay. Heavy feeder, and produces small, loose sprouts in poor soils. Lime soil if the pH is below 6.5. Lower pH if over 7.5.

Prepare soil the previous fall or early spring, adding a complete fertilizer that is high in phosphorus and potassium; rock phosphate and fine granite dust are good fertilizer ingredients. Add compost and manure for vigorous growth.

Rake seed bed smooth, removing surface debris.

Planting

Do not plant Brussels sprouts where other brassicas grew the previous two years. See "Crop Rotation", page 18.

Sow early variety seed 1/2-inch deep in flats or small pots indoors, or in a cold frame 6-8 weeks *before* the last average frost.

Harden-off seedlings in a cold frame, or by setting outside for a few hours daily. Transplant when 3-6 inches tall on 2-foot centers after the last frost. Set seedlings an inch or more deeper than they were in seed bed. Pack soil *firmly* around roots before watering-in.

Sow seed 1/2-inch deep directly into beds. Sow early varieties from April through July. Sow late varieties in June or July. Space seed on 3-inch centers in wide raised beds and thin to 24 inches apart when 6 inches tall.

Water seeds and seedlings regularly until established.

Cover seedlings with a floating row cover to keep flea beetles and cabbage root maggots out. Apply a dusting of diatomaceous earth, sawdust or a mix of lime and wood ashes to discourage root maggots.

Plant about 3-5 plants per person for an abundant supply of Brussels sprouts.

Crop Care

Weed seedlings by hand, and hoe lightly if space allows. Early crops may need protection from marauding birds.

Mulch after seedlings are 6 inches tall, apply mulch to check weed growth, cool soil, and retain moisture. Add more mulch as necessary.

Water deeply as needed. Wilting from water stress will stunt sprout formation.

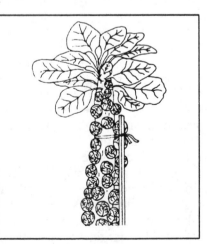

Fertilize with manure or compost tea every 2-4 weeks. Include some seaweed or kelp meal in the tea.

Watch closely for pests, and treat problems promptly. Pack soil around the base of plants if they are loosened by wind.

Stake tall plants if necessary, especially in sandy soils.

Do not stimulate tender new growth on overwintering varieties by fertilizing late in the fall. The succulent growth is very susceptible to frost damage.

In cold climates, where the temperature dips below 15° regularly, protect Brussels sprouts by bending the stock parallel to the ground and covering it with a thick mulch of (oak) leaves. To harvest, lift the mulch and pick sprouts as needed.

Harvesting

Harvest heads (buttons) as needed, starting from the base of the stock and progressing upward, when they are walnut sized, firm and tightly closed.

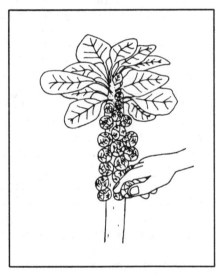

Use a sharp knife, or snap them off with in a quick downward motion.

Remove a few sprouts from each stem at each harvest, working up the stem. Remove and compost discolored bottom leaves and loose heads. The harvest should last for about two months.

After harvesting all the heads, uproot the stalk. Pound the tough woody stalk with a hammer to splinter and bruise or chip before tossing it on to the compost heap.

In the Kitchen

Note: This vegetable contains large amounts of vitamins A, C, B$_1$, B$_2$; and calcium, potassium, and iron.

Fresh: Soak in cold water (lightly salted) for ten minutes. Remove any loose outer leaves. Cut an "X" in the base of each sprout to ensure even cooking. Remember, sprouts are sweeter after being *nipped by frost* (see "Brassicas", page 41). If sprouts have not experienced a freeze, they might taste bitter. Steam for 10 minutes or drop into boiling water for 8 minutes - until tender. Or pressure cook at 15 lbs. for 3-4 minutes. Serve with butter, white, or cheese sauce.

Storage: Brussels sprouts keep for 2-3 weeks in a plastic bag in the refrigerator.

Freezing: After washing, cut an "X" in the base, boil blanch for 3-4 minutes, or steam for 3-5 minutes, dry, put in a plastic bag, and freeze.

Note: Brussels sprouts will grow through all but the coldest winters, and keep well in the garden.

Varieties

Early Varieties

Early varieties are generally short, with sprouts forming close together along thick stems. They start forming buds after they have reached a predetermined height, or after growing for a certain time. When sown earlier, they will mature earlier.

JADE CROSS (100 days), a popular early maturing hybrid, is heat tolerant. It produces medium round to oval sprouts on a 2 1/2-foot stem. Outstanding sweet flavor, and freezes well. Available (Bu, Fi, Jo, Ju, Le, Ma, St).

LONG ISLAND IMPROVED (Catskill) (108 days) is an old-timer that produces large, closely packed sprouts on a compact stem. Excellent variety for sustained production. Available (Gs, Ha, Le, Ma, Me, Ni, Sc, St).

OLIVER HYBRID (90 days) yields large, tight, flavorful sprouts on a sturdy, compact 2-foot bush. Extra-early variety that grows well in diverse climates. Available (Bu, Ha, Jo).

Late Varieties

Later varieties grow taller, with more distance between sprouts, and fall rains tend to rot them less frequently. Bud formation is triggered by longer nights and shorter days in the fall. If sown too late, they will be short and produce few sprouts.

ARIES (110 days) is bred for extreme-cold hardiness. Medium-sized sprouts are abundant, but tough and mediocre in flavor. It's the best variety for long, cold winters. Available (Te).

RUBINE RED (100 days) produces deep red, petite, round, flavor-packed sprouts on a tall stalk. Good producer. Sprouts retain their color after cooking and do not bleed. Available (Cg, Fi, Ha, Ni, Pa, Pi).

VALIANT (110 days) yields an abundance of large, rich-flavored sprouts on a tall vigorous stalk. Very frost tolerant, burst and rot resistant. Direct seed in midsummer for a long winter harvest. Available (She, St).

Cabbage (*Brassica oleracea*, Capitata Group)

Cabbage tastes great both garden fresh or lightly steamed. Long past are the days of eating limp, over-boiled cabbage with the life cooked out of it. The garden fresh cabbage harvest can last nearly all year round by picking the proper varieties and planting at the right time. Late-season varieties take up quite a bit of space, while early-maturing types require less room and can be spaced closer. Small-headed early varieties are normally best when eaten fresh, while larger types make good kraut or slaw. Chinese cabbage (*B. rapa*, Chinensis Group), including Bok Choi and Pak Choi, is rapidly gaining popularity because it is very quick to mature, and has an exotic flavor. Like most other cole crops, cabbage is a heavy feeder, with a shallow root system, requiring plenty of fertilizer and regular watering to form robust, tender heads. A covering of mulch helps retain moisture during dry weather.

Basic Facts

Germination time: 7-12 days.
Germination temperature: Minimum: 40° (5° C), Optimum: 85° (29° C), Maximum: 100° (38° C).
Approximate seeds per ounce: 7500.
Yield per plant: 1-5 pounds.
Life expectancy of stored seed: 4 years.
Estimated time between sowing and first picking: 9-12 weeks (early varieties), 11-12 weeks (mid season varieties) 14-20 weeks (late season), 7-9 weeks (Chinese).
Intercrop: Flowers, most other vegetables, except brassicas.
Effort to cultivate: Fairly easy if you follow basic brassica growing rules and keep abreast of pests.
Seed saving: Difficult, many brassicas readily cross, and as a biennial, it is normally grown for two years to produce seed..

Climate

Annual in all zones. Grows best in cool weather (60-75° (16-24° C)). Needs full sun, tolerates some shade in warm weather. Heads may split in hot heather. Immediately harvest heads that show signs of splitting.
Cold weather promotes a sweeter harvest. More sugar is drawn into leaves to protect possible freeze damage.

Soil Preparation

Cabbage is a *heavy* feeder, and must have nutrient-rich soil that drains well for the best crop. Lime soil in the fall or early spring if the pH is below 6.5. Lower pH if it is over 7.5. Lime also adds necessary calcium.
Prepare soil the previous fall or early spring, adding a complete fertilizer. Add compost and manure about a month before planting.
Rake seed bed smooth, removing surface debris.

Planting

Do not plant cabbage where other brassicas grew the previous two years. See "Crop Rotation" page 18.
Sow early variety seed 1/2-inch deep in flats, in small pots indoors, or in a cold frame 6-8 weeks *before* the last average frost.
Harden-off seedlings in a cold frame, or by setting outside for a few hours daily. Transplant when 3-6 inches tall on 12-inch centers for compact varieties and 18-inch centers for larger varieties, after last frost. Pack soil *firmly* around roots before watering-in.
Sow seed 1/2-inch deep directly into beds. Sow early and mid season varieties from April through July. Sow late varieties in June or July. Space seed on 3-inch centers in wide raised beds and thin to 12-24 inches apart, depending on variety, when 3-6 inches tall.
Water seeds and seedlings regularly until established.

Cover seedlings with a floating row cover to keep flea beetles and cabbage root maggots out. Apply a dusting of diatomaceous earth, sawdust or a mix of lime and wood ashes to discourage root maggots.
Chinese cabbage requires a little different planting and care. See "Chinese Varieties" below.

Crop Care

Weed seedlings by hand, and hoe lightly if space allows. May need protection from flea beetles and cabbage maggots. Use a floating row cover to exclude these pests.
Mulch after seedlings are 6-8 inches tall, apply mulch to check weed growth, cool soil and retain moisture. Add more mulch as necessary.
Regular surface watering is necessary for shallow-rooted cabbage. Wilting from water stress will stunt head formation. Mulch helps retain surface moisture. Fertilize with manure tea or fish emulsion every 2-4 weeks.
Watch closely for pests and treat problems promptly. Pack soil around base of plant if it is loosened by wind.
Do not stimulate tender new growth on overwintering varieties by fertilizing late in the fall. The succulent growth is very susceptible to frost damage.

Harvesting

Thin small, immature cabbages and cook as greens or use in a salad.
Harvest firm heads as needed knife by cutting them off at the base with a sharp knife. Cut an "X" 1/2-inch deep in the harvested stump; with luck, a secondary crop of smaller cabbages will sprout. Remove all but one of these newly formed heads. The second head is smaller but just as flavorful as the first.

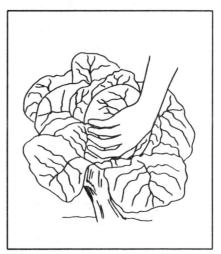

If too many cabbages become ripe at once, give mature plants a twist to split the stem. This will stop further development. Hot weather, and waiting too long after heads mature to harvest, promotes splitting. Harvest at first sign of splitting.

In the Kitchen

Fresh: Rich in vitamin C, cabbage tastes superb, fresh or cooked. To cook, peel away tough outer leaves, slam the base down hard against a strong counter top and remove the core. Cut the head into quarters. Steam for 10-20 minutes, or boil slowly for 5-10 minutes until tender-crisp. Savoy types take about 5 minutes longer. Or pressure cook at 15 lbs. for 3-5 minutes. Cooked leaves should be tender but retain crispness. Leaves can also be stir-fried or stuffed. Serve with butter or white sauce.

Kraut: Fresh kraut that does not have time to sour is delicious. Make in small quantities as needed throughout the year. When made without salt, kraut is very nutritious. Adding salt just wilts leaves to release water. The same result is accomplished by pounding the cabbage in a large plastic bucket before crocking.

Storage: Heads hold well for two weeks or longer under refrigeration, wrapped in a plastic bag. Wedges or slices can be cut from the head and cooked as needed.

Freezing: After washing, cut an "X" in the base, boil-blanch for 3-4 minutes or steam for 3-5 minutes, dry, put in a plastic bag, and freeze.

Note: Many cabbage varieties will grow through all but the coldest winters and keep well in the garden.

Varieties

Early Varieties

Smaller growing early varieties form a pointed head quickly and are bred for eating garden-fresh. Direct seed or transplant seedlings in spring for an early summer harvest. These types require the best soil, and need more insect protection. Space from 12-18 inches apart.

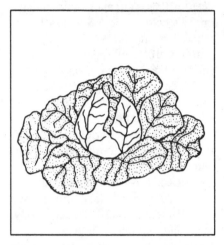

EARLY JERSEY WAKEFIELD (64 days) has a pointed head full of dark, waxy, green, compact leaves. Weighing in at 2-3 pounds, it offers rich flavor and holds well without splitting. Available (Bu, Cg, Fa, Fi, Gc, Gs, Ha, Jo, Ju, Ma, Me, Ni, So)

GOLDEN ACRE (73 days) types, including **PRINCESS** and **DERBY DAY** are a couple of the best varieties available, are a good space saver. They form firm, uniform, compact 3-4 pound heads on a small, short-stemmed plant. Resistant to many diseases. Plant for eating garden fresh. Mild and very sweet. Available (Fi, Gc, Ju, Ma, Me, So, St, Te).

GRENADIER (63 days) a Dutch hybrid, tastes superb fresh. Juicy, delicate, sweet leaves packed in small, dense, medium green heads that weigh about 2 pounds. Crack resistant and holds in the garden well. Available (St).

STONEHEAD (55-65 days), an AAS winner, yields stony firm, uniform, 3-pound, round heads with short cores on compact, space-saving plants. Good for kraut, but occasionally tough when eaten fresh. Resistant to cracking and yellows. Available (Bu, Fa, Fi, Ju, Le, Ma, Ni, Pi, St, Th, Sha).

Mid season Varieties

Mid season varieties are larger than early varieties, taking a bit longer to head up. Direct seed or transplant seedlings from early spring to midsummer. Mid season varieties are excellent fresh, cooked or stored.

COPENHAGEN MARKET (72 days) yields solid, round heads weighing about 4 pounds. Good tasting fresh or steamed. Holds in the garden and stores well. Available (Bu, Fi, Ma, Me, St).

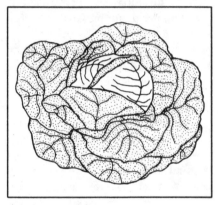

EMERALD CROSS (68 days) produces 7-inch heads on compact plants. Exterior leaves are bluish, and the interior blanched. Good flavor. Available (Bu, Fi, Ma).

TROPIC GIANT (75 days) produces large, round heads tipping the scales at 10-15 pounds. Available (Pa).

Late (winter) Varieties

These late-maturing varieties are grown during cool summers for a post-freeze harvest, or planted in mid to late summer for a winter or early spring harvest. Many are excellent fresh, and all make excellent kraut or slaw.

ATRIA (95 days) matures 6- to 8-pound round heads soon after mid season varieties. Tolerant to the

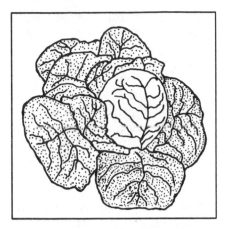

fungal disease yellows and lower fertility soils, Atria has good flavor, and stores well. Available (Jo, St).

DANISH BALLHEAD (100-125 days) types yield 6-8 pound, light green, mild, tender heads for cooking, kraut or slaw. Holds well into late fall. Available (Fa, Fi, Gc, Gs, Ju, Le, Ma, Te).

JANUARY KING (160-210 days) is a very cold hardy, producing 3-to 5-pound, light green, flattened heads on compact, purplish plants. Holds well through the winter. Available (Ni, Te, Th).

LATE FLAT DUTCH (100 days) grows vigorously to yield huge 20-30 pound crisp, tender, pale green heads. This cabbage lover's dream stores well after fall harvest. Available (Fa, Le, So).

Red Varieties

Red cabbages add splendid color to gardens and dinner plates. Depending on variety, they can ripen early to mid season. All are delightful additions to salads, eaten steamed in wedges, or stored to eat later.

LASSO (70 days) heads up early into a solid, compact, red ball weighing 2- to 4-pounds. It has few outer leaves, and stands in the field without splitting. Excellent in fresh salads. Stores well. Available (Gc, Gs, Jo).

RED ACRE (76 days) adds vibrant red to tossed salads. Compact mid season plants produce sweet, 2- to 4-pound heads that rarely crack when held in the garden. Available (Bu, Fa, Fi, Sc, So).

RUBY PERFECTION (86 days) is an excellent mid season choice. Bright, purple-red, uniform, 3- to 4-pound heads hold well, and taste swell. Available (Bu, Ju, St, Sha).

SCARLET O'HARA (72 days) a flashy red head, grows vigorously into an early-maturing 2- to 3-pound round sphere. The crunchy, mild flavor holds well in the garden or refrigerator. Available (Bu).

Savoy Varieties

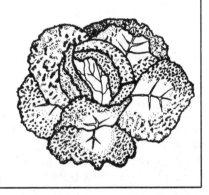

Savoy varieties are distinguished by their crinkly, puckered leaves. Developed from stock growing during the Middle Ages in northern Europe, the strong-tasting heads are surrounded by broad, fanning leaves. Maturing from early to late season, savoys are vigorous growers that taste best after a frost.

BLUE MAX (78 days) one of the earliest savoys, matures 2- to 4-pound, lime green heads. Excellent flavor after nipped by frost. Available (Jo, Gc, Hi).

ACE (90 days) an AAS winner, is both heat and frost tolerant. Compact 4- to 5-pound heads hold well for an extended harvest. Available (Bu, Ha, Ju).

SAVONARCH (Savoy Monarch) (110 days) grows vigorously to form light green, dense, uniform 7- to 10-pound heads. Great taste; a good late season variety, and holds well. Available (Te).

SAVOY KING (75 days) matures into uniform, 4- to 5-pound globe-shaped heads. Early to mid season, this AAS winner is good fresh and makes excellent slaw. Available (Fa, Ma, Ni, Pa, Th, Sha).

WALKING STICK GIANT CABBAGE (*Brassica oleracea longata*) Sow seeds just after first frost to harvest a 5-7-foot tall trunk that can be dried and used for a walking stick. It will grow to over 12 feet if left in the ground for two years!

Chinese Varieties

CHINESE CABBAGE (*Brassica rapa*, Chinensis Group) is growing rapidly in popularity because of its sweet taste and fast-growth habits. Heads mature in two months or less, but tend to bolt if planted late in the spring or summer when days are long, or daylight hours are increasing. It must be grown very rapidly, preferably in early summer or late summer to early fall, for heads to form without bolting. Seeds germinate well and plants require 18-inch spacing with *no crowding*. It's a heavy feeder that requires regular watering of the surface-feeding roots. Harvest as soon as heads fill out firmly.

MICHILI VARIETIES: GREEN ROCKET HYBRID is very early, producing uniform, sweet, crisp, cylindrical 4-5 pound heads. The JADE PAGODA HYBRID is vigorous and early maturing with mild, sweet leaves and a crinkly, creamy center. Available (Cg, Ma, Ha, Le, Pa, St).

NAPA VARIETIES: NERVA is super early and resistant to bolting. Dense rectangular heads are packed with thick, crisp, juicy leaves. CHINA EXPRESS heads up uniformly with mild, sweet, tender leaves. Barrel-shaped heads weigh in at 5-7 pounds. Available (Jo, Sc, Te).

BOK CHOI & PAK CHOI (45-55 days) sometimes listed as Chinese broccoli, Bok choi and Pak choi are members of the brassica family. Bok choi found in the supermarket is generally overgrown and tough. Homegrown

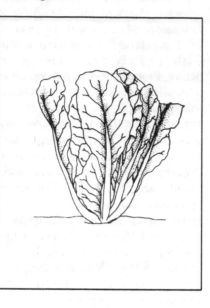

pak choi should be harvested when stalks are still young and succulent. Large plants become tough and fibrous after growing your own, you will never want to eat commercial Bok choi again. Bok choi has white stems with green leaves and Pak choi has green stems with green leaves. Both taste differently, bot both share the taste of minty licorice. The taste is superb raw, stir fried or steamed.

Bok choi and pak choi grow best when planted as a late summer or fall crop. Some varieties tend to bolt if they experience long cool days and nights followed by warm weather.

Grow this crop as fast as possible for the most succulent leaves and stems.

Cauliflower (*Brassica oleracea*, Botrytis Group)

Cauliflower is the fussiest member of the cabbage family, but the added cultivation difficulty is more than repaid with sweet, tender, creamy white curds. The soil must be deep and rich; growth must be rapid, and this brassica must *never* suffer drought. Do not buy seedlings that are potbound. Transplant seedlings when 4-5 weeks old, or growth will be checked. Seeds can also be sown directly in garden beds after last frost. If you don't provide these conditions, small "button" heads will result. However, heads can turn slightly pink or purple from stress and still taste good. Blanching, the practice of covering the head to shield sunshine to ensure tender head development, is customary. But self-blanching varieties (some taste a similar to broccoli) are easier to grow. With proper variety selection, the harvest can last up to 9 months, except during very cold winters or long, hot summers.

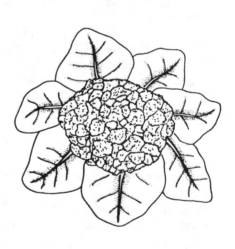

Basic Facts

Germination time: 7-12 days.
Germination temperature: Minimum: 40° (5° C), Optimum: 80° (27 C), Maximum: 100° (38° C).
Approximate seeds per ounce: 7500.

Yield per plant: 1-2 pounds.
Life expectancy of stored seed: 4 years.
Estimated time between sowing and first picking: 9-12 weeks (early varieties), 10-20 weeks (late season), 30-35 weeks (over-wintering).

Intercrop: Flowers, most other vegetables, except brassicas.
Effort to cultivate: Somewhat difficult, but easy if you follow basic brassica growing rules.
Seed saving: Difficult, many brassicas readily cross, and as a biennial, it must be grown for two years.

Climate

Annual in all zones. Seedlings produce larger heads if raised in 70° (21° C) weather. Temperatures below 60° (16° C) cause smaller heads to form. Older plants grow best in cool 60-65° (19° C) weather. Needs full sun but tolerates some shade in warm weather.

Soil Preparation

Cauliflower is a *very* heavy feeder and must have nutrient-rich soil that retains moisture but drains well. Lime soil the previous fall or early spring if the pH is below 6.5. Lower pH if over 7.5. Lime also adds necessary calcium.

Prepare soil the previous fall or early spring, adding a complete fertilizer, nitrogen-rich compost, and manure.

Rake seed bed smooth, removing surface debris.

Planting

Do not plant cauliflower where other brassicas grew the previous two years. See "Crop Rotation" page 18.

Sow early variety seed 1/2-inch deep in flats or small pots indoors, or in a cold frame 6-8 weeks *before* the last average frost. Harden-off seedlings in a cold frame or by setting outside for a few hours daily. Transplant when 4-5 weeks old, on 12-inch centers for compact varieties, and 18- to 24-inch centers for larger varieties, after last frost. *If seedlings are potbound, they will be stunted.* Pack soil *firmly* around roots before watering-in. Apply a dusting of diatomaceous earth, sawdust or a mix of lime and wood ashes to discourage root maggots.

Direct seed 1/2-inch deep. Sow early varieties from April through July. Sow late varieties in June or July. Space seed on 3-inch centers in wide raised beds and thin to 12-18 inches apart when 3-6 inches tall.

Water seeds and seedlings regularly until established. Mulch when seedlings are about 6 inches tall.

Cover seedlings with a floating row cover to keep flea beetles and cabbage root maggots out.

Plant about 4-6 plants per person.

Crop Care

Weed seedlings by hand and hoe lightly if space allows. After they are 6-8 inches tall, apply mulch to check weed growth, cool soil, and retain moisture. Add more mulch as necessary.

Regular surface watering is necessary for shallow-rooted cauliflower. Wilting from water stress, especially when young, causes "button" heads. Mulch helps retain moisture.

Fertilize the shallow root system with manure tea or fish emulsion every 2-4 weeks.

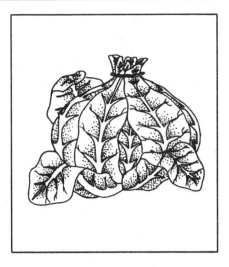

Blanching: When heads are about 2 inches wide, blanch by bending adjacent leaves to cover curd. Secure the leaves with twine or rubber bands. Watch closely for rot when heads are covered, especially during wet weather.

Self-blanching varieties need no special attention. Lots of sunshine causes heads to darken, but has little affect on taste.

Watch closely for pests, and treat problems promptly. Pack soil around base of plant if it is loosened by wind.

Do not stimulate tender new growth on overwintering varieties by fertilizing late in the fall. The succulent growth is very susceptible to frost damage.

Harvesting

Harvest compact heads as they begin to mature, until they become

ricey (curds separate) so you are not faced with an oversupply. Heads are substantially heavier
when harvested after curds are slightly separated. But if you wait too long, florets in curds become tough and bitter.

Use a sharp knife or pruners to cut heads off at the base.

If too many cauliflowers become ripe at once, give ripened plants a twist to break some of the roots to stop further maturation. Or store for up to 3 weeks by uprooting plant, shaking the soil off the roots and hanging upside-down in a cool basement or garage. Mist or dunk the plant in water every few days to keep curds fresh.

In the Kitchen

Fresh: Pare off any brown or discolored spots from curds. Cut off tough end of stem and soak in cold water (lightly salted) for 10 minutes. Cut garden-fresh florets into bite-size pieces and serve with a dip. Or steam for 10-12 minutes, or boil for 8-10 minutes - until tender. Or pressure cook at 15 lbs. for 3-4 minutes. Serve with butter, white, or cheese sauce. One medium to large head serves a family of four.

Storage: Cauliflower keeps for 3-4 days or longer in a plastic bag in the refrigerator.

Freezing: Steam blanch for 3-5 minutes, or boil blanch for 3-4 minutes, dry, place in a plastic bag, and freeze.

Varieties

Early Varieties

Transplant early varieties after first frost in spring, or direct seed in the garden in midsummer for a fall harvest.

RAKET (53 days) is a very early Dutch hybrid with robust, vigorous growth. Mild, sweet curds are reliable on this easy-to-grow variety. Available (She).

SNOWBALL (55 days) varieties are very popular and early maturing. Tight, compact heads average 2 pounds each. Choose from many reliable performers: **EARLY SNOWBALL**, **SNOW KING**, or the AAS winner **SNOW CROWN**, known for versatility and it's easy to grow. Available (Fa, Fi, Gs, Ju, Ni, Pa, Pi, Sc, So, Te, Th).

Late Varieties

RAVELLA (70 days) forms vigorous, snow-white heads that are well wrapped (self-blanching) to protect against frost and rain. Sow from March through June for a summer to fall harvest. Available (Pa, St).

WALCHERIN VARIETIES (210-270 days) including **ARMANDO APRIL**, **ARMANDO MAY**, **ARMANDO CLIO**, **ARMANDO TARDO**, and **PENNACLE** all originated in Holland. They will overwinter in climates that stay above 10°. Plant in midsummer for a concentrated early-to-late spring harvest of fine, sweet curds. Once you grow overwintering cauliflower, you will probably find space for it every year. Nothing beats having fresh cauliflower early in the spring. Available (Te).

Self-blanching Varieties

ANDES (68 days) performs well as an early summer or a fall crop. The heavy, well-domed curds are sweet and consistent. Leaves keep the head well-wrapped. Available (Jo, Hi, St, Th).

MONTANO (58 days) an early-maturing type, has tall wavy leaves that protect the succulent head, and resists purpling. Available (Jo)

WHITE ROCK (80-100 days) matures into sweet, compact, well-wrapped florets for good rain and frost protection. Transplant in June for a fall harvest. Available (She, St, Te).

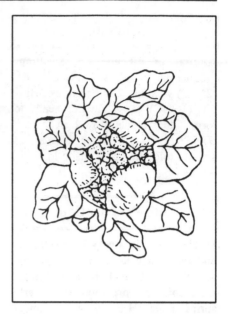

WHITE TOP (70 days) matures in mid season, yielding large, tasty, tight, firm, snow-white curds. A vigorous, sturdy grower. Available (St).

Colored Varieties

Colored varieties brighten dinner plates and salads. Purple cauliflower is actually a cauliflower-broccoli cross which is easier to grow than pure cauliflower. They do not wrap their heads with leaves, and can suffer frost damage once curds develop. Purple-head varieties have much lower pest and disease incidence than white types.

ALVERDA (64 days) is one of the increasingly popular green-headed varieties. Bright yellow green, medium-sized heads that are scrumptious raw or steamed. No blanching and easy to grow. Available (Jo).

PURPLE HEAD (56 days) varieties look like deep purple broccoli, with a similar flavor. These types are easier to grow than white types. Available (Bu, Ju, Pi)

ROYAL PURPLE (96 days) yields a compact 6-inch purple head that turn green when cooked. Very easy to cultivate. Good taste and freezes very well. Available (Fa).

Problems

Kale is the only member of the cabbage (brassica) family that is virtually trouble free. The others can fall victim to numerous pests and diseases. Most pests are relatively easy to control, and diseases are avoidable. Covering seedlings for the first month or two of growth with floating row covers will prevent cabbage fly root maggots, flea beetles and cabbage loppers from attacking. A three-year crop rotation plan is *extremely* helpful in preventing the accumulation of overwintering insects and diseases. The key is to pay attention and catch problems *before* they get out of hand. Strong healthy plants are the best form of problem prevention. Healthy plants usually grow faster than menacing problems. Brassicas are heavy feeders and need regular fertilizing with a complete mix. Make sure to read and follow the guidelines for each brassica to ensure high yields.

BRASSICAS	SYMPTOM	PROVABLE CAUSES
Seedlings	eaten	2, 4, 6, 10
	falling over	14
	numerous small holes	6
	cut off at soil line	4, 9
Stems	tunneled	3
	black near soil	14
	cut off at soil line	4, 9
Leaves	dark leaf edges	19
	distorted, curled	21
	white	18
	yellowing	13, 16
	yellow between veins	12, 20
	holes	2, 6, 8, 9
	aphid infestation	1
	caterpillars	2
	dark mold	1
	chewed, holes	22
	spots, cottony or dark	15
Roots	swollen, galls	13
	tunneled	3
Plants	wilts in hot sunshine	13
	wilting, dying	8, 11
Brussels spts.	small or loose heads	17, 19
Cabbage	no hearts	17, 19
	split hearts	lack of water
		sudden frost
Cauliflower	small heads	transplant too late
		lack of fertilizer
		lack of water
	brown heads	21

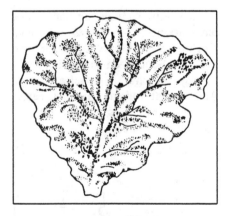

1. Aphids, about the size of a pinhead, are found on leaves, especially young succulent growth. This pest is a most serious problem as weather warms. The clusters of gray pests puncture soft foliage, feeding on plant fluids, and excrete a sticky honeydew that promotes sooty mold. Leaves yellow and tend to cup; growth is stunted.
Control: Smash aphids between fingers and blast off with a jet of water every 3-4 days. Spray with insecticidal soap, ryana, sabadilla, nicotine sulfate or pyrethrum.
Prevention: Ladybugs, lacewings and hover flies all prey on aphids. Cover plants with a spun fiber to exclude pests. Inspect weekly for aphids, and control as soon as possible.

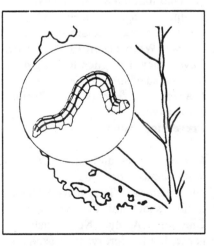

2. Cabbage loopers are pastel green to brownish-gray worms with vertical stripes and measure up to 1 1/2 inches long. They loop or double up as they crawl around riddling leaves with holes. The adult, a white mothlike butterfly, flutters from plant to plant depositing one egg at each stop.
Control: Hand-pick; spray infestations with insecticidal soap, lime spray; dust with *Bacillus thuringiensis* or as a last resort use rotenone.
Prevention: Install floating row covers. Encourage natural enemies: trichogramma wasps, birds, frogs and toads. If particularly bad in your area, apply *Bacillus thuringiensis* weekly as long as butterflies are about.

3. Cabbage fly root maggots are a major pest, cutting dingy channels and burrowing into the stems and roots. Legless 1/3-inch-long larvae are white. Infested crops slowly wilt and produce deformed or no heads.

Feeding wounds foster fungal diseases.

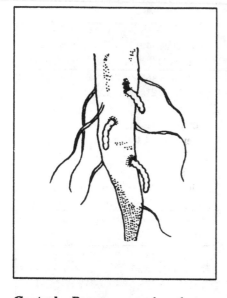

Control: Remove and destroy heavily infested plants.

Prevention: Cover young crops with floating row covers or a 2-inch plastic collar with a slit for the stem placed around the base of each plant to keep egg-laying, houseflylike adults out. Sprinkle diatomaceous earth, sawdust or a lime and wood ash mix around the base of plants.

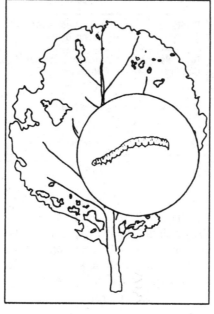

4. Cutworms are plump, gray, light green, or brown worms, smooth-skinned gray to brown (some have stripes or spots), 1/2 to 1 1/2 inches long, that live in the soil, and coil when disturbed. They feed on the base of a plant, cutting it off near soil level. Adults are night-flying moths.

Control: Sprinkle cornmeal, diatomaceous earth or *Bacillus thuringiensis* around the base of plants. Promptly search under the soil surface around the dead plant for the lingering pest, and destroy.

Prevention: Encircle plants with a stiff 3-inch-wide barrier of cardboard or plastic anchored an inch deep in the soil. Birds, firefly larvae, braconid wasps, Nc nematodes, tachinid flies, moles and toads are predators.

5. Diamondback moth larvae are 1/2-inch long, green-and-yellow caterpillars that eat small holes in leaves. When disturbed from under leaves, they may glide to the ground on a thread of silk.

Control: Apply *Bacillus thuringiensis.*

Prevention: None.

6. Flea beetles are dark, 1/16-inch-long beetles that bound like fleas when disturbed. They make hundreds of tiny "shot holes" in leaves.

Control: Apply Nc nematodes, garlic, hot pepper, ryana, sabadilla or rotenone sprays.

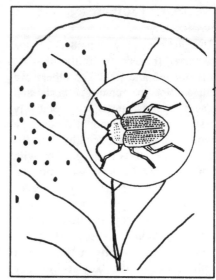

Prevention: Plant and harvest the crop in cool weather. Cultivate the soil frequently to destroy eggs, and clear weeds that provide a source of food. Set out small containers full of a half-and-half mix of lime and wood ash around plants. Or sprinkle small amounts of wood ash around plants several times a week.

7. Harlequin bugs are black with red markings. About 1/2-inch long, they're flat and easy to see. Worst in the South, an infestation can destroy an entire brassica crop. Adults eat foliage. Nymphs cause wilting, browning, and death by sucking plant juices.

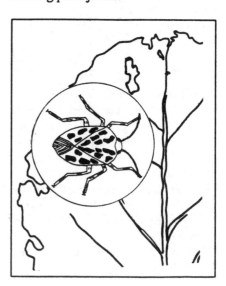

Control: Hand-pick, apply insecticidal soap, sabadilla, or pyrethrum sprays.

Prevention: Destroy small white columnar eggs that are neatly lined up in two rows on foliage. Keep a vigil for this pest. Fall cleanup and tillage.

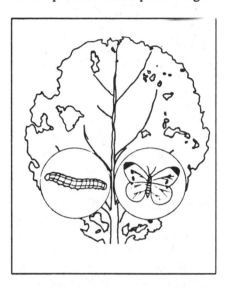

8. Imported cabbage worms chew ragged holes in leaves and burrow into cabbage heads. They are an inch or longer, pale green with short hairs and a yellow-green stripe running down its back. The adult is a pale white butterfly with black-spotted wings.

Control: Spray with insecticidal soap, a lime spray, or both. Use *Bacillus thuringiensis* on large infestations; as a last resort, use rotenone.

Prevention: Cover crop with a floating row cover to exclude egg-laying butterflies. Till soil in the fall. Interplant brassicas in the flower garden to make them difficult for butterflies to find. Braconid and trichogramma wasps are predators.

9. Mole crickets are a 1 1/4-inch-long pest that burrows into the soil to eat roots by day, surfacing at night to sever stems at the soil line, pulling the plant into its hole. Worst in the South during warm, moist weather.

Control: Insecticidal soap sprays or dust with sabadilla.

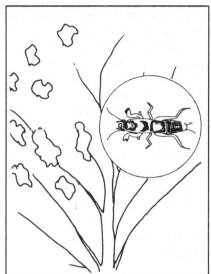

Prevention: Cover plants with a floating row cover. Many birds, insects, snakes, frogs and toads prey on this pest. Fall cleanup and tillage.

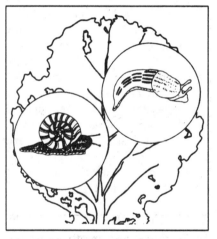

10. Slugs and snails can cause severe damage in wet weather. They slither from hiding places at night or on rainy days to eat foliage, leaving a silvery trail of slime. These pests prefer young succulent plants.

Control: Hand-pick. A thin layer of lime, diatomaceous earth or salty beach sand around individual plants, beds, or the entire garden, dissolves and repels mollusks. Or dust with dolomite lime or diatomaceous earth. Pour a jam-and-water mix into a small plastic bowl. Pests are attracted to the mix, enter, and drown. Spray slugs with a half-and-half mix of ammonia and water.

Prevention: Encourage natural predators: birds, frogs, toads, salamanders and small snakes.

11. Black leg causes small, dark spots, that continue to enlarge on foliage. Leaf edges wilt and discolor. The plant may wilt or fall over. The disease is transported in water.

Control: Remove and destroy infected plants.

Prevention: Use seed produced in arid Western regions, such as California. Keep garden free of debris. Do not work among wet plants. Surface irrigate rather than overhead sprinkle. Three-year crop rotation.

12. Black rot first causes yellow, triangular areas with darker veins on leaves. As the rot progresses, leaves wilt, and heads may fail to form or rot. This disease is carried by insects and water.

Control: Remove and destroy infected plants.

Prevention: Use seed produced in arid Western regions, such as California, where disease is very uncommon. Keep garden free of debris. Do not work among wet plants. Surface irrigate rather than overhead sprinkle. Three-year crop rotation.

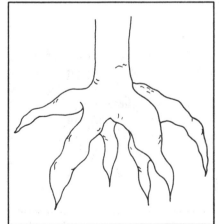

13. Clubfoot causes leaves to yellow, causing plants to wilt during hot days, and sometimes when the weather cools.

when weather cools. Plants become stunted, and die. Roots swell, become clublike, and eventually rot.
Control: Lift, burn or destroy infected plants. *Do not compost!*
Prevention: Three-year crop rotation and lime soil to raise pH to 7.2 to 7.5. Add compost and manure to improve drainage.

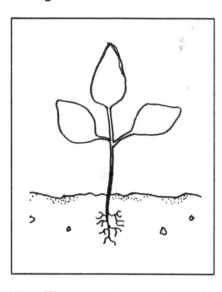

14. Wire stem, like damping-off, causes the stem of seedlings to blacken and shrink. Seedlings that don't die will be stunted for life and have stems that snap easily.
Control: Remove and destroy affected seedlings.
Prevention: Three-year crop rotation. Do not grow seedlings in wet, cold compost or soil. Avoid overcrowding.

15. Watery soft rot attacks many garden vegetables, stunting growth. Cottony white patches grow into black hard bodies, which fall to the ground and lay dormant until the following year.

Control: None. *Destroy infected plants immediately. Do not compost!*
Prevention: Destroy affected plants before cottony growth turns black. This keeps the fungus from wintering over in soil. Fall cleanup.

16. Yellows (fusarium or wilt) is a widespread warm-weather fungus, but inactive when the average soil temperature stays below 60° (19° C). Lower leaves turn yellow and brown before dropping. Plants and heads become stunted, but seldom rot.
Control: None. Remove and *destroy infected plants*.
Prevention: Plant disease-resistant varieties.

17. Small heads, open Brussels sprouts and heartless cabbages can be caused by too little fertilizer, and organic matter in soil. Before planting, use a complete fertilizer, not just a high-nitrogen mix, and lime soil with dolomite. Failure to pack soil firmly around seedlings may be the problem. Lack of water and sunlight are also likely causes. Water deeply during dry weather, and use plenty of mulch to conserve water. Insufficient hardening-off, and transplanting root-bound plants, causes small "button" cauliflower heads. See: "Hardening-off, page 5.

18. Whitened leaves are caused by frost. Once blanched by frost, leaves are soon attacked by fungus. Hardy brassicas can withstand frost after they are established. Seedlings or plants not well-anchored in the soil can be affected by frost and die. A sudden cold snap during normally warm weather will also cause frost damage.

Control: Remove affected leaves and "hot" compost.
Prevention: When transplanting, pack soil firmly around seedlings, and plant an inch below seed container soil level. Mulch to insulate roots. Keep well watered and fertilized.

19. Calcium deficiency symptoms include stunted growth and "burned" or dark leaf edges. Brussels sprouts and cabbage heads turn dark inside and are punky - not full.
Control: Apply a small dose of wood ash, or hydrated lime diluted in water.
Prevention: Add agricultural or dolomite lime to soil before planting.

20. A magnesium deficiency causes leaves to yellow between veins. Older growth is most affected.
Control: Foliar-feed with liquid seaweed.
Prevention: Incorporate plenty of compost into soil before planting. Add seaweed to the supplemental fertilizer mix.

21. A boron deficiency is signaled by small, bitter heads with brown patches on curds, and distorted leaves. Cauliflower is extremely sensitive to a short supply of boron.
Control: Foliar-feed with liquid seaweed.
Prevention: Incorporate plenty of compost into the soil before planting. Add seaweed to the supplemental fertilizer mix.

Other brassica pests may include:

22. Anthracnose: page 77
23. Vegetable weevil: page 60

The average garden contains 6,000 slugs! These members of the mollusk family consist of 90% moisture. Snails are similar to slugs except snails have an outer protective shell that lets them live in arid climates.

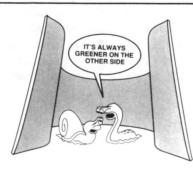

IT'S ALWAYS GREENER ON THE OTHER SIDE

The Slug & Snail DeFence provides a slug and snail barrier around garden beds. Hold the fence in place with soil or staple it to raised bed frames. The fence is made from 50% recycled plastic and 50% table salt. Slugs will not cross it!

Carrot *(Daucus carota var. sativus)*

After a long germination, up to 3 weeks in cool weather, tiny fernlike carrot greens pop through the soil. They prefer warm soil and ample water for quick growth to yield sweet, tender roots. The secret to growing this crop is deep soil preparation and rapid growth. The seed bed should be fine, and raked smooth. Seeds won't be able to push through a crusty, compacted surface. Some gardeners sow radishes along with carrots. The radishes germinate first to "break ground" for the carrots. Prepare the soil well, up to a foot deep, removing any stones or debris that will cause roots to fork. Carrots also grow well in a container full of loose potting soil. All of the soil preparation pays off; in deeply cultivated, fertile soil, carrots can grow so closely together that weeds have a hard time getting started. Young, sweet carrots are harvested first, making more room for their neighbors. The short varieties are the earliest, sweetest and easiest to grow. Intermediate sizes are good all-round varieties. When immature, they are sweet; when mature, they are still very tasty and store well. Long-rooted varieties are frequently more fibrous, but store well in the ground during winter.

Basic Facts

Germination time: 17-21 days.
Germination temperature: Minimum: 40° (5° C), Optimum: 80° (27° C), Maximum: 95° (35° C).
Approximate seeds per ounce: 20,000.
Yield per 4 X 4 raised bed: 10 pounds (early), 15-20 pounds (maincrop).
Yield per 10-foot row: 8 pounds (early), 12 pounds (maincrop).
Life expectancy of stored seed: 4 years.
Estimated time between sowing and first picking: 12 weeks (early), 16 weeks (late).
Intercrop: Flowers, most other vegetables, except brassicas.
Effort to cultivate: Easy if soil is properly prepared.
Seed saving: Readily crosses with wild carrots (Queen Anne's Lace) and other carrot varieties. Easier to buy seed.

Climate

Annual in all zones. Need full sun. Mature carrots are somewhat frost tolerant.

Soil Preparation

The ideal soil to grow long, straight carrots is slightly acidic, deep, fertile, sandy loam. If your soil is clayey or full of rocks, grow shorter varieties such as Chantenay or round-rooted types. Do not grow in soil full of rich compost and manure, or the roots will be very "hairy".
Cultivate the soil deeply, to a depth of one foot in the spring, adding peat moss and soft phosphate. Prepare a seed bed with fine, light topsoil before sowing. Deep, loose soil can double carrot yields.
Add (soft) rock phosphate, wood ash, and blood meal when preparing soil. Add dolomite lime if the pH is lower than 6.5.

Planting

To give seed a quick start in the spring, soak overnight in water, drain, and place them in the freezer for a week. Before freezing, dry the seeds out on a paper napkin or towel so they do not form clumps. Handle these tender seeds carefully while planting.
For the earliest harvest, sow short-rooted varieties under a plastic tunnel or in a cold frame 6-8 weeks before the last average frost.
For an early crop, sow short-rooted carrots in a sunny spot after last frost.
Intermediate- and long-rooted, late summer crops can be sown for a month or two after the last frost.
For a late fall and winter harvest sow short- and intermediate-rooted varieties in July through mid August.
Raised Beds: Broadcast tiny seeds evenly over the surface of raised beds. Mix seed with sand or well-rotted, sifted compost to distribute it

more evenly. Sprinkle a fine layer of peat or soil on top and lightly rake in. Seedlings can't break through crusty soil. Keep evenly moist until they sprout. A layer of newspaper or burlap on the soil's surface will help retain moisture. Remove the cover as soon as seeds sprout.

Rows: Sow seed 1/4-inch deep, 1/2-inch apart in rows spaced 4-6 inches apart. Keep moist until they sprout.

An alternative method is to sow carrots in clumps, thinning to 6-8 roots. The entire clump is dug at the same time so adjacent roots are not disturbed. This method also works well in containers.

Plant 20-50 carrots per person.

Crop Care

Thin seedlings after 6-8 weeks to 1- to 1 1/2-inch centers. Immature roots are succulent garden-fresh and tops add early flavor to salads and soups. Take care when thinning to not damage other roots. Firm soil around remaining plants. Thinned-out immature plants left by the planting patch, and bruised roots, attract destructive carrot flies and scavenger pests.

Deep-water regularly. Drought followed by moist soil conditions promotes splitting.

Weed young carrots by hand. Once tops grow tall enough to shade the ground, there will be little competition from weeds.

No supplemental fertilization is necessary in fertile ground. Apply a complete liquid fertilizer monthly in less fertile soil.

Mulch will check weed growth, conserve water, and keep exposed root "shoulders" from becoming green and bitter.

Harvesting

Harvest immature carrots as thinnings after 6-8 weeks of growth. Once the roots enlarge, carefully slip a fork or hand trowel alongside carrots to loosen moist soil.

To harvest maincrop carrots, use a fork to loosen moist soil before lifting roots. Damaged roots should be used quickly.

Cut the tops off an inch or two above the root to prevent nutrient loss; the root tries to supply the top with nutrients which dries out the root.

Leave fall and winter carrots, that are resistant to cracking, in the soil, and dig as needed. In cool climates, mulch the soil heavily with oak leaves or conifer needles to add a layer of protection (avoid straw mulch, which harbors mice). Roots will stay sweet, even after left in the ground when maturing. If the ground freezes, carrots will rot.

Harvest the crop if ground is likely to freeze and, follow the storage methods outlined below.

In the Kitchen

Carrots, like spinach, are more nutritious when cooked. Even though heating causes some nutrient loss, it makes nutrients more available for the body to absorb.

Fresh: Wash carrots in cold water, lightly scrubbing off tiny feeder roots. Unless badly scratched or deformed, refrain from peeling. Slice off the bitter tip and tops. Cook "baby" carrots whole; slice larger roots into uniform bite-size pieces that will cook faster and evenly. Steam for 10-15 minutes or add to boiling water,

then simmer for 10-12 minutes. Serve with butter, or add cooked carrots, butter, and honey or marmalade to a skillet and lightly saute-simmering until the carrots are well glazed. Or pressure cook whole carrots 4 minutes. Set 2 1/2 minutes if sliced. Carrots also make a wonderful and nutritious addition to stews, soups, or baked dishes.

Storage: Carrots keep for up to 14 days in a plastic bag in the refrigerator.

Store harvested carrots by cutting off tops 1/2-inch above the crowns. Let carrots set out in the air for a few hours before storing, to dry root hairs and induce dormancy. Do not wash carrots; the water could initiate new growth. Place the roots in layers between sand or dry peat in a box. Prevent rotting by keeping the carrots from touching. Store the box in a cool (35-45° (2-7° C)) basement or garage. Inspect periodically, and discard any rotten roots. They will keep until early spring.

Freezing: Slice or keep whole - blanch by steaming 3-5 minutes or boiling 4-6 minutes, dry, place in a zip-lock bag and freeze.

Note: Carrots keep very well in the ground when mulched to prevent freezing.

Juice: Carrot juice is very nutritious and delicious. Juicers on the market today cost much less than just a few years ago.

Note: The deeper the orange color, the higher the beta carotene and vitamin content. Medium and long varieties are packed with fiber.

Varieties

Short-rooted Varieties

Round or finger-sized, succulent, short-rooted varieties are the first sown and the first harvested. They are short in size but long on flavor. Sow every 2-3 weeks from early spring until June or July for a steady supply.

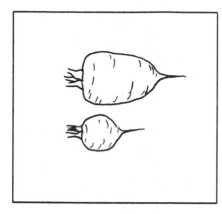

AMSTERDAM FORCING types produce small, early sweet roots. MINICOR yields, slender, blunt-tipped 6- to 7-inch succulent roots that are perfect to grow as "baby" carrots. BABY SPIKE. Roots mature early into slender, blunt-tipped 3- to 4-inch sweet, tender orange "baby" roots. Available (Cg, Fi, Jo, Hi, She, St).

CYLINDRICAL NANTES types, including BABY NANTES, have a high sugar content with little fiber. They are sweet and tender if harvested regularly. Available (Fi, St).

KUNDULUS (68 days) is fairly fast maturing, and grows well in heavy soils. Also grow this sweet, round carrot in containers or flats. Available (Pa, Th).

PARMEX (50 days) matures extra early into 1- to 1 1/2-inch round carrots. A good companion with garden-fresh peas. Sweet, mild roots grow very well in heavy soil. Available (Cg, Jo, Hi).

Medium-rooted Varieties

Sow these versatile varieties a couple of weeks after short varieties. Plant them in loose soil to promote long root development. Harvest when succulent and immature as thinnings, or uproot when mature to eat fresh, store, or juice.

DANVERS HALF LONG (75 days). A good choice for heavy soil, slightly tapered, 6- to 7-inch roots, and bright orange flesh. Good producer

for canning and storing. Sweet flavor, tender and crisp. Available (Bu, Fa, Fi, Gc, Gs, Le, Ma, Me, Pi, So).

NANTES HALF LONG (Scarlet) (70 days) is exceptionally popular among discriminating gardeners. The tender, crisp, sweetness is at it's peak when harvested young. Grows cylindrically, 6-7 inches long with the characteristic Nantes blunt tip and a very small core. Available (Bu, So).

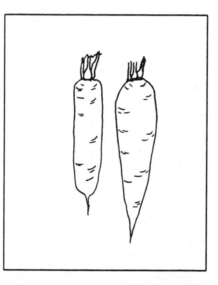

RED CORE CHANTENAY (65-70 days) is a favorite for flavor. The 4- to 5-inch, stocky roots with a blunt tip matures in mid season. Excellent fresh or cooked. Available (Bu, Fa, Fi, Ju, Ni, Pi, So, St).

ROYAL CHANTENAY (70 days) matures into a delicious, stump-shaped, 6- to 7-inch long carrot that is reddish-orange to the core. Available (Bu, Fi, Gc, Ha, Ma, Me, Pa, St, Te).

NANTES SLENDERO (70 days) matures into 6- to 9-inch-long, smooth, tender, juicy, and very sweet carrots. Holds well in the soil without splitting. Available (Te).

NANTES TIP-TOP (73 days) is a good all-round variety that matures early, stays slender and crisp after maturity. Excellent flavor. Available (She).

Long-rooted Varieties

These types are just a little longer than medium-rooted varieties, but more spectacular. They require a longer growing season, but are weighty and hold in unfrozen ground until needed.

A PLUS (72 days) a very popular variety, develops 8-inch-long roots containing a megadose of vitamin A. The deep orange color is the result of the high beta carotene content. Uniform growth and tasty. Available (Bu, Ha, Jo, Ju, Ni, Pa, Pi, St).

GOLD PAK types, such as NEW RED INTERMEDIATE and ST. VALLERY are somewhat scarce. They are the long, perfectly tapered, smooth-skinned varieties grown mainly for show. They require perfecting soil conditions for an impeccable root. Available (Bu, Fa, Fi, Ju, Sc, St).

KING MIDAS (65 days) an Imperator type, is packed full of flavor, size, and vigor. Relatively quick to mature 8- to 9-inch roots, are nearly coreless, deep orange in color, and fine-textured. Available (She).

SAVORY (68 days) is similar only in size and shape to its supermarket relative, IMPROVED IMPERATOR. Savory is very crisp and retains its sweet, rich flavor well in the field. Packed with vitamin A. Available (She).

Problems

Beets are remarkably easy to grow and are normally trouble free. The leaves may discolor with unsightly irregular spots from their extreme sensitivity to a lack of boron. Even though the leaves demonstrate mineral deficiencies, roots are seldom affected. After beets hold in the garden a few weeks, the skin becomes tough. The skin helps deter pests and disease. Peel the skin before preparing.

CARROTS	SYMPTOM	PROVABLE CAUSES
Seedlings	poor gemination	17
	falling over	20
Leaves	yellowing	1, 2, 6, 7
	yellow/red	4
	distorted	4
	holes, chewed	3, 5
	spots, yellow or greasy	8
Root	split	13
	forked or "hairy"	13
	tunneled	2, 6,
	rot	1, 7, 10
	small	11
	eaten	cutworm page 54 or slugs page 55
	galls or swelling	9

1. Carrot rust fly larvae (maggots) hatch from eggs deposited by the adult around the crown. The legless, 1/3-inch long, yellowish maggot cuts rusty tunnels in roots. Carrots and parsnips are stunted; tops yellow, and roots may develop soft-rot. Dry soil leads to the worst attacks.
Control: remove roots, cut away damaged parts before eating; compost damaged parts.
Prevention: Practice a 3-year crop rotation. Harvest the crop August and do not replant until summer the following year, after maggots have died of starvation. Flies are repelled by leeks, onions, sage and coriander.

2. Carrot weevil grubs are legless, 1/3-inch long, brown-headed pests that burrow into roots. Tops yellow, and growth is stunted.

Control: Remove and compost affected roots.
Prevention: Practice a 3-year crop rotation. Avoid planting celery, parsley and parsnips. Fall cleanup and tillage.

3. Carrotworm (celeryworm or parsleyworm) is the larvae of the beautiful swallowtail butterfly. The 2-inch long green caterpillar is encircled with yellow-dotted black bands, and when disturbed, projects two orange horns and emits a sweet odor. This pest is easy to spot munching away on green tops.

Control: Hand-pick when they are most active in the mornings. Apply

Bacillus thuringiensis if infestations occur.
Prevention: None

4. Sixspotted leafhopper (aster leafhopper) causes young leaves to yellow, and older leaves may twist or turn reddish. The greenish, 1/8-inch-long leafhopper has six tiny spots.
Control: Apply pyrethrum.
Prevention: Cover plants with floating row covers and do not plant carrots near lettuce or asters.

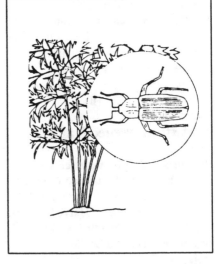

5. Vegetable weevils chew holes in the foliage of numerous vegetables. The nocturnal, beige, 3/8-inch weevil and their creamy-white 1/2-

inch long larvae can be menacing in southern gardens.
Control: None
Prevention: Rotate crops; keep garden free of debris; destroy eggs and nests by fall tilling.

6. Wireworms dig tunnels in the roots or seeds of many plants, causing sickly growth and yellowing of foliage. The many species of wireworms can be light yellow to brown and all have jointed bodies that resemble wires. Wireworms are the larval stage of the click beetle, that "clicks" when it jumps in the air or if laid on its back.
Control: Skewer several potatoes on sticks (cut the "eyes" out to prevent sprouting) and bury them around the garden. Lift the wireworm-infested potatoes after several days and dispose of them.

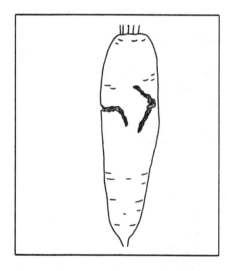

Prevention: Spring and fall tilling. Watch closely for damage if crops are planted where sod grass grew the previous two years.

7. Damping-off, a soil-borne disease, can attack young seedlings. It causes soft-rot at the soil line. Roots may rot and foliage may turn yellow before dying. Tops fall over in advanced stages.
Control: Use fungicide-treated seed. Diatomaceous earth is just starting to be used as a fungicide on seed in place of Captan.

Prevention: Allow good air circulation around seedlings. Make sure the soil is damp but not soggy and drains freely.

8. Leaf blight causes white or yellow spots on leaves. The irregular spots soon turn a greasy brown. The spotting may also attack roots.
Control: None
Prevention: Crop rotation. Tillage, adequate spacing to promote the growth of strong, healthy plants that can fight the disease.

9. Root knot is caused by minute nematodes (eelworms) feeding on roots. Small knots, galls or swelling, form on the root causing it to enlarge. Plants are stunted and leaves yellow.
Control: Apply *Bacillus thuringiensis* (Dipel or Thuricide).
Prevention: Plant French marigold *(Tagetes patula)*, black or white mustard to repel destructive nematodes. Rotate crops using a 3 year schedule. Many fungi found in healthy *living soil* prey on nematodes.

10. Vegetable soft rot causes soft, slimy rotting of the root. The unique sulfurous odor will help you identify this disease. Leaves yellow and wilt when the underground rot progresses. This soil-borne disease is worst in hot, humid weather.
Control: None. Remove and destroy affected plants.
Prevention: Crop rotation. Do not store bruised roots.

11. A boron or manganese deficiency turns carrot cores black.
Control: None
Prevention: Incorporate rock phosphate and (dolomite) limestone when planting. Add fish emulsion and kelp to the supplemental fertilizer.

12. Rabbits and gophers love carrots. They can devastate a garden in just a few nights of dining.
Control: Introduce a hungry cat or medium to large snake. Traps are

very effective, but require experience to become proficient.
Prevention: Bury a poultry wire fence 1 foot deep and 3 feet above the ground all the way around the carrot patch. If gophers are a real problem, line a raised bed with wire buried one foot deep.

Electronic noise and vibrators work very well to drive the rodents away, but the electric units may short out during wet weather. Rabbits can be driven away easiest by a dog. Euphorbia, also known as the "gopher plant" is planted to drive the pest out.

13. Small roots can be caused by insect or viral attacks. But more than likely the problem lies in poor, compacted soil. Compost and manure must be added one or two years prior to planting to discourage forking roots.
Control: None
Prevention: Cultivate soil deeply. Apply soft phosphate before planting, and a regular feeding of liquid seaweed or manure tea in poor soils.

14. Forking and "hairy" roots are caused by incorporating too much manure and compost in the soil up to a year before planting. Another cause is growing carrots or parsnips in heavy clay or stony soil so that root development is impaired.
Control: None

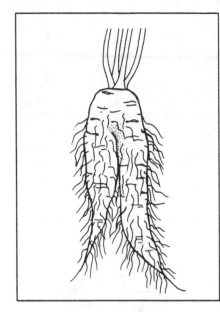

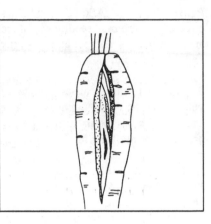

Prevention: Regular watering, and apply a mulch to hold moisture in the ground.

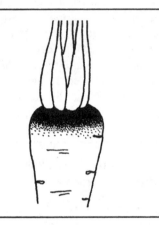

Prevention: Use peat moss or very well-rotted compost to improve soil texture; remove rocks by screening soil if necessary and do not pack down the soil in the seed bed.

15. Splitting roots can be a serious problem which is easily avoided. It is caused by heavy rains or watering following a period of drought.
Control: None. Use split carrots soon, as they rot quickly if stored.

16. Green shoulder is caused by the top of the root being exposed to sunlight. The green top is bitter and inedible.
Control/Prevention: Brush soil or compost over the green root. Within about two weeks the root will turn orange.

17. Poor Germination is caused by old seed or a hard crust of the soil surface. Pounding rain on the soil makes a hard crust form. This crust is too difficult for tender carrot sprouts to penetrate.
Control: sprinkle a fine layer of sifted compost or peat moss on top of the planted seeds. Or lay a moist newspaper on top of the planted seed bed. When the first sprouts show, remove the newspaper.
Prevention: same as control above.

Other problems that may affect carrots include:

18. Cutworm: page 54
19. Slugs and snails: page 55
20. Damping-off: page 61

Celery (*Apium graveolens var. dulce*) and Celeriac (*A. fraveolens var. rappaceum*)

Celery is probably the most demanding of all garden vegetables. If you can grow celery well, you should have no trouble with other crops. Celery and celeriac (also called root celery) are close relatives, requiring similar conditions for growth. Nonetheless, celeriac is easier to grow because it is less sensitive to temperature. Celery that needs blanching is uncommon in seed catalogs, and less nutritious than self-blanching types. Self-blanching celery is the type found in the supermarket, and requires less work to grow. Blanching, earthing up, or placing a dark cover around stems to tenderize and whiten the stalks also works on self-blanching celery. Celery and celeriac are heavy feeders and need rich organic soil. The small diameter, deep root system is adapted to grow in wet, bog soil, drawing in a lot of water. Regular deep watering is a must to harvest tender, succulent produce. The temperature *must stay between 55° and 85° (14-29° C)* for a successful crop. Bolting is caused by seedlings being exposed to temperatures below 55° (14° C), followed by warm weather.

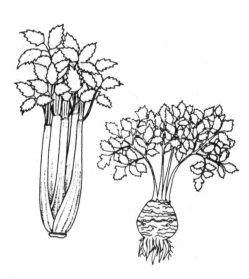

Basic Facts

Germination time: 12-20 days.
Germination temperature: Minimum: 40° (5° C), Optimum: 70° (21° C), Maximum: 85° (29° C).
Approximate seeds per ounce: 70,000.
Yield per 4 X 4 raised bed: 15-20 pounds.
Yield per 10-foot row: 10-12 pounds.
Life expectancy of stored seed: 5 years.
Estimated time between sowing and first picking: 25 weeks.
Intercrop: Coriander, lettuce, radish, flowers.
Effort to cultivate: Difficult, must keep soil temperature between 55 and 85° (14-29° C). Needs regular feeding and watering.
Seed saving: This biennial is forced to bolt by temperatures below 55° (14° C) followed by warm weather. Collect seed regularly.

Climate

Annual in all zones. Needs intense sunlight, with mild nights and cool days. *Celery must have a temperature range of 55-85° (14-29° C) or it will not produce.*

Soil Preparation

Rich organic soil that holds ample water but drains well is ideal. Incorporate generous amounts of compost and manure into the growing bed when preparing the soil in the spring. Add dolomite lime if the pH is above or below the ideal 6.0.
Add a complete fertilizer to soil when preparing. Rake the surface smooth removing surface debris.

Planting

To hasten germination, soak seed in water for a couple of hours drain, then freeze for a week. Before freezing, dry the seeds out on a paper napkin or towel so they do not form clumps. Handle these tender seeds carefully while planting.
To start seed indoors, sow seed in a flat of fine, rich soil 1/8- to 1/4-inch deep. Seeds emerge in 2-3 weeks. Transplant when the soil has warmed. Transplanted seedlings develop more surface roots, with a short taproot. They *require more frequent watering* and fertilizing.

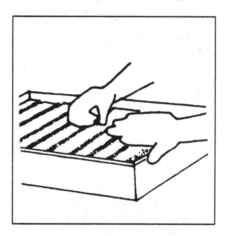

To direct seed after the soil has been prepared, sow seed 1/4- to 1/2-inch deep, 8-12 seeds per inch in rows 6-12 inches apart. To sow seed in a wide, raised bed, place seeds on 2-4 inch centers. Thin when 3-4 inches tall to 9- to 12-inch centers. Direct-seeding germination rates are low, but plants develop a much deeper root system than seedlings grown in containers.
Transplant seedlings after the last frost when soil has warmed to above 55° (14° C). Water-in heavily.

Crop Care

Deep water direct-seeded crops regularly, especially during dry weather. Surface-water transplanted seedlings regularly. Water constitutes 94% of celery's weight and it must have an abundant supply.
Fertilize every 2-4 weeks with a complete liquid fertilizer. Apply the fertilizer close to the roots.
Mulch around plants when they are 6-8 inches tall to conserve water and keep the ground from heating above 85° (29° C).
Pull weeds by hand, because roots grow near the soil's surface and will be damaged by a hoe.

Harvesting

Harvest a few leaves from the top of stalks to enjoy as a seasoning in salads or soups.

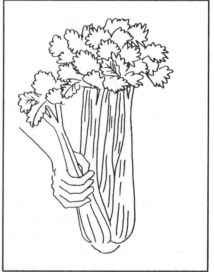

Harvest a few outside stalks of self-blanching plants as needed when they are 6 inches or taller. Entire plants can also be harvested and stored in a canning jar half full of water in the refrigerator for up to a month.
Continue harvesting until first frost. Once the temperature drops below 55° (14° C), celery growth virtually stops. Mature celery and celeriac are somewhat cold-tolerant, surviving under a cloche well past first frost in milder climates. Harvest all plants before a hard, killing frost strikes in cold climates.
Celeriac: Harvest entire celeriac plants as needed. Uproot the surface bulb when it is 2 or 3 inches across; larger roots become pithy and woody. Cut roots and leaves off, and compost. Mature celeriac can be coaxed along after frost under a cold frame, or by mounding soil or compost around plants for insulation.

In the Kitchen

Fresh: This crop is high in fiber and vitamin A. Celery sticks are excellent when eaten fresh, and when spread with peanut butter, or various soft cheeses. The leaves, chopped finely, add a delightful garnish to soups and sauces, or when added to salads.

Celeriac makes a delightful addition to fresh salads, soups, or sauces. Slice the difficult-to-peel bulbs before peeling away the tough skin. Blanch slices for 1-2 minutes adding lemon juice to the water to retain whiteness.

Storage: Celery keeps in a canning jar half full of water in the refrigerator for several weeks. Place celeriac in a plastic bag in the refrigerator for up to a week.

Freezing: Slice and blanch for 3 minutes in boiling water, or 3 1/2 minutes steamed. Dry put into a plastic bag and freeze.

Celery Varieties

GOLDEN SELF-BLANCHING (85 days) is the most popular variety. The stalks turn a golden yellow when they mature to a height of nearly 2 feet. Crisp, tender stalks with relatively few strings. Available (Bg, Bu, Fa, Fi, Gc, Ju, Ma, Me, Ni, Pi, Sc, Te, Th).

UTAH VARIETIES 100-110 days) **UTAH**, **TALL UTAH** and **CRISP UTAH** are similar, all maturing deep, green stalks about the same time. Each of the above varieties has slightly different qualities. Check seed catalogs for one that grows best in your area. One particular standout is **UTAH 5270 IMPROVED.** The stalks grow very vigorously to 12 inches tall. Available (Bu, Gc, Ju, Le, Pa, Pi, Te)

VENTURA (80 days) the quickest to mature, grows long, crisp stalks that are a deep, glossy green color. It's a Tall Utah type with better developed hearts and more upright growth. A good choice. Available (Jo, St).

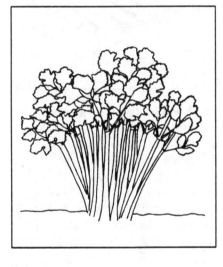

FRENCH CELERY DINANT (120-140 days). An unusual variety that sends out numerous thin, narrow stalks. It is resistant to light frosts and has a fuller celery flavor. Great in soups, salads and stews. Available (Ni).

Celeriac Varieties

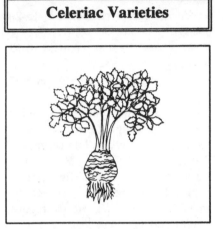

AVARI (110 days) has a very vigorous growth habit, producing white fleshy root bulbs that don't discolor when cooked. Most popular variety grown in Europe. Great flavor. Available (Te).

JOSE (110 days) produces large, round roots that are white and flavorful. Resistant to pithiness and hollow heart. Available (Cg, Jo).

MARBLE BALL (110 days) yields large, high-quality roots with a celery mint-like flavor. Available (Ha).

Problems

The difficulty of celery and celeriac cultivation can be compounded by bolting, aphids, slugs, snails, damping-off, and lack of water. But all of these maladies are easy to avoid with just a little care. Inisect and disease problems are most common in areas where celeriac and celery are grown commercially.

CELERY & CELERIAC	SYMPTOM	PROVABLE CAUSES
Seedlings	falling over	14, 15
Leaves	spots, brown	3, 8
	spots, greasy	4
	yellowing, wilted	16 or lacks boron
	eaten	2, 14
	chewed, folded	1
	aphid infestation	9
Stalks	bitter, stringy, tough	5
	pithy	lack of water
	split horizontally	7
	split vertically	7
	holes or divots	1, 2, 12
	moldy, rotten base	5
	darkened joints	3
Hearts	single central stalk	6
Roots	eaten	10
	tunneled	10, 11, 13

1. Celery leaftiers chew holes in leaves and stalks, folding and tying leaves over with their webs. Night-flying adult moths lay fish scalelike eggs on the undersides of leaves. The green-to-yellow caterpillars with a white stripe grow to 3/4-inch long.
Control: Hand-pick caterpillars and destroy damaged leaves. Use *Bacillus thuringiensis* or pyrethrum if infested.
Prevention: Luck!

2. Southern armyworm, most common in the deep South, are yellow with dark markings on black caterpillars. They may attack *en masse*, cleaning out all vegetation in a wide swath.
Control: Encourage natural predators: birds, frogs, toads and tachinid flies. Use *Bacillus thuringiensis* on infestations.
Prevention: Encourage predators.

3. Tarnished plant bugs are reclusive 1/4-inch long, green-to-brown, with tarnished wings. While feeding on an assortment of plants, they excrete a toxin that causes celery joints to blacken. Other signs of attack are brownish divots in foliage near the top of the plants.

Control: Spray in the early mornings, while insects are inactive, with sabadilla.

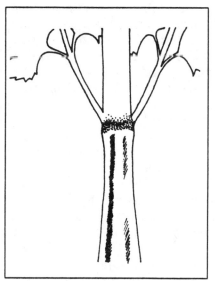

Prevention: Regular garden and fall cleanup.

4. Blight may appear as small yellowish green spots on seedlings that turn dark and fuse together as they grow. A later blight can also cause small greaselike spots on seedlings or mature plants. The disease spreads fast in wet weather.
Control: Destroy affected plants.
Prevention: A 118° (47° C) water bath for 30 minutes will stop this seed-borne disease. Avoid overcrowding, use blight-resistant varieties and buy certified, disease-free seed.

5. Pink rot causes greasy, water-soaked spots and a pink, fuzzy, cottonlike growth near the bottom of stalks. Stalks taste bitter. This fungus lives in the soil for years and can also cause damping-off.
Control: Remove and destroy affected plants.
Prevention: Crop rotation; do not follow celery with lettuce or brassica crops.

6. Bolting is probably the most serious problem, and most common in hot, dry weather. Bolting causes the development of just one bitter, tough stalk in the heart as the plant runs to seed. Drought, transplanting seedlings that have grown too large, and seedlings that have been checked by cold weather (below 55° (14° C)) are all provable causes.
Control: None
Prevention: Keep well watered. Do not set plants out if severely rootbound or if they have suffered cold shock.

7. Boron deficiency is noted by cracked stems that ultimately become brittle, and leaves that develop brown spots.
Control: None
Prevention: Add plenty of compost when planting. Fertilize with a fish emulsion and kelp meal tea.

8. Splitting is caused by lack of water, or excessive nitrogen in the soil. The stalks split vertically.
Control: None
Prevention: Keep well watered, especially when young. Feed regularly with a high-potassium, low-nitrogen fertilizer.

Other pests that might attack celery and celeriac are:

9. Aphids: page 53
10. Carrot rust fly: page 60
11. Carrot weevil: page 60
12. Celeryworm (carrotworm or parsleyworm): page 60
13. Nematodes (eelworms): page 61, number 9.
14. Slugs and snails: page 10
15. Damping-off: page 61
16. Fusarium wilt (Yellows wilt): page 56

Sweet Corn (*Zea mays*)

Corn, a type of maize, is a major American contribution to the agricultural world. Sweet corn is bred for a low-starch, high-sugar content. When picked, the sugar stored in kernels converts to starch at a *very* rapid rate. This is why corn is sweetest when eaten within minutes of picking. However, super-sweet corn contains twice the sugar, and the sugar-to-starch conversion is much slower.

Cobs are 6- to 10-inches long. One to three cobs grow on 4- to 15-foot-tall stalks. The tassels on the top of the stalk contain male flowers that fertilize the female flower silks which grow out of the cob. Tassels form only after corn has received enough days of heat. In fact, breeders classify corn by "heat units" (HU); that is, the number of hours over 50° (10° C) that each variety needs to mature. This explains why corn planted early may mature at the same time as seed sown later, during warmer weather.

Be careful when planting sweet and super-sweet types close to one another or the male flowers from one type may fertilize the female flowers of the other, which reduces quality. Always plant the same variety of corn in a patch containing several rows rather than one long row, to ensure pollination. If the weather is calm and windless, shaking the stalks after the silk has set will cause male pollen to rain downward and pollinate the female silk. Complete pollination ensures that a cob full of kernels will develop. Short cobs are common to fast-maturing, varieties. Long ears on both short and tall stalks are the norm in later varieties.

Basic Facts

Germination time: 7-10 days.
Germination temperature: Minimum: 50-60° (10-16° C), Optimum: 95° (35° C), Maximum: 105° (40° C).
Approximate seeds per ounce: 200-300.
Yield per 4 X 4 raised bed: 20-60 ears.
Yield per 10-foot row: 10-20 ears.
Life expectancy of stored seed: 2 years.
Estimated time between sowing and first picking: 10-13 weeks.
Intercrop: Clover, pole beans, squash, leaf crops, flowers.
Effort to cultivate: Easy.
Seed saving: Must be isolated from other varieties by 100 to 500 feet. Open-pollinated varieties yield about half as much as hybrid seed.

Climate

Annual in all zones. Needs full sun and *must have* warm weather - over 50° (10° C) both day and night; growth stops below 50° (10° C). Super-sweet varieties need a little warmer soil to germinate and grow well.

Soil Preparation

A heavy feeder, corn benefits from rich organic soil. Prepare the soil in early spring by adding plenty of compost, manure and a complete fertilizer mix.

Good drainage and water retention are essential. Compost and mulch will help hold water longer and improve drainage.

Planting

Soak seeds in water until they swell to hasten germination. Sprout seeds by soaking in a glass of water before sowing. See Bean Planting, page 29 for details.

Sow sweet varieties after the soil has warmed, about a month after the last frost. If the seeds are planted in cool ground they tend to rot before sprouting.

Sow super-sweet varieties when the soil has warmed to 60° (16° C). These varieties do not germinate well in cold soils found in many regions of America. Growing under plastic tunnels in a "hot bed" will make early and cold-climate planting more reliable.

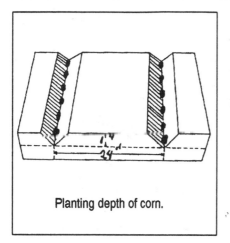

Planting depth of corn.

In rows spaced 18-36 inches apart, sow seed 1 inch deep and 2 inches apart. Corn grows tall, casting a shadow. Plant on the north or east end of the garden so undesirable shadows are not cast on other crops.

In raised wide beds, sow kernels on 4-inch centers, 1-inch deep. Each stalk develops just 1 or 2 ears, but the overall yield per square foot is *much higher* than when planted in rows.

A succession of plantings at 2-4 week intervals assures a steady supply of corn for several months. Plant early varieties first and later-maturing or super-sweet corn in midsummer.

Crop Care

Keep well watered at all times. After the corn has grown a foot tall, remove large weeds by hand or very carefully with a hoe.

A heavy layer of mulch will smother small and new weeds. The mulch will also cut water usage substantially.

For most vigorous growth, do not remove side shoots (suckers) growing from the base.

Hot weather makes corn grow up to a foot a day. Fertilize every 2-4 weeks with a manure tea or sidedress with a high-nitrogen complete mix monthly. Add more mulch and keep well watered in hot weather, especially when ears form.

When silk appears on ears, shake stalks to ensure pollination, which fills out ears with kernels.

Harvesting

When the ears bulge within the husk and the silk turns dark, peel back the outer leaves on larger ears. A sweet, creamy-white juice will squirt from ripe kernels when pinched. Unripe kernels spew out a watery liquid.

Carefully twist ripe ears off the stalk. Husk in the garden and toss peeled husk on the compost pile. Eat raw in the garden or cook immediately. Cool ears rapidly to 33-35º (1-2º C) if you plan to store them for a day or two. Cooling slows the sugar-to-starch conversion.

In wide raised beds that are intensively planted, remove harvested cornstalks every few days to make room for other stalks.

In the Kitchen

Corn contains vitamin A, some of the B vitamins, minerals and protein. It is rich in carbohydrates.

Fresh: Have the water boiling in the kitchen when you go out to pick corn. As explained in the introduction, once picked, the sugar converts to starch *very* rapidly, except in *sugary enhanced* and *extra-sweet* varieties. Steam fresh cobs for 5-10 minutes or boil, setting single ears into the water so that it remains boiling, for 4-6 minutes. Serve with butter and season to taste.

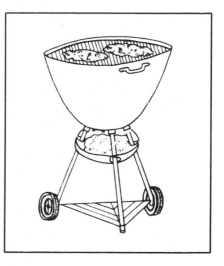

To barbecue, peel back the husk but do not remove entirely. Discard the silk. Place 1-2 pats of butter on kernels and cover with the husk. Wrap each ear in aluminum foil and set on the barbecue grill for 5-10 minutes per side. Season to taste.

Cut kernels from the cob with a knife or with a corn cutter, which is available from many seed suppliers. Use the corn in salads, for pastry filling, or add to soups and stews.

Storage: Do not store sweet corn at all. Store super-sweet and sugar-enhanced (SE) varieties for up to 3 days in the refrigerator, wrapped, husk and all in a plastic bag.

Freezing: Super-sweet varieties are the best to freeze, since they retain sugar better than sweet types. Blanch cobs in boiling water 3-5 minutes or steam 7-11 minutes, pat dry with a towel and store in a plastic bag. Blanch kernels 3-4 minutes in boiling water or steam 4-8 minutes before sealing in a plastic bag and freezing.

Varieties

There are hundreds of corn varieties to choose from. Listed below are some of the most popular for the home gardener.

Sweet Varieties

These varieties taste best when eaten within minutes of harvest. Sweet corn is classified in three basic groups, according to the sugar content. The first group is called SU, which refers to *normal sugary*. Most sweet corn is in this group. The second group contains an extra gene. It is *sugar enhanced* (SE), with about 25 percent more sugar than *normal* sweet corn. The SE group is also called EH which stands for Everlasting Heritage types. The SE (EH) sweet corn is more tender and sweeter than *normal*. A third group, called SE+ (*fully sugary enhanced*) is even more sweet and tender. The extra sugar creates a slower conversion of the sugar to starch after harvest, which helps retain the sweet taste longer.

Yellow Sweet Varieties

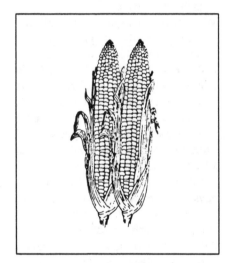

EARLY SUNGLO (63 days) grows vigorously, even in cool weather, for an early harvest. Uniform 7-inch ears yield tasty yellow corn on 4- to 5-foot stalks. Trouble-free and consistent. Stalks are often multiple. Available (Bu, Fa, Fi, Me, Ni, Pa, She).

GOLDEN BANTAM (81 days) is a favorite hybrid that tastes great fresh or cooked. The uniform, long ears are packed with juicy kernels. Very popular for canning and freezing. Available (Bg, Cg, Gc, Fi, Jo, Ju, Ma, Me, Th)

IOCHIEF (89 days) an AAS winner, has 8- to 10-inch ears packed full of narrow, juicy, sweet, yellow kernels. The drought-resistant quality helps Iochief through a long growing season. Available (Bu, Fa, Fi, Ma, Me).

KANDY KORN (84 days), the first variety with the EH (SE) gene factor, set a new standard. It holds sweetness 1-2 weeks after ripening. Very sweet and tender yellow kernels on 9-inch ears are great fresh, frozen or canned. Available (Bu, Fi, Gc, Ju, Ma, Me, She, St).

MIRACLE (85-100 days) is an improved GOLDEN JUBILEE type with SE genes. Sweet, large 9- to 10-inch ears mature on 6-foot stalks near the end of the season. Excellent eating, and probably the best all-round choice in this group. Available (Bu, Fa, Hi, Ma, Ni, St, Te).

White Sweet Varieties

COUNTRY GENTLEMAN (93 days) has small, sweet, flavorful, tightly packed, round white kernels arranged irregularly rather than in rows. Cut kernels off the 8-inch cobs of this turn-of-the-century variety to make creamed corn, eat fresh, or freeze. Available (Bg, Fi, Gs, Le, Ma, So).

PLATINUM LADY (75 days) matures relatively early. The delicious, sweet kernels are packed all the way to the tip of a 7- to 8-inch-long cob. Husks are green and purple. Available (Bu, Cg, Gc, Ni, Pi, St).

SILVER QUEEN (92 days) sets the standard for white sweet corn. This old-fashioned variety yields high-quality, 8- to 9-inch-long ears with tightly packed rows of kernels. Excellent taste. Available (Bu, Fa, Fi, Ha, Jo, Le, Ma, Me, Pa, St).

Bicolor Sweet Varieties

HONEY & CREAM (Butter & Cream) (85 days) yields stocky, 7- to 8-inch cobs packed full of broad yellow and white kernels. Smooth texture and sweet flavor. Available (Bu, Ju, Ma, Me, Pi).

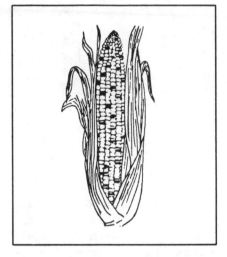

PEACHES 'N CREAM (70 days) an early maturing EH gene variety, yields luscious, long ears of succulent yellow and white kernels on 6- to 8-foot stalks. Available (Fi, She, St).

Super- or Xtra-sweet Varieties

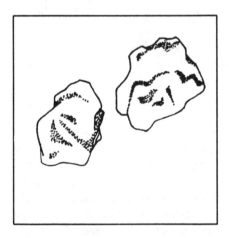

The genetic makeup of these varieties gives them about twice the sugar content of *normal* sweet corn. This creates much sweeter taste and slower conversion of the sugar to starch after harvest. Super-sweet varieties hold up to two weeks on stocks after ripening, and retain a sweet taste longer after harvest. Also called a *shrunken* variety, which refers to the genetic affect on the dry kernel, which is smaller and appears shriveled or shrunken. Super-sweets do not germinate well in cool soils. They grow best where the weather is hot all summer. Do not plant *super-sweet* varieties close (within 500 feet) to *normal* sweet corn. The cross-pollination between the two types creates tough, starchy kernels.

Yellow Super-sweet Varieties

EARLY XTRA-SWEET (71 days), an AAS winner, is 2 weeks earlier than Illini and more uniform. Five- to 6-foot stalks produce 7- to 9-inch ears full of extraordinarily sweet, yellow kernels. Available (Bu, Fa, Ju, Ma, Me, Th).

FLORIDA STAYSWEET (87 days) preforms well in southern gardens and northern climates with hot summers. Succulent yellow kernels on 7- to 8-inch ears are sweetest fresh. Available (Jo).

ILLINI XTRA-SWEET (85 days) has broad, sweet, tender, yellow kernels on a plump 7-inch cob. Excellent fresh, frozen, or canned. Available (Bu, Fa, Ju, Ma, Me)

White and Bicolor Super-sweet Varieties

HOW SWEET IT IS (85 days), an AAS winner, yields ultra-sweet white kernels on 8-inch ears. Harvest 6- to 7-foot stalks in mid season. Available (Bu, Fi, Ha, Jo, Ju, Le, Ma, Me, Ni, Pa, Pi, St, Th).

STARSTRUCK (92 days) is the original yellow/white bicolored super-sweet. Long 8- to 9-inch ears yield fat, juicy kernels that are great fresh, or frozen on the cob. Available (Jo).

Ornamental Varieties

This corn is left to dry in the field on the stock and later suspended in a sheltered area to finish drying. Most varieties of ornamental corn require a long growing season.

INDIAN CORN (90-100 days) is available in many varieties: Fingers, Rainbow and Squaw are a few. Red, blue, yellow and white kernels are left to sun-dry on long slender cobs. Several ears can be tied together by the husks and hung for fall decorations. Available (Da, Fi, Gs, Jo, Ma, Pi, Pl, St).

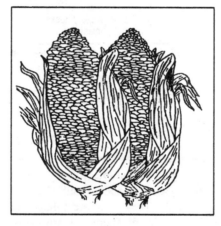

STRAWBERRY CORN (105 days) ears are plump, and only 3 inches long. Small mahogany-red kernels are decorative, and good for popping too. Strawberry is an early-maturing variety for northern climates. Available (Bu, Cg, Da, Fa, Fi, Ha, Hu, Ju, Le, Me, Ni, Pa, Pl, Th).

Popcorn Varieties

These types of corn have deep, pointed kernels with a very soft hull. They cross-pollinate with other corn,

so grow them at least 500 feet away. Let the kernels dry on the plant for the ideal moisture content (14%), and fluffy popcorn. Check popcorn for moisture content by rubbing a few kernels from an ear and popping. At least 8 out of 10 kernels should pop. Store harvested popcorn in an airtight container so it will retain the desired moisture content.

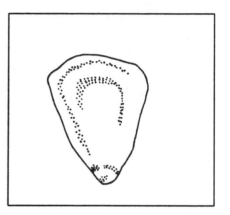

CROCKET SEEDS, P.O. Box 237, Metamora, OH 43540, grows nothing but popcorn. Their two favorites are P-305 and P-410. Both varieties are tender, with a good popping volume.

BURPEE'S PEPPY HYBRID (90 days) matures in 3 months. Short 4-inch ears on 4- to 5-foot stalks are packed with white kernels. Good popper. Available (Bu).

JAPANESE YELLOW and JAPANESE WHITE HULL-LESS (83-110 days) varieties make excellent popcorn. The White matures 2 weeks sooner than the Yellow. Good expansion, and fluffy. Available (Fi, Le).

TOM THUMB (85 days) bears one or two 3- to 4-inch ears on dwarf 3 1/2-foot-tall stalks. This early-maturing popcorn is an excellent choice for northern climates. Available (Bg, Gc, Jo).

Problems

Corn is easy to grow, but can be plagued with many different pests, especially if your garden is in commercial corn country. Planting after the weather is warm, and ample fertilizer and water, will keep the crop growing faster than many insects can eat. Insects that attack kernels and cobs present the gravest threat. Humid, rainy weather when ears are maturing sets the stage for fungal and disease attacks. Keep your eyes peeled for these pests and conditions. Remember to actually open ears of corn to inspect for insects.

CORN	SYMPTOM	PROVABLE CAUSES
Seed & Seedlings	riddled with holes	2
	poor gemination	7 or too cold
	uprooted, missing	13
Stems	tunnels	2, 5
	darkened	8
Leaves	aphid infestation	1
	wilt	5
	discolored, streaks	9
	eaten	19, 22
	spots, dark	11
	spots, gray or dark	12
Roots	channels	2, 20, 23
	rotten	21
Ears	small, deformed ears	1, 15
	eaten kernels	4, 6, 22
	rot, dry husks	10
	missing	14
Plants	wilt, dwarf, dying	3
	wilts in hot sunshine	9
	small, stunted	16

1. Aphids that attack corn are normally green, and found on the upper leaves and tassels. The pest sucks life-giving juices from plants, exuding a sticky, dark honeydew. The honeydew attracts corn earworm moths, and fungus. Growth slows, and full ears may not develop.
Control: Blast aphids off with a jet of water. Use insecticidal soap or pyrethrum if severely infested.
Prevention: Release and encourage ladybugs and lacewings, which prey on aphids. Attract hover-flies, whose larva eat aphids, by growing flowers in the garden.

2. Billbugs are football shaped, black to mahogany-red in color, with whitish grubs. The adults play dead when disturbed, and puncture young stems, which riddles unfolded leaves with holes. Grubs favor roots, boring up through the stem.
Control: Apply insecticidal soap, or as a last resort, rotenone
Prevention: Crop rotation, good drainage, fall cleanup and tillage.

3. Chinch bugs have a 1/8- to 1/4-inch long reddish-black body with white wings, and smell bad if squished. They puncture foliage to feed on plant fluids. Corn wilts, dwarfs, or dies from attacks. This pest is worst during hot, dry summer weather.
Control: Dust with diatomaceous earth or spray with insecticidal soap.
Prevention: Remove grassy weeds around the garden. Fall cleanup and tilling.

4. Corn earworms, also known as tomato fruitworms or cotton bollworms, are probably the worst corn pest, and can be found anywhere corn is grown. A gray adult moth with dark blotches on its wings, it lays eggs which grow into 2-inch-long, brown, green, or yellow caterpillars with both light and dark stripes running the length of its body. The caterpillars are found on young plants, or inside ears feeding on kernels. They leave a trail of taletale moist, sawdustlike castings. The caterpillars also attack beans, broccoli, cabbage, and lettuce, but they like tomatoes the most, tunneling through one fruit after another.
Control: Hand-pick. Dust with the *Bt* strain called *Baculovirus heliothis* (Elcar is the trade name) or use a rotenone spray as a last resort.
Prevention: Plant resistant varieties. Seal off ears by wrapping rubber bands around the open end of the husk, which prevents the pest from entering.

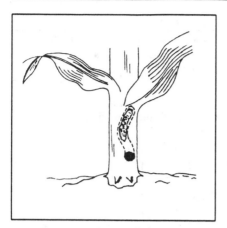

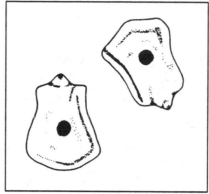

11. Leaf spot causes leaves to spot with dark, thin , fungal growth similar to sun scorch. Damage occurs in late season after wet weather.

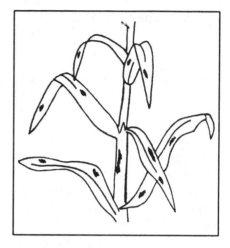

5. European corn borers are inch long tan caterpillars, with a dark head, and body spots. The adult is a night-flying, yellowish-brown moth that appears in the garden from May to June. Their preferred food is corn, but they will attack numerous other plants as well. The pest tunnels into stems or canes, causing leaves to wilt. Look for a small entry hole and moist sawdust castings on canes and stems.
Control: Hand-pick with a knife or fingernail. Apply *Bacillus thuringiensis* or ryana.
Prevention: Release or encourage natural enemies: ladybugs, lacewings, tachinid flies and trichogramma wasps. Fall cleanup.

6. Sap beetle's larvae are dark, inch-long maggots that attack ears of corn. Look for small, round entry holes in the husk. When you open the husk, maggots scatter and hide.
Control: Hand-pick. Dust with *Bacillus thuringiensis* or use a rotenone spray as a last resort. Remove and destroy infested ears.
Prevention: Fall cleanup. Crop rotation.

7. Seedcorn maggots are 1/4-inch-long, pale yellow worms with a pointed head that drills into planted seeds. The seeds fail to germinate, or produce sickly, stunted plants. They are most destructive in cold, wet weather.
Control: None.

Prevention: Sow seed when soil is warm. Remove and destroy affected seed and replant new seed.

8. Stalk borers are slender, 1 1/2-inch-long, white to pastel-purple caterpillars with or without stripes and a dark band. These pests bore into stalks, destroying the interior. Stems darken or fold, and growth is stunted. Look for their entry holes.
Control: Hand-pick with a fingernail or knife. Bind the split stem back together with twine. Loosen or remove the twine after the wound has healed.
Prevention: Remove debris around garden. Fall cleanup.

9. Bacterial wilt makes leaves wilt on hot, sunny days. Most common in eastern and southern states, this disease causes long discolored streaks in leaves. The flea beetle is a common vector of this disease.
Control: Destroy infected plants.
Prevention: Fall cleanup and tillage. Control flea beetles (page 54) that spread the wilt.

10. Ear rot appears on the tip of ears, or at the base of the outer husk, before spreading through the ear. Husks become dry and stick together. Affected growth is moldy, with black spots.
Control: Remove and destroy infected plants.
Prevention: Practice a 3-year crop rotation and plant resistant varieties if ear rot is a problem.

Control: None.
Prevention: Keep plants strong, and well fertilized. Avoid planting late-maturing varieties.

12. Smut, a fungal disease, appears as large galls (smut balls) on foliage. In early stages, smut is light gray, and gets darker later in the season. Wet weather, followed by a dry period, gives this disease perfect growing conditions.
Control: Remove and destroy affected foliage when galls are seen. Remove before they ripen, bursting open, spewing black spores which infect other plants.
Prevention: Three-year crop rotation. Use disease-resistant seed. Keep garden area clean. Cleanup in the fall and till soil.

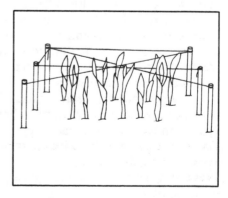

13. Birds, usually crows, eat and uproot seedlings, searching for the attached seed. Other birds attack ripe ears.
Control: Camouflage seedlings with mulch. Cover small patches with protective wire. Stretch dark thread between stakes a few inches above seedlings in straight rows.
Prevention: A dog or cat will keep birds away. Scarecrows and garden mobiles are marginally effective.

14. Raccoons raid corn patches at night. This is their favorite food, and they can clean out a crop in just a few raids.
Control: Fence the patch with poultry wire. If raccoons climb the fence, electrify it, turning it on at night. Protect individual mature ears by covering them with a paper bag, and cover the bag with poultry wire. Live animal traps are an alternative when raccoons become a serious nuisance.

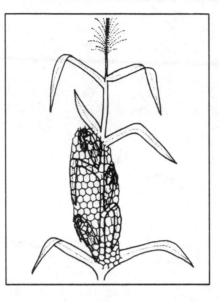

Prevention: A large, barking dog helps but be careful; raccoons can kill dogs that attack.

15. Small, deformed ears are caused by poor pollination due to wet weather, drought, or lack of nutrients.
Control: None

Prevention: Shake each plant after the silk sets to ensure pollination. Do not plant varieties of sweet and super-sweet corn within 500 feet of one another or they will cross-pollinate. Fertilize and water regularly. Mulch heavily.

16. Small plants are caused by drought, and lack of nutrients in the soil.
Control: None
Prevention: Regular fertilization and irrigation. Mulch plants to conserve water.
Other problems that affect corn are:

17. Cutworm: page 54
18. Flea beetle: page 54
19. Grasshoppers: 120
20. Cabbage fly root maggots: page 53
21. Root rot: page 72
22. Southern Armyworm: page 65
23. Wireworm: page 61

Cucurbitaceae Family

Cucurbits, or the cucurbitaceae family, includes cucumbers, melons, and squashes. They all love warm weather and sandy soil. They grow poorly in cool, damp climates, and are sensitive to frost. Cucurbits, in descending order of frost tolerance, are squash, pumpkin, cucumber, cantaloupe, and watermelon. A deep taproot is encouraged in many varieties by deep watering of this family that originated in desert climates.

The seedlings are susceptible to powdery mildew, especially when germinating. For best gemination results, water seedlings only once, just after sowing in moist climates.

Cucurbits develop separate male and female flowers. Male flowers develop first and are easily distinguished as a plain flower on a long stem, having only stamens. The female flower forms large ovaries that look like small fruit. After the first female flowers are pollinated, the vines develop alternating male and female flowers.

Some melons, many squashes, and all cucumbers cross-pollinate with one another. When cultivating a seed crop, grow only one variety of each type. Hand-pollinate by removing a male flower and shaking it inside a female flower on another plant to ensure vigorous seed. To prevent further pollination, close the female bloom with a piece of string, or twist-tie for a few days.

Cucumber *(Cucumis sativus)*

This warm-weather vine or bush crop is a favorite in salads, fresh from the vine, or when preserved as pickles. When started early indoors under a cold frame, cucumbers ripen early enough to enjoy with cool-weather lettuce in a salad. Cucumbers come in all shapes and sizes. Pickling "cukes" are short and stubby; slicers are long and slender; apple or lemon cucumbers are spherical and yellow. Armenian cucumbers are really a long, slender melon that grows up to three feet in length. Each type of cucumber has its own distinctive flavor. The short pickling varieties are bitter when eaten fresh, and when used to make pickles, should be picked when only a few inches long. Some slicing varieties possess a tough, bitter skin that is peeled before eating the sweet creamy flesh within. Since cucumbers are mostly water, many commercial growers cover them with a thin layer of wax after harvesting to retain moisture. To enjoy the peak flavor of cucumbers, they should be eaten within a few hours of harvest.

Basic Facts

Germination time: 6-10 days.
Germination temperature: Minimum: 60° (16° C), Optimum: 95° (35° C), Maximum: 105° (40° C).
Approximate seeds per ounce: 175.
Yield per plant: 10-50.
Life expectancy of stored seed: 5-6 years.
Estimated time between sowing and first picking: 10-14 weeks.
Intercrop: Lettuce and flowers.
Effort to cultivate: Easy in warm climates, requires cold protection in cool climates.
Seed saving: Best to hand-pollinate. See "Cuculbrits" above.

Climate

Annual in all zones. Needs full sun and *warm* weather, above 70° (21° C). Cold temperatures slow vine growth, stop flowering and fruit set.

Soil Preparation

Prepare soil in early spring or the previous fall. Incorporate plenty of compost and manure. Add dolomite lime to neutralize the pH and keep cukes from "bubbling" and turning pithy on one end. Add a complete organic fertilizer. Soil should hold moisture, but drain well.

Planting

Do not plant where cucumbers, melons or squash grew the previous two years.
Indoors: Plant seeds 1/2-inch deep in small containers of fine potting soil. Transplant to mounds or rows after all danger of frost is past.

The soil temperature must be at least 60° (16° C) for gemination and strong growth.

In mounds: Sow four to six seeds 1 1/2 inches deep in mounds or "hills". Drench the mound with water and do not water again until after sprouting, unless absolutely necessary.
In rows: Sow seeds 1 1/2 inches deep, 1 to 2 inches apart. Thin to 6 inches apart when seedlings are 4-6 inches tall.
Pickling varieties: Plant several dozen plants, so that many become ripe at the same time, and an entire batch can be processed at once.
Build a trellis for vines to climb. This saves precious garden space and keeps the fruit off the ground, which discourages insects and rot. The fruit develops straight and makes them easier to spot when picking. Trellised fruit is protected from sunburn, which causes bitterness.
Replant seeds if the first sowing does not germinate rapidly, or is slowed by spring rains.
Plant 5-10 plants per person.

Crop Care

Keep seedlings moist enough to avoid wilting, but be careful not to overwater, which promotes damping-off.

Mulch with dark compost or black plastic to heat soil after plants are 6 inches tall, and the soil is well warmed. Continue adding mulch as needed.

Deep-water as needed to encourage a long taproot. The crop consumes more water when fruit sets, and surface watering is necessary. Fruit is over 90% water and must have an adequate amount to form large fruit.

Water stress will cause deformed cucumbers, and a smaller crop.

Side-dress with complete low-nitrogen soluble fertilizer as soon as flowers set, and twice a month thereafter until the end of season.

Removing side or lateral shoots will send all the nutrients to remaining fruit, which makes them larger, and mature them faster.

Pinch off the end of vines about 2 weeks before the first frost so all of the fruit that has set will mature.

Harvesting

For maximum production, harvest cucumbers as soon as they become ripe. When left too long on the vine, they yellow, become sour, and slow other fruit from ripening.

Pickling varieties should be harvested when they are 3-6 inches long. When longer, they preserve poorly and become mushy.

Slicing varieties are picked when they are from 6-10 inches long. If slicers get too long, or start to yellow, they become bitter and pithy.

Apple or lemon cucumbers should be picked when they are the size of a small lemon!

In the Kitchen

Fresh: The skin is the most nutritious part. It is packed with vitamins A and C. The skin should be peeled only if it is too bitter. Slice and serve soon after picking for the fullest flavor. Incorporate into green salads, or use as the main ingredient in a menagerie of dishes. Or slice and let set in a bowl of olive oil, rice vinegar, a few sprigs of French tarragon, and a dash of lemon juice in the refrigerator for an hour or two before serving. The refreshing dish is cool as a cucumber. Sandwiches made of cucumber slices are popular in some parts of the world. Some cooks hollow out the seedy centers and stuff them with cream cheese.

Storage: Wrap in a plastic bag or cellophane. A cucumber that is not allowed to dry out will last for up to a week in the refrigerator.

Pickling: Grow specific pickling varieties. Plant more than you plan to use. Pick the cukes when they are very small and succulent to make the best pickles.

For more information on making dill and sweet pickles, check your favorite cookbook.

Varieties

Cucumbers fall into three main categories: pickling, slicing, and novelty, most of which are available in both vine and bush varieties. Small slicing cucumbers can also be used for pickling, but most pickling "cukes" are much too bitter to be eaten raw. A new all-female category is also listed below. These types produce small, bumpy cucumbers that ripen many fruit at once and 1-3 weeks earlier than most slicers.

Pickling Varieties

GERKIN TYPES (55-65 days) (*Cucumis aguria*) are slightly different than cucumbers, but they are grown the same. Plants yield short two-inch, pale green fruit covered with stubby burrs. Developed to make superb sour little pickles (cornichons). Available (Gs, Jo, Pi, She).

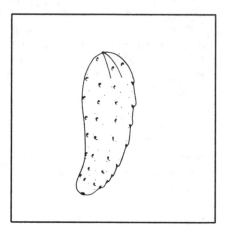

NORTHERN PICKLING (48 days) sets heavily and early on short vines. Resistant to scab, and a good choice for short summer climates. Available (Bu, Gc, Jo, Hi, Ni).

SMR 58 (60 days) an open-pollinated variety, is an excellent choice for temperate, moist climates. Available (Fi, Ju, Ma, Ni, Te).

Slicing Varieties

BURPLESS HYBRID TYPES (60-65 days), **TASTY GREEN**, **SWEET SLICE**, **GREEN KNIGHT** and **SWEET SUCCESS** (an AAS winner), came from the Orient, and grow best during long, hot summers. They are easier to digest, but peeling away the bitter skin is advised. **SUYO LONG** is the best choice for Northern climates. Available (Bu, Cg, Fa, Fi, Ha, Le, Ma, Pi).

MARKETMORE TYPES (67 days) is an excellent all-round choice for all climates. An open-pollinated variety, it yields well and is very resistant to diseases. Good crisp flavor from 8-inch-long fruits. Available (Bu, Fa, Fi, Gc, Ha, Hi, Ju, St, Te)

MIDDLE EASTERN VARIETIES (Beit Alpha cucumbers) (60-70 days) such as **AMIRA, HYLARES, SARIA** and **SWEET ALPHEE**, are the *highest quality* for salads. They have a thin skin, sweet flavor, and smaller size. They grow best in very warm, long-season climates such as in the Southwest, but do well under cover in cooler climates. Available (Jo, She).

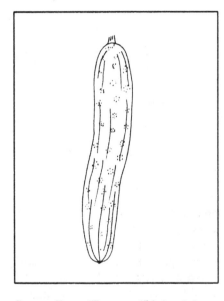

SALAD BUSH HYBRID (56 days) is an AAS winner that yields 8-inch long fruit on compact vines; ideal for a small trellis in containers, on a deck or patio. Good tasting and good yield. Resistant to most diseases. Available (Bu, Fi, Ha, Ju, Le, Ma, Ni, Pa, Pi).

All-Female Varieties

The "greenhouse" (parthenocarpic) cucumber produces only female flowers. They *must not* be pollinated or the resulting fruit will be an inedible gourd. The other all-female cucumber (gynoecious) also produces only female flowers. Pollination is accomplished by adding just a few seeds in the packet that produce male flowers. These hybrids produce earlier cucumbers, but should be avoided if you are only able to plant just a few cucumbers, because you can't ensure male flowers.

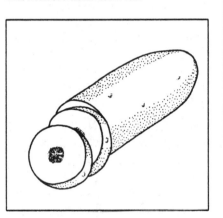

ELITE HYBRID (60 days) (parthenocarpic) is an exceptionally heavy producer of sweet, 8-inch fruit. Yields early and is very disease resistant. Available (Te).

EURO AMERICAN (52 days) is one of the best burpless slicers available. This European greenhouse variety yields foot-long fruit that is tender through and through. Resistant to many diseases. Available (Pa, Te).

STREAMLINER HYBRID (60 days) (gynoecious) yields 10-inch-long slender fruit over a long season. Flesh is crisp and tasty with few seeds. Resistant to mildew and mosaic. Available (Bu)

Novelty Varieties

APPLE OR LEMON (60 days) cucumbers are open-pollinated vintage varieties. The mild, white-to green-flesh with a crisp texture and sweet skin sours if allowed to overripen. (Bg, Cg, Fi, Gc, Gs, Ju, Ni, Pi, Pl, She, St, Te).

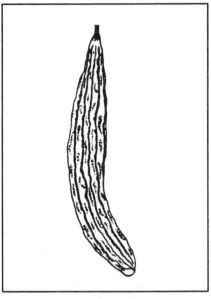

ARMENIAN OR SERPENT VARIETIES (65-75 days) grow ribbed fruit up to 3 feet long. Light green skin and flesh are not bitter. No peeling, but needs a long, hot summer. Available (Bu, Fi, Gs, Ni, Pl, Sc, She).

Problems

Most problems with the Cucurbitaceae family, **cantaloupe, cucumber, squash** and **watermelon,** can be avoided by planting in rich organic soil, and watering adequately throughout the season. Cucumbers, gourds, pumpkins and squash are prone to rot and insect damage when left on the ground. All are remarkably trouble-free except for gray mold and powdery mildew, which usually affects them near the end of the growing season or during prolonged wet weather. Avoid working in the garden during wet weather, which spreads disease. These crops can suffer grave losses if mosaic virus is not checked.

1. Aphid: Several species of aphids infest cucumbers and squash. Typically they are green, but can range from black to yellow in color. Found on leaf undersides, they cause foliage wilting and curl, or, if severe, stunting and death.

Control is normally not necessary. A jet of water will blast many of them from their homes on leaves. Several applications of insecticidal soap if the crop is infested.

Prevention: Release and encourage ladybugs and lacewings, which prey on aphid adults and larvae. Attract hover-flies, whose larva eat aphids, by growing a large selection of flowers in the garden.

CUCUMBER	SYMPTOM	PROVABLE CAUSES
Seed & Seedlings	stem rots at soil line no germination	9 26
Stems	holes, tunnels rot at soil line	5 25
Leaves	wilt, leaf curl holes chewed small dark spots yellowing yellow spots fuzzy purple growth fuzzy white/gray patches stippling, small spots	1, 5, 8, 10, 12, 2, 3, 4, 19, 20, 21 6, 14 9, 13, 21 11 11 11 18
Flowers	holes chewed poor yield	2, 3, 4 17
Plant	stunted sudden wilt	1, 10 5, 7
Fruit	tunnels discolored, dropping bad taste, bitter deformed poor yield	1, 10 6 12, 15 17 16

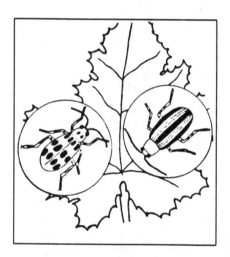

2. Cucumber beetles (southern corn rootworm) measure 1/4 inch long. These slender beetles are yellow-to-orange, with black spots or stripes. The adult consumes foliage and the 1/3-inch-long white larvae feed on roots and stems. Both carry bacterial wilt and mosaic virus, which does more damage than the holes beetles chew.

Control: Apply pyrethrum or rotenone.

Prevention: Cover crop with floating row covers. Mulch heavily. Plant late in the season. Encourage predatory braconid wasps, Nc nematodes, soldier beetles and tachinid flies.

3. Melonworm attacks are worst in the Gulf States. The slender caterpillar has thin white stripes running down its body. It eats foliage and burrows into fruit.

Control: Hand-pick, use rotenone for infestations.

Prevention: Encourage predatory birds and reptiles.

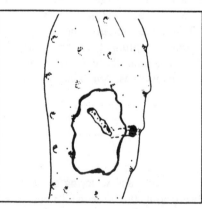

4. Pickleworm causes most damage in the South, but is found further north late in the season. The green-to-copper-colored worm grows to 3/4-inch long as it tunnels into flower buds, fruits, and vines.

Control: Apply pyrethrum, rotenone, or grow a trap crop of squash. Make sure to remove the squash before the worms leave the blossoms.

Prevention: Prevent overwintering by tilling or hot composting. Grow resistant varieties.

5. Squash bug adults are murky brown-and-black insects just over 1/2-inch long. They are green, with a red head shortly after hatching. They feed on sap, and discharge a toxin that wilts foliage. When squashed, the insect stinks.

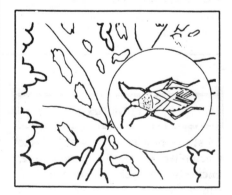

Control: Apply sabadilla.
Prevention: Encourage tachinid flies, garden sanitation, crop rotation and fall tillage.

6. Squash vine borer, an inch-long worm, burrows into stems, which causes sudden wilting. Look for yellowish sawdust at their entrance holes, usually near ground level. The wasplike adult lays eggs near ground level in early summer.
Control: *Bacillus thuringiensis. Bt* can also be applied with a syringe *Bt* is injected into the stem where the borer is living.
Prevention: Garden sanitation and fall tillage. Plant in mid summer in the south. Mound soil, or wrap a nylon stocking around the base of vines. Encourage trichogramma wasps.

7. Anthracnose is a fungal disease that lives in the soil. Foliage develops numerous small, dark spots that enlarge. Advanced stages are signaled by fruit discoloring and dropping. Warm, moist conditions help it disseminate.
Control: Remove and destroy affected plants.
Prevention: Three-year or longer rotation with nonmelon crops.

8. Bacterial wilt causes foliage to wilt rapidly. This disease is carried by cucumber beetles. Identify the wilt by cutting open a stem. A gooey, white sap will be secreted.
Control: Remove and destroy affected foliage.

Prevention: Control cucumber beetles with pyrethrum or rotenone.

9. Damping-off, a soil-borne disease, attacks young seedlings. It causes soft-rot at the soil line. Roots may rot and foliage may turn yellow before dying. Seedlings fall over in advanced stages.
Control: Use fungicide-treated seed. Diatomaceous earth is just starting to be used as a fungicide to replace Captan.
Prevention: Allow good air circulation around seedlings; make sure the soil is damp but not soggy, and drains freely.

10. Fusarium wilt, causes sudden wilt, stunted growth; yellowing, rolled leaves and a meager harvest. Roots gradually turn dark when attacked by this soil-borne disease. Cucumber beetles are the vectors of this fungal disease.
Control: Remove and destroy *all* affected plants.
Prevention: Cover young plants, which are most susceptible, with floating row covers to prevent cucumber beetles from entering. Grow wilt-resistant varieties; rotate crops.

11. Downy mildew, a fungus prevalent in the South and Eastern seaboard, causes yellow spots on the tops of leaves, and fuzzy purple growth on leaf undersides. It's worst in humid, wet weather.
Control: Remove and destroy affected plants.
Prevention: Plant resistant varieties.

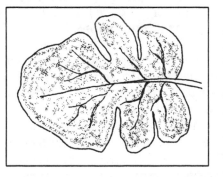

12. Powdery mildew causes a white powdery growth on foliage. Plants grow weak and foliage becomes brittle before dropping. Fruit may become disfigured and taste bad. Powdery mildew is most common during humid weather late in the season.
Control: Dust lightly with sulfur. Be careful not to burn foliage. If fungus appears a month before the first frost, no control is necessary.
Prevention: Grow resistant varieties.

13. Mosaic virus makes leaves curl, yellow, and die. Fruit turns a pale green and grows "warts". The virus is spread by aphids and cucumber beetles.
Control: Destroy affected plants.
Prevention: Fall cleanup and tillage. Control aphids and cucumber beetles.

14. Scab causes dark, dribbling spots on fruit that later dry, leaving a gray fungus covering the wound. This fungus is worst in cool, wet weather.
Control: Destroy all affected plants.
Prevention: Plant disease-resistant varieties. Crop rotation.

15. Bitter fruit can be caused by sudden fluctuations in temperature or ground moisture. Heavy pruning can also cause bitterness. All-female parthenocarpic varieties may become bitter if pollinated.
Control: Drop bitter fruit in boiling water for one minute. Cut away the bitter ends and skin before eating.
Prevention: Keep evenly watered, and protect from rapid temperature change.

16. Poor yield is normally caused by a lack of fertilizer or water. If fruit is allowed to mature too long on the vine, new fruit will not develop.
Control: Fertilize every two weeks after flowering starts, keep evenly moist and harvest regularly.

17. Deformed fruit is the result of water stress. If fruiting cucumber plants suffer an inconsistent water

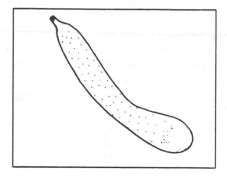

supply, one end of the fruit bulbs and turns pithy.

Control: Remove badly affected fruit.

Prevention: Mulch regularly. Water regularly, making sure to let it penetrate deeply to encourage deep root growth.

Other pests that may attack these vegetables include:

18. **Beet leafhopper (whitefly)**: page 39
19. **Imported cabbageworm**: page 55
02. **Mexican bean beetle**: page 34
21. **Onion thrips**: page 106
22. **Slugs & snails**: page 55
23. **Curly top**: page 100
24. **Root Rot**: page 72
25. **Wirestem rot**: page 56
26. **Damping-off**: page 77

The Solanum Family

Eggplants, peppers, and tomatoes are all members of the solanum family. Potatoes are also a member of the tomato family. Most potatoes grow best in cool-to-warm weather. The other members of the family are semitropical or tropical, and grow as an annual in most regions of North America. In greenhouses and in the warmest winter climates, they can be grown as perennials when cutback for the winter and fertilized regularly.

Deadly nightshade, the common weed whose red berries are poisonous, is a member of the solanum (belladonna) family. The toxic berries were confused with peppers and tomatoes by gardeners when the Spanish discovered the plant in the New World. Consequently, tomatoes were not eaten for centuries! Finally an Italian gardener made the distinction that native Americans had made for centuries, and tomatoes became a basic ingredient of European cuisine.

Tomatillos are sometimes listed in seed catalogs as tomatoes, while others call them peppers. The confusion arises since they are members of the same family.

Tomatoes, peppers, and to a lesser degree eggplants, can come in all shapes, sizes and colors: red, green, white, yellow, oblong, pear-shaped, pickle-shaped, etc.

The solanums *must have* warm weather in all stages of life to produce well. Nighttime temperatures above 55º (14º C) are necessary for eggplants and most peppers to survive, but some varieties of tomatoes, such as Oregon Spring, tolerate freezing temperatures for short periods. They all produce much better at warmer temperatures, and setting them out before the weather warms can be very disappointing.

Starting or buying seedlings and transplanting them under a cloche in moderately cool climates will increase fruit set substantially. Be careful to pamper transplants and not expose them to cold soil or weather. Let them harden-off slowly.

Avoid fertilizing these plants when the weather is cool. Only heat will speed growth. Additional fertilizer applied during cool weather will only toxify the plant!

Eggplant (*Solanum melongena*)

Eggplant, also called aubergine, needs daytime temperatures of 60-95° (16-35° C), and minimum nighttime temperatures of 65° (19° C), to yield fruit. *If the temperature dips below this point, they will not produce fruit.* For earliest production in northern latitudes, grow seedlings indoors and transplant them into a cold frame, or to under plastic tunnels until the temperature has warmed.

The oblong (egg-shaped) purple fruit is most common, but varieties are available in green, yellow, white and striped that can be oblong, round, or cylindrical in form.

Basic Facts

Germination time: 4-10 days.
Germination temperature: Minimum: 60° (16° C), Optimum: 85° (29° C), Maximum: 95° (35° C).
Approximate seeds per ounce: 5,600.
Yield per plant: 3-6 fruits (large varieties), more when grown under cover and in warm southern climates.
Life expectancy of stored seed: 5 years.
Estimated time between sowing and first picking: 10-12 weeks.
Intercrop: Radishes, onions, garlic, lettuce
Effort to cultivate: Somewhat difficult. Must have warm weather (above 65° (19° C)) and adequate water to bear fruit.
Seed saving: Self-pollinated. Harvest seed from fruit that has over matured, and has a tough skin.

Climate

Annual in climates with days and nights above 60° (16° C) over 90 consecutive days.. *Must have* daytime temperatures from 60-95° (16-35° C), and nighttime temperatures *must stay above 65° (19° C) to set and grow fruit.* Needs full sun.

Soil Preparation

Prepare soil in early spring or the previous fall. Incorporate plenty of compost and manure. Incorporate a complete organic fertilizer, and adjust the pH with dolomite lime if it is out of the 5.6-6.8 range.

Planting

Indoors: Plant seeds 1/2-inch deep in small containers of fine potting soil. Harden-off gradually, preferably under a cold frame. Transplant outdoors into a cold frame or under plastic tunnels.

The temperature must be at least 60° (16° C) for gemination, and 65-90° (19-32° C) for strong, rapid growth.

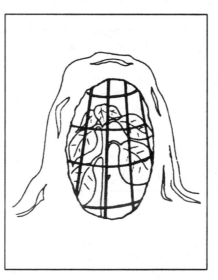

In rows: Sow seeds 1/2-inch deep 1-2 inches apart. Thin to 6-12 inches when seedlings are 4-6 inches tall.
In raised beds: Space seedlings on 12-24-inch centers, or sow seed on 2-inch centers and thin to 12-24-inch centers.

Replant seeds outdoors if the first sowing does not germinate rapidly or is slowed by spring rains.
Once the soil warms, mulch seedlings with black plastic or dark compost to raise soil temperature.
Plant about 3-4 plants per person.

Crop Care

Keep seedlings moist enough to avoid wilting. Be careful to keep from overwatering.
Mulch with dark compost or black plastic to heat soil after the soil has warmed or plants are 6 inches tall.
Deep-water as needed to encourage a long taproot, but do not let plants wilt. Water stress causes deformed fruit and lower yield.
Sidedress with a complete soluble fertilizer as soon as flowers set, and twice a month thereafter until the end of season.

Harvesting

Harvest when the fruit has stopped expanding, while the skin is still glossy and thin. This is just before peak maturity, when eggplants are succulent and the most flavorful.
Use pruners to cut each fruit from the plant as it matures. Keep fruit picked. Letting fruit overdevelop will retard the ripening of subsequent fruit.

Harvest all fruit late in the season. Once the sun intensity diminishes and weather starts to cool, fruit development virtually stops.

In the Kitchen

Fresh: Slice and eat succulent young eggplants raw, fresh from the garden. Or saute in olive oil and garlic for a few minutes before serving. Or roll slices in eggs and bread crumbs before frying or baking.

Storage: Wrap eggplants in cellophane or a plastic bag, and put in the refrigerator. They will keep for 2 weeks.

Freezing: Eggplant freezes best when cooked in dishes such as casseroles. However, they always become brown and mushy.

Pickling: Pickle small varieties whole. Slice larger types before pickling.

Eggplants offer little in the way of nutrient value, a modest amount of fiber, but best of all they are low in calories.

Varieties

Standard Purple Varieties

DUSKY HYBRID (65-75 days) is one of the best producers in all climates.

Large 6-7-inch-long, rich, tasty fruit. Available (Fa, Fi, Ma, Ni, Pi, Te St, Sha).

EARLY BLACK EGG (65-75 days), a Japanese variety, is the earliest producer in Northern latitudes. Yields 5-inch fruits on a compact plant. Available (Gc, So, Te).

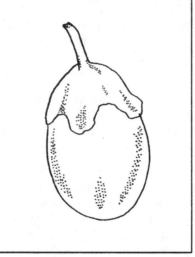

EARLY BIRD (75 days) yields slightly smaller fruit, but ripens a week or two earlier than Dusky Hybrid. Available (Pa, Te).

Other Varieties

CASPER (70 days) grows into a medium-sized plant that matures mild-tasting snowy white fruits.

Harvest fruit when 6 inches long for the best flavor. Available (St).

EASTER EGG (52 days) bears numerous 2-3-inch fruit, shaped like large white eggs. The fruit turns yellow when mature. Good flavor and compact plant, grows well in containers. Available (Pa, Pi).

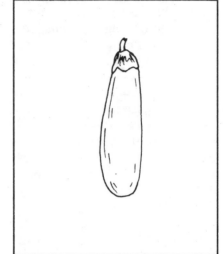

ICHIBAN (58 days) yields very early, deep purple, long, slender fruits with a sweet taste. Good slicers. Available (Pa, Pi).

TYCOON JAPANESE (61 days) will yield up to 75 twelve-inch, slender fruits per plant in ideal conditions. Bears mild, sweet flavored fruit early, and throughout a long season. Available (Fi, Le, Ni, Sha).

EGGPLANT	SYMPTOM	PROVABLE CAUSES
Seedlings	missing	8
Leaves	yellow patches	1
	dark spots	1, 3
	curled, wilt	6
	chewed	7, 9, 10, 12
	stippling, light spots	11, 13
Plants	cut off at base	8
	stunted	2
	sudden wilt	4
Fruit	slow development	2
	dark spots	3
	small or no fruit	5

Problems

Healthy eggplants rarely have any problems with pests or disease. The main problems they have are cool weather and a lack of nutrients. In fall, when the weather cools and the sunshine is less intense, growth slows notably.

1. Lace bugs that attack eggplants are gray to light brown, and flat with transparent lacy wings. A problem in the South, large groups of these insects feed on leaf undersides covering foliage with spots of excrement. Leaves turn pale yellow in patches. Infestations are often fatal and can devastate a garden.

Control: Early in the season you can squash them by hand or blast them off with a jet of water. Apply insecticidal soap or pyrethrum on infestations.
Prevention: Keep plants healthy, and growing rapidly.

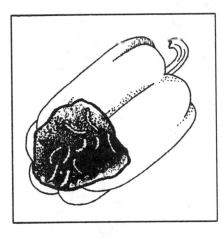

2. Pepper maggots first appear as translucent white, and gradually yellow, as they feed on fruit. The yellow adult fly lays eggs in the fruit.
Control: Remove infested plants and hot compost.
Prevention: Dust for adults with diatomaceous earth or rock phosphate during July and August when adults are laying eggs.

3. Fruit rot (blight) causes brown-to-gray spots on leaves, and large bands of spots on fruits. Damage is worst in warm, damp weather.
Control: None
Prevention: Select rot-resistant varieties. Rotate crops.

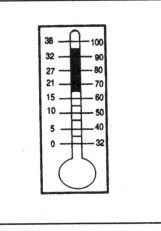

4. Small or no fruit is caused by temperatures below 65° (19° C), lack of water or fertilizer.

Control/prevention: Grow under a plastic tunnel or cloche. Keep well watered and fertilized during active growth.

5. Verticillium wilt causes leaves to wilt in the heat of the day, and recover when weather cools. Leaves eventually dry up and die.
Control: None
Prevention: Rotate crops; do not plant where tomatoes, peppers or potatoes have grown for the previous two years.

Other pests that may attack eggplants include:

6. Aphid: page 137
7. Colorado potato beetle page 120
8. Cutworm: page 137
9. Flea beetles: page 137
10. Harlequin bug: page 54
11. Spider mite: page 137
12. Tomato hornworm: page 138
13. Whitefly: page 137

Endive (*Cichorium endiva*) and Chicory (*Cichorium intybus*)

Typically, when someone thinks of endive, a vision of a white miniature lettuce heart comes to mind. Popular in gourmet restaurants, Belgian or French endive (it's usually chicory) is blanched by withholding light for 2-3 weeks, which lessens bitterness. Endive varieties have curly leaves, and escarole is the name given to broad-leafed varieties of endive. Radicchio is the name of various red-leafed chicories. Chicory forms slender, tall heads while endive forms looser heads similar to leaf lettuce.

Whatever name you know this leafy green by, it is growing in popularity rapidly. Endive may look similar to lettuce, but it is really a biennial cousin of chickory. Endive is an excellent crop for cool climates, and will overwinter, even if temperatures dip down to 10°! In fact, like its relative, Brussels sprouts, endive loses bitterness when gradually exposed to freezing temperatures. Warm weather increases bitterness. A great addition to salads, and one of the few greens available in the winter.

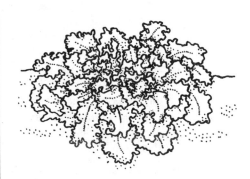

Basic Facts

Germination time: 10-14 days.
Germination temperature: Minimum: 30°, Optimum: 60°, Maximum 90°
Approximate seeds per ounce: 3,000.
Yield per 10-foot row: 3-6 pounds.
Life expectancy of stored seed: 5 years.
Estimated time between sowing and first picking: 12-14 weeks.
Intercrop: Basil, chives, garlic.
Effort to cultivate: Fairly easy, but needs protection from hot weather.
Seed saving: Trick this biennial into flowering. Plant early in the spring. Collect seeds from dry flower pods after plants bolt during hot weather.

Climate

Annual in all zones. Tolerant to both heat and cold (down to 10°). Grows well in cool weather. Heavy winter rains can cause rot damage. Plant summer crops in partial shade.

Curly endive is the most cold tolerant. Escarole grows broad, flat leaves best during hot weather.

Soil Preparation

To prepare soil before planting, incorporate plenty of compost and manure. Add a complete, high-nitrogen fertilizer when planting. Kelp meal will help poor soils become more fertile.

Most of the roots only penetrate the soil 8 inches, so cultivation can be shallow. The pH should be near 6.0 for the best growth.

Planting

In rows: Sow seed 1/4-inch deep, 3-4 seeds per inch in rows spaced 18 inches apart.
In raised beds: Broadcast seed 1/4-inch deep on 2-4-inch centers. Cover small seed with fine compost for best germination.
Plant early in spring or late winter for a spring crop. Leaves may taste bitter when allowed to mature in warm weather.
Note: If germination temperatures are too cold (near the minimum) the chances of bolting in warm weather are increased.

For a fall and winter crop, sow seed from August through September in warm climates, and from June through August in northern regions. It can be sown later if planted in a cold frame. The later seeds are sown, the closer they may be spaced.
Plant 4-6 plants per person.

Crop Care

Thin plants as they mature. Thinnings may be used for early salads. When sown for a spring and summer crop, plants should ultimately be thinned to 12-18 inches apart.
Do not let leaves of plants touch one another in wet climates. This will cut down on rot significantly.
Rapid growth enables endive to produce lush, succulent, tender growth. A side dressing of soluble high-nitrogen fertilizer encourages broad, succulent leaves.
Mulch and water regularly. Plants can take some water stress, but there are numerous surface roots. Plants need about 1 inch of water weekly.

In warm weather, cover plants with shade cloth to lessen bitterness and help prevent bolting.
To blanch, once the plants have reached full size, slip a rubber band around the outer leaves so that a head is formed. The outer leaves block light from the center of the rosette. Blanching turns the internal leaves white and makes them tender. Or blanch by inverting flowerpots over well-formed heads. Late fall and winter heads can be blanched by gently digging root ball and storing the uprooted plant in a cool, dark garage or basement for several weeks.

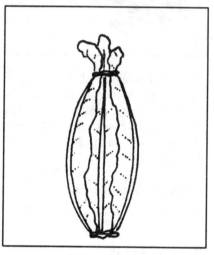

Note: Blanching lowers the nutritional value of green leaves.
In wet climates, use the flowerpot method (above) to blanch endive to guard against rot.

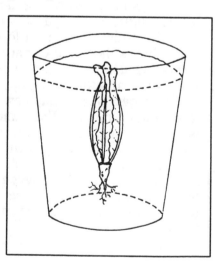

To "force" endive, dig up the long, carrotlike root after first frost. Cut off the leaves, leaving about 2 inches above the roots. Place the roots upright in a bucket with drainage holes, and cover the roots with at least 8 inches of sand or sawdust. Drench the roots weekly with water. After 3 weeks, the heads will sprout blanched heads. Cut the heads, and put the roots back in the bucket to sprout another crop of smaller heads.

Harvesting

In the fall and winter, cut individual leaves from the outside of the rosette. The smaller leaves will continue to grow.

Harvest entire plants that have been blanched by cutting them off at ground level. Both the outer leaves and the tender center may be included in salads.

Harvest roots after the leaf harvest by uprooting. Wash and dry on a screen, or hang in a dry location.

If about an inch of stem is left on the root stock after the initial harvest, new smaller heads will form in warm weather. This is called the "cut and come again" method. Harvest the heads as they mature.

In the Kitchen

Fresh green leaves added to salads enhance flavor immensely. Add chopped green leaves to soups for a

savory flavor. Serve in salads with a squeeze of lemon.

Storage: Keeps in the refrigerator in a plastic bag for up to 2 weeks.

Roots can be dried, roasted and chopped to be used as a coffee substitute.

Green leaves are high in vitamins A, B_1, and C.

Varieties

Chicory Varieties

Chicory (*Cichorium intybus*) grows fast and is a good choice for any garden.

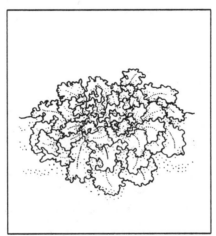

ARUGULA (Roquette or Rocket) (*Eruca vesicaria*) (35 days) is native to western Asia and has been popular in Europe for centuries. Arugola adds a strong, distinctive flavor to spring salads. Long, dark green leaves thrive in both hot and cold weather to yield loose, open heads with a peppery bite. Available (Bu, Ca, Ha, He, Hi, Hu, Jo, Ni, Pa, Ric, Th Sha).

RADICCHIO (80 days) varieties including are red-leafed chicory, including **ALTO, AGUSTO, GIULIO** and **RED VERONA.** They form heads of loose rosettes in the winter and during hot weather. They can also be forced like Witloof chicory. The "Chioggia" (round red-heading) Radicchio forms heads without forcing. Available (Bu, Hi, Pa, Sha).

Endive (escarole) Varieties

Endive (*Cichorium endiva*) is slower to mature and is more cold hardy than chicory.

FLORIDA DEEP HEART (85 days) leaves are slightly curled in this late, broad-leafed, heat-tolerant variety. Excellent flavor, and blanches well. Available (Ha, Sha).

FULL-HEARTED BATAVIA (Escarole) (90 days) has thick, broad, slightly kinked lettucelike leaves with a deep white buttery heart. Heads grow up to 16 inches across. Available (Gc, Hi, Le, Me, Ni, St).

GREEN CURLED (Giant Fringed Oyster) (90 days) is a popular open-pollinated variety that matures late into thick 12- to 16-inch diameter plants. Hearts easily blanch to a creamy white. Available (Bu, Le, Ma).

Problems

Endive and chicory are almost pest-free when grown in the cool months. The major problems they have are aphids, slugs, snails, rot and bolting. All of these problems are compounded during hot weather.

ENDIVE & CHICORY	SYMPTOM	PROVABLE CAUSES
Seedlings	missing	2
Leaves	yellowing, curl	1
	chewed, holes	2
	dark patches	3
Plant	stunted	1, 2
	premature flowering	4

1. Aphids about the size of a pinhead are found on leaves, especially on young, succulent growth. This pest is a most serious problem as weather warms. The clusters of yellow-to-brown aphids puncture soft foliage, feed on plant fluids, and excrete a sticky honeydew that promotes sooty mold. Leaves yellow, and growth is stunted.
Control: Blast off with a jet of water. Spray with insecticidal soap, ryana, sabadilla, nicotine sulfate, or pyrethrum.
Prevention: Ladybugs, lacewings and hover-flies all prey on aphids. Inspect weekly for aphids and control as soon as possible.

silvery trail of slime. These pests prefer young, succulent plants.
Control: Hand-pick. A thin layer of lime, diatomaceous earth, or salty beach sand around individual plants, beds, or the entire garden dissolves and repels mollusks. Or dust plants with dolomite lime or diatomaceous earth. Pour a jam- and-water mix into a covered coffee can with a slot cut in the side to form a slug and snail hotel. The pests are attracted to the mix, enter and drown. Spray slugs with a half-and-half mix of ammonia and water.
Prevention: Encourage natural predators: birds, frogs, toads, salamanders and small snakes.

Control: Pick off rotten leaves, and compost them.
Prevention: Harvest closely spaced plants before leaves overlap on adjacent plants. Space seedlings 12-18 inches apart.

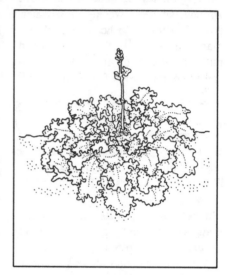

2. Slugs and snails can cause severe damage in wet weather. They slither from hiding places at night or on rainy days to eat foliage leaving a

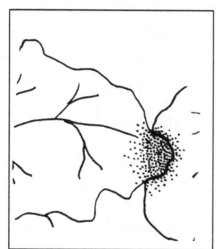

3. Rot or fungus can become a problem when plants are spaced so closely that leaves overlap and moisture is trapped between them.

4. Bolting, or running to seed, is common in warm weather.
Control: Harvest plants as soon as they start to bolt. You can eat the leaves if they are not too bitter.
Prevention: Cover plants with a shade cloth; plant where shaded from midday sun; plant in coolest section of the garden.

Other pests that may attack endive and chicory also attack lettuce. See Lettuce "Problems" page 95

Allium Family

Chives, garlic, leeks, onions, scallions and shallots are all members of the allium family. Alliums are frost-hardy biennials grown as annuals. In fact, some alliums are so tolerant to freezing temperatures, gardeners in most climates can enjoy them fresh all year-round.

This family is very sensitive to the length of days and nights (photoperiodic). That is, they will bulb or flower when the length of day commands. But since alliums are biennial, some, such as garlic and shallots, will only bulb after exposure to cold winter temperatures, and the increasing length of days and shortening of nights in spring. Flowering is triggered in the majority of alliums by longer nights and shorter days of autumn. This means that vegetative growth before flowering must be rapid and consistent, since bulbs quit growing once flowering starts. It also means that fertilizer will be wasted if applied after vegetative growth and bulb formation is completed.

Allium roots are coarse, thick, shallow and do not spread far or grow deep. They hold water well, which makes transplanting nearly fail-safe, but roots do not spread out to look for water and must be kept moist. The ideal soil for alliums is a sandy loam; they do not expand or bulb well in heavy clay nor coarse sand.

Starting onions from seed is easy. Seeds sprout in cool, moist soil within about two weeks. When growing from seed, keep the soil from forming a crust, which the weak seedlings can't penetrate. Also apply a liquid soluble fertilizer to feed the small roots. The seedlings are easy to transplant, even if the roots are entirely bare.

Garlic, some shallots, and nonbulbing onions, have been propagated so long from bulbs or cloves that seed is unavailable.

Saving and growing your own seed is possible. However seeds tend to cross-pollinate, varieties must be separated by 500-1,000 feet.

Garlic (*Allium sativum*) and Shallots (*Allium cepa aggregatum*)

All gardeners should plant garlic! The compound bulb consists of 6-12 individual segments (cloves), and a leaf stock, which produces seeds and bulblets, both of which can be planted. A perennial grown as an annual, garlic boasts insecticidal and antibiotic qualities in the garden plus numerous health benefits when consumed. A very aromatic and savory food flavoring, garlic also aids the circulatory and digestive systems. All gourmet cooks would be lost without this essential culinary ingredient. The delectable aroma of garlic hung to dry in the kitchen is mouth watering. Garlic takes up so little space, it can be interplanted with numerous vegetables and flowers. The narrow, bluish-green, bladelike leaves add subtle color and texture to diverse garden designs.

An excellent insecticide and fungicide when minced or juiced and mixed with water. As a fungicide, garlic helps control downy mildew, various rusts, bean anthracnose, some leaf spots, and blights.

Shallots are sweet, savory gourmet onions that grow just like garlic. The cloves of shallots' compound bulbs are planted and cultured the same as garlic.

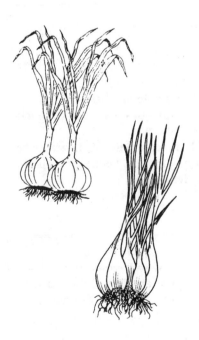

Basic Facts

Germination time: 5-14 days.
Germination temperature: Minimum: 40º (5º C), Optimum: 75º (24º C), Maximum: 95º (35º C).
Approximate cloves per ounce: 30-50 (regular), 10-15 (Elephant garlic & shallots).
Yield per ounce of cloves: 3/4 pound.
Life expectancy of stored cloves: 1 year.
Estimated time between sowing and first picking: 38-40 weeks (overwintering), 14-16 (summer).
Intercrop: With any plant that will not shade it.
Effort to cultivate: Easy!
Seed saving: Save the largest cloves for planting the next year. Immature flower bulbs that grow from the top of plants can also be saved and planted.

Climate

Annual in all zones. Seedlings require cool temperatures to develop leaves, and hot weather to promote bulb growth. Frost-hardy. Elephant garlic is *extremely* hardy.

Soil Preparation

Ideal soil is a fertile sandy loam well amended with organic matter. The soil should be loose and fine with a slightly acidic pH. Soil that is rich in sulfur tends to make garlic taste sweeter.
Add a complete fertilizer when working the soil. Garlic grows best in very fertile soil.
Rake seed bed smooth before planting.

Planting

Seeds are rare. If you do find seeds, plant them the same as onions page 103.

Cloves, including flower bulblets: Plant the largest cloves one-inch deep with the blunt (root) end down and the pointed end up. The cloves can also be set halfway into the soil and covered with a 1/2- to 1-inch layer of rich compost.

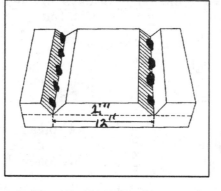

In wide raised beds, space cloves on 3-4-inch centers. In rows, space cloves 3-4 inches apart in rows spaced at 12-18 inches.
Interplant several cloves of garlic with flowers and vegetables. Garlic takes up little space and deters many insects.
Plant from August through November in mild climates. In cold climates, start cloves indoors, and transplant outdoors 4-6 weeks before last frost. Garlic can also be planted outdoors in the fall if mulched for protection from severe freezes.

Crop Care

Keep well watered during warm weather. Garlic and shallots have a small, but pulpy root system that holds water well.
Mulch heavily to retain moisture, cool soil, and stifle weeds.
Weed by hand, especially when garlic is young. Competition from weeds greatly reduces yield.
Remove flower heads when they form. This will allow all the plant's energy to develop larger bulbs.
The bulblets in the flower head can be allowed to develop. Once flower bulblets are fully mature, they are planted.

Harvesting

When the tops start to yellow, initiate the harvesting process. Stop watering and bend the tops over to accelerate bulb curing.

Three to six days after knocking over tops, lift the bulbs using a spading fork.
Store bulbs in a cool, shady location to dry for several weeks.
Trim off the excess stem and roots before hanging the dry bulbs of cloves in a mesh net sack that provides good air circulation.
An alternative method of harvesting and drying is to lift mature bulbs. Braid the tops together when they are still green. Start with three garlic or shallots; each time a braid crosses, add one more plant. Tie the end of braided foliage off with a string and hang the braided string of garlic or shallots in a cool dry location to cure.
Note: When harvesting, it is difficult to dig out all of the cloves. Those left in the ground will ensure an early planting for the following year! Save enough of the largest cloves to plant for subsequent crops.

In the Kitchen

Fresh: Garlic can be used to enhance the flavor of salads, meat dishes, soups, casseroles, and just about anything else. Separate cloves from the bulb by rubbing the papery outer skin off. Lay a clove on a counter top. Use a flat utensil to press down lightly on it to separate the skin. Remove the papery skin. Either mince the garlic with a knife or squeeze it with a garlic press.

Shallots are used the same as onions in cooking. (page 104).

Storage: Hang garlic and shallots bulbs in braids, a net sleeve or a bag, or keep them in a cool dry container in the kitchen.

Varieties

Garlic and shallots are normally sold at nurseries in the fall and spring, but you can buy them just as easily at the grocery store, often for less than they cost at nurseries. Look for bulbs with well-formed cloves that show no sign of rot.

Garlic Varieties

ELEPHANT GARLIC (*Allium scorodoprasum*) (days) is actually a type of leek developed in Albany, Oregon by Nichols Nursery that produces large multiple bulbs (cloves) that are 5-6 times larger than true garlic. It is milder than "normal" garlic and considerably more cold tolerant. A very good choice in any climate. Available (Bu, Cr, Da, Fa, Fi, Ha, Me, Hi, Pa, Ric, Sha, St, Th).

EUROPEAN (pink, red or purple) types have been bred into some new, and into numerous regional varieties. Many produce strong, full-flavored cloves that store very well. Available (Gs, Se)

MEXICAN (white) varieties produce sooner than European varieties. They have a robust, garlic flavor and large cloves, but they do not store as well as European types. Available (Fi, Gs, Ju, Sc)

OPHIO GARLIC (*A. S. var. ophioscorodon*) descended from the ancient varieties of South Central Asia. Ophio Garlic is easy to identify by the top-setting bulblets on a coiled seed stock. (Available (Gs, Se).

Shallot Varieties

DUTCH YELLOW SHALLOTS (77 days) yield 6-8 bulblets from each bulb. The mild, savory bulbs are a golden yellow. Very good fresh in any soup or salad. Available (Ric, Th).

FRENCH SHALLOTS bulblets divide into a cluster of 5-8 mild, delectable bulblets. Also use as scallions early in the season. Make sure to request **FRENCH SHALLOTS** and do not settle for the yellow type (multiplier onions) Available (Jo, Ni, Ric, Sc).

GIANT RED SHALLOT (70 days) forms deep red bulblets that keep well in the garden or after harvest. The harvest continues for several months. Crisp, crunchy bulbs are rich in flavor. Available (Th).

Problems

The only problems normally associated with garlic are poor vigor and meager harvests. These problems are due to a lack of nutrients (they are relatively heavy feeders), moisture, or not cutting the flower tops off as soon as they set.

For additional problems that might befall garlic and shallots, see "Onion Problems" page 106.

Kale (*Brassica oleracea*, Acephala Group)

Ben Franklin brought the first kale seeds to America. He carried them from Scotland over two centuries ago. Today garden-fresh, homegrown kale is a far cry from tough, bitter, supermarket types. A member of the brassica family (page 41), kale is so hardy it will overwinter when temperatures dip below 0. It will grow all year round in most climates, but grows best in cool weather. Warm temperatures induce mild dormancy and make leaves quite bitter and leathery. As with many brassicas, kale tastes best after being nipped by frost. There are several edible ornamental varieties that are popular in flower beds and containers to provide winter color. The ruffled leaves add to the circular bands of color in these ornamental types. One of the few salad greens available in winter, kale is packed with vitamins, and low in calories.

Basic Facts

Germination time: 6-10 days.
Germination temperature: Minimum: 40° (5° C), Optimum: 72° (22° C), Maximum: 95° (35° C).
Approximate seeds per ounce: 7,000.
Yield per plant: 1-2 pounds of leaves.
Life expectancy of stored seed: 5 years.
Estimated time between sowing and first picking: 12-14 weeks.
Intercrop: Plant in mid summer among soft annuals and vegetables. After the soft vegetation is frozen, kale plants are well established!
Effort to cultivate: Easy. Plant so that it matures in cool weather.
Seed saving: Biennial kale crosses with other brassicas. Requires 1, 000 feet of isolation from other brassicas.

Climate

Annual in all zones. Cold hardy to 10° below zero. A hard freeze increases sugar content of leaves, which makes them delightfully sweet.
Grows slowly at 40° (5° C) or less. Foliage gets tough and bitter if temperatures climb above 75° (24° C). The ideal temperature for fast growth is 60-65° (16-19° C).

Soil Preparation

Like other brassicas, kale is a heavy feeder with a shallow root system. It develops best in rich loamy soil. Flavor and texture suffer in sandy or heavy clay soils.
Add plenty of rich compost and manure up to a month before direct seeding or transplanting seedlings.
Lime soil when preparing to buffer the pH and add necessary calcium.

Planting

Spring Crops: Sow as soon as the soil can be worked in spring. Sow seed 1/4-inch deep, at 2-4 inch intervals in rows spaced 24-30 inches apart.
In raised, wide beds, sow seed on 3-4-inch centers.
Thin plantings to 12-18-inches apart.
Winter crops: Sow seed from two months to two weeks before the first killing frost of winter. Sow seed 1/4-inch deep, slightly closer than for spring crops.
Thin seedlings to 12 inches apart when they are about 6 inches tall. Thinnings make excellent greens for salads.

Crop Care

A heavy feeder, kale needs supplemental fertilization for the best crop production.
Fertilize with a manure tea or soluble high-nitrogen fertilizer every two-to-four weeks.

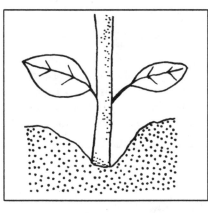

Mulch is especially beneficial to kale. Mulch helps keep the surface root system cool and moist. Mulch also allows feeder roots to absorb nutrients near the soil surface. When mulching, take care to keep it 1-2 inches away from the stem to lessen the possibility of stem rot.
Water regularly. Kale has a shallow root system which requires surface watering.
In the winter, when watering is unnecessary, brush the mulch away from the stem to guard against mouse damage. The mice are attracted to the warm bed of mulch and gnaw at the stems.

Harvesting

Spring crops can be harvested as soon as plants size up. Harvest individual leaves starting at the bottom of the plant or cut the entire plant, at ground level. Harvest all plants before the hottest weather of July and August. Overripe, heat-stressed kale is tough, stringy, with much of it's nutritional value lost.

After the first frost, harvest individual outer leaves or entire plants. Continue harvesting throughout the winter, even in the snow!

In the Kitchen

Note: Kale is renowned for its high vitamin A, C, and iron content.
Fresh: Add leaves to salads or steam greens and serve with freshly squeezed lemon juice and butter, like spinach. Save the cooking water for use as soup stock, or add to drinks. Or chop and saute leaves in olive oil. Chopped kale leaves make a tangy garnish on soups and egg dishes. Kale is an excellent ingredient in numerous stir-fry dishes.
Storage: Kale stores very well during the cool months of winter in the garden; harvest it a leaf at a time, starting at the bottom. Kale also stores up to 3 weeks when wrapped in plastic in the refrigerator.

Freezing: Simply wash leaves, pat dry with a towel and pop into a plastic bag. The kale will store in the freezer quite well.

Varieties

The best varieties of kale grow low to the ground, and have thick, crinkled leaves that spread to form a dense mass of foliage.

DWARF BLUE CURLED VATES (55 days) matures very quickly into productive low, compact plants with tightly curled blue-green leaves. This variety is not as cold tolerant as SIBERIAN. Available (Bu, Em, Fi, Ha, Ju, Ma, Me, Ni, Pa, Pi, St).
PEACOCK TYPES (70 days) including RED PEACOCK and WHITE PEACOCK ornamental kale, produce rose pink or white, finely-fringed centers with ruffled crimson or green outer leaves on a 16-inch plant. Available (Bu, Pa, St, Th)
RED RUSSIAN (55-65 days), an American heirloom, grows large 2-3-foot wavy leaves. The leaf veins turn an exquisite red that illuminates the winter garden. Amazingly sweet and succulent, even in warmer weather. Available (Gc, Ni, She).
SIBERIAN (70 days), also available in a dwarf variety, grows slightly ruffled, blue-green leaves up to 2 feet across. It is extremely hardy and very tender with a delicate flavor. Bu, Hi, Te).
WINTERBOR HYBRID (60 days) has one of the mildest flavors before frost. The frilly, deep blue-green leaves are very ornamental in the garden or as a garnish. Hybrid vigor makes this variety very early and productive. Available (Jo, Pa, Te).

Problems

Typically, kale is trouble-free when supplied with adequate nutrients and the surface root system is kept mulched and moist. Pests that may attack kale include aphids and flea beetles.

See "Brassica Problems" page 53 for more information about Kale problems.

Kohlrabi (*Brassica oleracea*, Gongylodes Group)

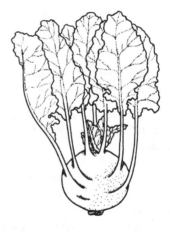

This member of the brassica family (page 41) looks like a turnip growing above ground on a cabbage root! Kohlrabi's bulbous stem has the taste of the most delicate cabbage, with the consistency of a turnip. It tastes good either raw or cooked. A biennial, grown as an annual, kohlrabi is very easy to culture, and has few problems with disease or insects. Like most cabbage, kohlrabi grows best when planted early in the spring and harvested before warm weather makes bulbs hot and woody. Mid- to late-summer plantings can be harvested after frost has killed most other plants in the garden.

Basic Facts

Germination time: 7-14 days.
Germination temperature: Minimum: 40° (5° C), Optimum: 72° (22° C), Maximum: 95° (35° C).
Approximate seeds per ounce: 8,000.
Yield per 10 foot row: 10-30 pounds
Life expectancy of stored seed: 3 years.
Estimated time between sowing and first picking: 8-9 weeks.
Intercrop: Plant during midsummer among soft ornamentals and vegetables. When a freeze kills the soft vegetation, kale plants are well established!
Effort to cultivate: Easy. Grow in cool weather.
Seed saving: Difficult. A biennial, kohlrabi is grown 2 years before good seed can be produced.

Climate

Annual in all zones. Prefers cool temperatures of spring and fall. The ideal temperature range for growth is 60-65° (16-19° C). Hot weather turns the bulb tough, woody and hot.

Soil Preparation

A heavy feeder, kohlrabi benefits much from fertile soil that drains well.
Prepare the soil up to a month before planting. Add plenty of compost and manure to increase fertility and tilth. A heavy phosphorus feeder, kohlrabi benefits from greensand and wood ashes added to the soil.

Add a complete fertilizer when preparing the soil, and lime if the pH is out of the acceptable 6.0-7.0 range.

Planting

For an early summer harvest, sow seed on the last average frost date. Sow small quantities of seed, because spring-sown kohlrabi does not hold in the garden without losing flavor or turning woody. Plan successive plantings at two-week intervals through mid spring.

For a fall harvest, sow seed July through August. Sow a larger patch for the fall or winter crop. The kohlrabi holds in the garden much better in cool weather.

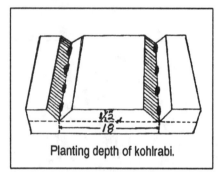

Planting depth of kohlrabi.

In rows, sow seed 1/2-inch deep, 3-4 seeds per inch, and space rows 18 inches apart.

In wide raised beds, broadcast seed over the bed, or space seed on one-inch centers and cover with 1/2 inch of fine topsoil or well-rotted compost.

Thin when seedlings are 6 inches tall. Place them 3 inches apart in rows with 6-inch centers in wide raised beds. *Overcrowded kohlrabi does not bulb well.*

Plant approximately 4-6 plants per person.

Crop Care

A weak shallow root system is typical of kohlrabi and it needs regular watering for best production. The most succulent growth is achieved when growth is rapid.

Fertilize with a soluble, all-purpose mix when bulbs start to form.

Mulch plants about 2 weeks after the last thinning. Mulching is essential to retain surface water and keep roots cool.

Weed by hand before mulching.

Harvesting

Harvest entire plants when the bulbs have sized up to 2-3 inches in diameter. If the bulbs grow too long, especially in hot weather, they turn woody, tough, and hot.

Cut plants off at the base, or uproot. Trim leaves and root off and discard in the compost pile.

In the Kitchen

Fresh: Kohlrabi is delicious when harvested at the size of a walnut fresh from the garden. If the bulb grows to a 3-inch diameter, it becomes fibrous.

Steam kohlrabi just as you would any other vegetable and serve with butter.

Storage: Just pop trimmed roots into a plastic bag. They will keep in the refrigerator up to two weeks.

Freezing: Blanch entire bulbs for 1-2 minutes, pat dry, and put into a plastic bag.

Varieties

Inexpensive, poorly performing varieties are grown for the-home garden trade in the U.S. Be careful not to select one of these varieties: PURPLE VIENNA or WHITE VIENNA. Select varieties grown in Europe for best flavor and production.

Varieties

GRAND DUKE (45-50 days), an AAS Winner, yields early, succulent round bulbs with white flesh. Bulbs can grow to 4 inches for peak yield. Available (Bu, Fa, Fi, Le, Na, Ju, Ma, Pa, St, Th, Ri)

GIANT WINTER (62 days from transplant) yields an 8-inch bulb that is tender throughout. This variety may set the new standard for kohlrabi. Resistant to root maggots. Good choice for late season and overwintering in temperate climates. Available (Ni, So)

WINNER (60 days) grows uniform, mild, sweet-fleshed bulbs. Grows well in cool, moist climates. Available (Te).

Problems

The cabbage fly root maggot (page 53) is the biggest pest that kohlrabi faces. The only other maladies are small harvests and tough woody bulbs. Small harvests can be remedied by growing in rich, fertile soil, regular watering, and mulching to conserve water and keep roots cool. Tough woody bulbs are caused by letting the bulb mature too long during hot weather.

Other problems that might occur with kohlrabi are discussed in detail under Brassica "Problems" page 41.

Leek (*Allium ampeloprasum*, Porrum Group)

Leeks, like garlic, have flat leaves. The flat leaves distinguish leeks from other members of the onion family. Leeks need a long growing season. Autumn leeks are tender and sweet. Overwintering varieties are very frost hardy, which may keep you in garden fresh "onions" year round. Most bulb onions are harvested in the fall and stored for the winter. Leeks, on the other hand, can be stored in the garden and used throughout the winter when needed, even when there is snow on the ground. This quality is especially attractive in damp climates where bulb onions do not store well.

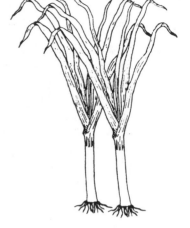

Basic Facts

Germination time: 10-18 days.
Germination temperature: Minimum: 40º (5º C), Optimum: 70º (21º C), Maximum: 95º (35º C).
Approximate seeds per ounce: 9,500.
Yield per 10-foot row: 1-30 pounds
Life expectancy of stored seed: 1-2 years.
Estimated time between sowing and first picking: 10-12 weeks (summer), 15-30 weeks (overwintering).
Intercrop: Carrots, celery, and onions
Effort to cultivate: Fairly easy, requires a long season and special planting technique.
Seed saving: Difficult. As a biennial, leeks must be grown for two years to produce seed.

Climate

Annual in all zones. Seedlings need temperate weather to germinate, and produce most succulent growth in hot weather. Leeks grow best during 60-70º (21º C) days and 50-60º (10-16º C) nights. As they mature, leeks become very cold-hardy, growing well in cool weather.

Soil Preparation

Ideal soil is a fertile sandy loam, well amended with organic matter. The soil should be loose and fine with a slightly acidic pH.
Add a complete fertilizer when working the soil and lime if the pH is out of the acceptable 6.0-7.0 range.
Rake seed bed smooth before planting seed or transplanting.

Planting

Autumn leeks can be sown indoors in northern or wet climates very early in the spring; they are transplanted outdoors 2-4 weeks after the last frost date. In warm southern climates, sow seed outdoors in early spring as described below.
Winter leeks are sown outdoors after the last frost date through early summer as described below.
To sow leek seed, prepare a nursery bed in the garden by spreading one to three inches of compost and a complete fertilizer. Cultivate the bed 6-8 inches deep so that it is free of clods. Broadcast about 5 seeds per square inch and cover the seed with finely sifted compost, peat or soil. Keep the top layer of compost/soil moist so that it does not develop a crust.
Thin the seedlings if extraordinarily overcrowded, but lanky seedlings are the most desirable for transplanting.
Transplant the seedlings when they are 8-10 inches tall. Dig and separate the seedlings. Place them in a bunch and cut off the top half of the green leaves; place the seedlings in a moist plastic bag or jar of water to keep them from drying out.

Dig a narrow trench 8-12 inches deep in a fertile, well-prepared bed. Carefully place the seedlings about 2 inches apart in the bottom of the trench and backfill to just below the first joint of leaves. Dig more trenches 12-18 inches apart, parallel to the first trench. Once all seedlings are transplanted, water them thoroughly.
Backfill the trench, and later, gradually mound soil around the leek to blanch the bottom part throughout the growing season. Do not backfill soil beyond the first leaf joint or soil will become trapped inside the leek.

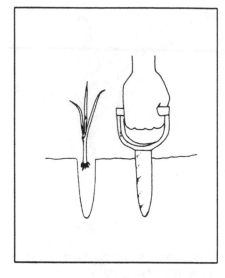

A very easy alternative to digging a trench is to use a long, slender staff called a dibble, to make individual holes, and plant the leeks in the holes. The holes are drilled 6-9 inches deep, and the leeks set in them. The first set of leaves hold the seedling in place. The leeks grow to fill the hole, making backfilling unnecessary.

As a winter onion substitute, plant leek seeds in midsummer and harvest from September through April. Eat the leek seedlings as green onions. **Plant 10-20 leeks per person.**

Crop Care

Keep well watered during warm weather.

Weed with a hoe, scraping a little soil into the trench during each weeding. Take care to keep soil out of the leaf grooves.

Mulch to conserve moisture, to keep weeds at bay, and to guard against cold damage. Mulch also helps to blanch the edible root.

Thin the leeks if they become overcrowded and eat them as green onions. In fact, many gardeners enjoy succulent young leeks all winter.

Cut off any flower spikes before they flower. Producing flowers draws energy away from stem production.

Harvesting

Autumn leeks can be harvested for 2-3 months. Dig every other leek in the row. This will allow better air circulation which lessens disease and pest occurrence. Start harvesting when leeks are about an inch in diameter.

Winter leeks can be harvested throughout the winter until they bolt in spring. Apply a band of high-nitrogen fertilizer along both sides of the crop in late winter to encourage spring growth.

In the Kitchen

Fresh: Garden-fresh leeks harvested all winter long taste much better than stored onions. Use them just as you would onions in salads, soups, and all cooking.

Storage: Autumn leeks store very well in the refrigerator for up to a month when wrapped in plastic. Winter leeks store best in the garden and dug as needed.

Varieties

Autumn Varieties

KING RICHARD (75 days), Foot-tall white stems are normal when properly cultured. Very early to produce, this variety yields exceptionally well. Available (Jo, Hi).

TITAN (70 days) is a favorite for summer cultivation. Six-inch-long white stems grow fat for the earliest harvests. Available (Bu, St, Sha)

Winter Varieties

ALASKA (105 days) is a commercial Dutch leek that is cold-tolerant to zero. Alaska has thick white stems up to 8 inches long and they keep in the ground very well. Available (St).

GIANT MUSSELBURGH (110 days) has massive stems that are extremely hardy, tender, and mild. Available (Ni).

CARINA (105 days) is an improved Catalina variety. This Dutch hybrid yields thick 10-inch-long stems. Good tolerance to frost. Available (She, St).

Problems

Leeks are remarkably trouble-free. Rot or fungus are the only problems that may affect leeks. To circumvent mold and rot, leave adequate spacing between plants.

See Onion "Problems" page 106 for more information about leek problems.

Do you have some good recipes that you would like to share with us? We would love to know about them. Maybe we'll add them to our next book. Write down your recipe and mail it to Van Patten Publishing, 4204 S.E. Ogden St., Portland, OR 97206. If we use your information, we'll note your name in the book and send you a free copy of the book your information was used in.

Lettuce (*Lactuca sativa*)

This is one crop all gardeners can grow with very little effort when the weather is cool. The onset of hot weather turns lettuce bitter and induces bolting, but there are several heat-tolerant varieties. The real challenge to growing lettuce is maintaining a constant supply all summer long. This requires successive sowing. Since lettuce is a light feeder and requires little direct sunlight, it is a perfect crop to interplant throughout the season. Leaf varieties are the easiest to cultivate, and much more nutritious than the tricky head lettuce. There is a variety for all tastes and climates. Growing the proper variety for your climate and season will keep you in lettuce as long as relatively warm weather allows. Many varieties tolerate frost to 20° if hardened-off gradually. Lettuce can be nurtured indoors when it's too cold to grow outdoors. It also grows well under glass in an insulated cold frame, or in a plastic tunnel.

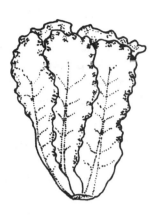

Basic Facts

Germination time: 3-7 days.
Germination temperature: Minimum: 35° (2° C), Optimum: 75° (24° C), Maximum: 85° (29° C).
Approximate seeds per ounce: 20,000.
Yield per 10 foot row: 10-20 plants.
Life expectancy of stored seed: 2 years.
Estimated time between sowing and first picking: 9-12 weeks.
Intercrop with any flower or vegetable.
Effort to cultivate: Easy, requires moderate temperatures.
Seed saving: Isolate seed crops 200 feet from other varieties. Harvest seed stocks when dry.

Climate

Annual in all zones. Needs full to partial sun. Starts to bolt when temperatures climb beyond 85° (29° C). Locate summer crops where they are shaded from midday sun.

Soil Preparation

Ideal soil for lettuce cultivation is a rich, well-drained loam that is near neutral on the pH scale (5.8-6.8).

Incorporate plenty of compost and well-rotted manure in the soil 4-6 weeks before planting. Add lime if the pH is too high or low.
Lettuce has a dense but shallow root system. The soil will have to hold enough water near the surface to reduce daily maintenance.
Rake the seed bed smooth to a fine consistency and free of clods.

Planting

Sow seed by broadcasting over wide raised bed or space 2-4 seeds per inch in rows. Sow two or three different types that mature at different rates to ensure a longer harvest.

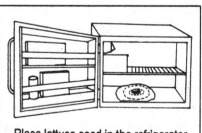

Place lettuce seed in the refrigerator for 5 days to hasten germination in hot weather.

Sow seed on soil surface, then gently rake in, so that the seed is lightly covered with fine soil. Or cover seed with a 1/4-inch layer of peat moss or a layer of newspaper, which will hold moisture until the seeds sprout in a few days. *Remove the newspaper as soon as the first seeds sprouts.*
In hot weather, ensure germination by wrapping seed in a moist paper towel and store in the refrigerator for about 5 days. The ideal temperature range for growth is 65-70° (19-21° C), and can dip to 45° (7° C) at night with no ill effects.

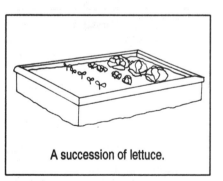

A succession of lettuce.

Sow only enough seed to last a week or two in the kitchen. Plant successive crops every two weeks.
Indoor crops can be sown in flats or small containers if the outdoor weather is too cold. Seedlings need more intense light and more room for root growth. Then move them outdoors under a cold frame or transplanted into the garden. A cold frame will extend the lettuce season over a month in each spring and fall.

When transplanting seedlings, set them at the same depth as they were in the seedling pot. Planting too deep may cause rot around the base of plants.

Crop Care

Thin seedlings to a spacing of 6-12 inches when they are 2-4 inches tall. The thinnings can be transplanted or composted. Water the day before thinning or transplanting.

Protect from cutworms, slugs and snails.

Water regularly in the mornings to keep the small surface root system moist. Watering in the evening promotes fungus.

Fertilize with a soluble high nitrogen mix every 2-4 weeks or if the leaves begin to yellow.

Mulch during hot weather to conserve moisture and retain cool soil. Keep the mulch 2-3 inches away from the plant to discourage rot.

Shade in hot weather with other, taller plants; shade cloth; or lattice. Oakleaf types are the most tolerant of hot weather.

Harvesting

Harvest thinnings by uprooting the entire plant.

Harvest larger outer leaves of maturing looseleaf and romaine varieties. Remove 2-4 outer leaves from each plant.

Head lettuce: Harvest the entire plant when head is well formed.

Harvest all plants that start to bolt. Symptoms of bolting include sudden growth from the central leaves (heart), and bitterness.

Wash lettuce thoroughly to clean off any slugs, snails and dust.

In the Kitchen

Fresh: Looseleaf and romaine varieties are rich in vitamin A and good sources of vitamins B, C and calcium. All lettuce is excellent in fresh salads, or when used as a garnish on numerous dishes. Wilted lettuce is even more tender. Make wilted lettuce, soak it in a vinegar solution, then spinning the lettuce in a centrifugal food drier.

Storage: Head lettuce can be stored up to three weeks wrapped in plastic in the refrigerator. Looseleaf and romaine types will remain crisp for up to two weeks in the refrigerator wrapped in plastic.

Varieties

One of the problems with lettuce is that the entire crop matures at the same time. Grow several different varieties of lettuce at the same time, and plant a few more seeds every two weeks to ensure a perpetual harvest. One seed company, The Cook's Garden, P.O. Box 535, Londonderry, VT 05148, specializes in lettuce. They offer over 50 varieties of lettuce and many other culinary delights.

Butterhead Varieties

These types are the hardiest. The heads mature quickly (40-50 days) into loose, succulent heads of thick leaves.

BIBB (75 days) is a favorite of greenhouse growers and home gardeners alike. Small, loosely formed heads are packed with sweet tender leaves. Bibb is one of the most flavorful varieties. Available (Bu, Le, Me, Ni, Pa).

BUTTERCRUNCH (60-65 days) is a big favorite everywhere. The vigorous, dependable growth is of excellent quality. The leaves are delicious, and the heart of the loosely folded leaves is sweet and tender. Grows robustly, and holds in the garden well. Readily available.

CONTINUITY (Merveille des 4 Saisons) (75 days) produces loosely formed heads a foot or more in diameter. The green heart leaves are bordered with a bronze/red fringe and outer leaves. Available (Bg, Bu, Ni, Te).

NORTH POLE (50 days) is extremely resistant to cold. Sow this lettuce 2-3 weeks before the first average frost date for a spring crop, or plant in late summer for a winter harvest. A great variety for winter gardens, and poor performer in hot climates. Available (Ni).

TOM THUMB (52 days), an heirloom variety, yields a miniature butterhead plant that is crisp and sweet. The loosely formed tennis ball-sized heads can be served whole as individual salads. An ideal variety for window box or kitchen gardens. Available (Gs, Le, Pi, She).

Looseleaf Varieties

Maturing in 60-80 days, these types offer a long, consistent harvest when outer leaves are picked through the season.

RED SAILS (45-55 days), an AAS winner, produces attractive red-bronze, frilly leaves with a great flavor and high nutritional value. This bolt-resistant variety really adds color to salads. Available (Bg, Bu, Cg, Fi, Jo, Ju, Ma, Ni, Pa, Pi, Sha, So, Te).

GRAND RAPIDS (45 days) is a good variety to sow early in the spring. Quick growth of tasty looseleaf heads. Available (Bu, Fa, Fi, Ju, Ma, St).

PRIZEHEAD (48 days) yields frilly, red-tinged leaves. Super-tender, sweet leaves form a loose head. Available (Fa, Ju, Hi, Ma, Me).

SLOBOLT (65 days) has been cherished for generations. The loose, leafy heads remain compact even when over-mature or in hot weather. Harvest outer leaves for weeks, while inner leaves continue to grow. Grows well outdoors or under cover. Available (Bu, Fa, Fi, Jo, Ju, Ma, St, Te).

OAKLEAF (45-55 days) has been a gourmet favorite for decades. The delightful light green, oakleaf-shaped leaves are thin, tender and always sweet, even late in the season. It is exceedingly *heat tolerant* and slow to bolt. Available (Cg, Em, Fa, Fi, Gc, Ha, Hi, Jo, Le, Ma, Ni, Pi, Sc, She, So)

RED SALAD BOWL (60 days) is very slow to bolt in hot weather. The deeply cut dark green leaves are

tasty and add diversity to the salad plate. Available (Bu, Cg, Em, Fi, Gc, Jo, Hi, Me).

Crisphead or Iceberg Varieties

ITHACA (72 days) heads up into a well-wrapped ball with outer-frilled green leaves. It grows well during both cool and relatively warm weather. Resistant to tip burn, brown rib, and is slow to bolt. Very crisp. Available (Fi, Gc, Ha, Le, St, Th)

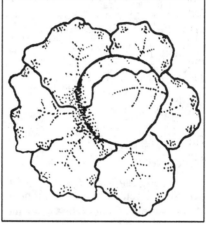

ROSA RED (80 days) produces beautiful 5-6-inch red heads. Excellent iceberg texture and flavor. Slow bolting. Available (Te).

ICEBERG (82 days) forms large dense, crisp heads with outer wrapper leaves. The flavor is a far cry from supermarket produce. Available (Fi, Me, Th)

Romaine or Cos Varieties

These types are heat tolerant and mature in 75-85 days. Harvest over a long season by picking outer leaves every few days.

VALMAINE (80 days) grows tall, upright, loosely formed heads full of dark-green, crinkled leaves. An excellent flavor in all dishes. Available (Bg, Ju, Pa, St, Th, Te).

PARIS ISLAND (70 days) yields 12-inch-long, thick, tasty leaves. Resistant to bolting and tip burn. **PARIS ISLAND COS 318** is taller, heavier, and just a little earlier. Available (Em, Gc, Ha, Hi, Jo, Le, Ma, St).

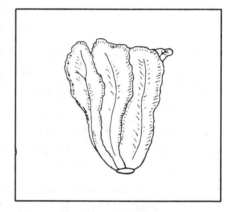

LITTLE GEM MINI ROMAINE (56 days) is an English heirloom with dense crunchy leaves, crunchy texture and sweet romaine flavor. The compact miniature heads grow to 5-6 inches tall, just perfect for individual servings. Available (She)

Problems

Lettuce is very easy to grow, but there are a few problems a crop might encounter along the way. Slugs and snails love tender, succulent seedling, and mature plants. They easily hide between the leaves. Keep an eye peeled for cutworms and flea beetles that favor seedlings. Hot weather causes bolting, and plants need ample water supply for their surface root system.

LETTUCE	SYMPTOM	PROVABLE CAUSES
Seedlings	rotting at soil line	18
	missing	13, 18
Plants	cut at soil line	13
	wilting	5
	no heads form	5, 9
	overall yellowing	6
	premature flowering	8
Leaves	rotting, dark spots	1, 7, 10
	yellow vein margins	2, 7
	blisters	3
	yellow patches	4, 11
	curled leaves	11
	fuzzy mold	4
	stippling, small spots	16
	chewed, holes	12, 14, 15, 17

1. Bacterial soft rot is a soil-borne disease that causes the fringes of lower leaves to rot. As it progresses, the entire plant turns slimy.
Control: Remove affected foliage immediately.
Prevention: Protect plants from splashing rain; irrigate soil; do not sprinkle overhead.

2. Big vein originates from diseased soil, and symptoms of yellowing vein margins and brittle, thickened, crinkled leaves. Heads are smaller and lower quality.
Control: Destroy affected plants.
Prevention: Rotate crops on a 3-4-year schedule. Plant in virus-free soil.

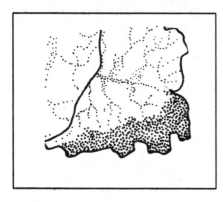

3. Bottom rot enters through bottom leaves that touch the soil. It causes recessed blisters on petioles and ribs. Rot develops on lower leaves that spreads through the head while ribs and stems stay solid.
Control: Remove and destroy affected plants.
Prevention: Practice a 3-4-year crop rotation with such plants as onions and sweet corn. Plant in well-drained soil. The upright growth habit of romaine varieties make the disease difficult to transmit from the soil.

4. Downy mildew causes older leaves to turn light green to yellow in spots. Later spots develop the characteristic fuzzy gray mold that eventually turns dark. This fungus is most common in humid climates.
Control: Remove affected growth from each head, and you may eat the balance.

Prevention: Remove wild lettuce near the garden and plant resistant (Imperial) varieties.

5. Fusarium yellows is transported by leafhoppers. Leaves wilt, growth is stifled, and heads may fail to form.
Control: Control leafhoppers with an application of pyrethrum (page 60).
Prevention: Remove nearby weeds and refrain from planting asters, carrots and other plants vulnerable to yellows.

6. Mosaic induces blotchy green-yellow growth and an overall yellowish appearance. Growth is checked, heads fail to form, and leaf margins may turn dark. Most common in warm, humid weather. Infected seed is the main source of the disease. This ailment is spread by aphids.
Control: Remove and destroy diseased plants immediately. Control aphids (page 84).
Prevention: Remove adjacent weeds that harbor aphids. Don't replant ground with lettuce for a few months. Clean out lettuce and debris after the crop is harvested.

7. Tip burn is most common where lettuce is grown outdoors under cover. Symptoms include enlarging yellowish leaf margins that darken, and veins that darken and rot. Wet conditions yielding succulent growth followed by hot, dry days encourage the condition.
Control: Remove the affected plants immediately. Damaged portions may be removed and the remainder eaten.
Prevention: Maintain an even irrigation and nutrient regimen. Do not promote super-succulent growth by using excessive nitrogen.

8. Bolting is caused by hot weather. The central leaves of the heads elongate to form a seed stalk. Leaves turn bitter. To check for early signs of bolting, tear a leaf; if it exudes a milky sap rather than a watery liquid, bitterness and bolting are evident.

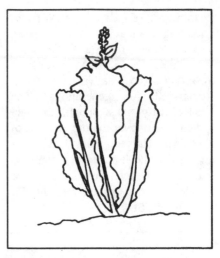

Control: Harvest if prolonged hot weather occurs.
Prevention: Build a shade awning, or plant in shady spots. Grow heat-tolerant (Oakleaf) varieties.

9. Failure to head is caused by disease and insect damage, hot weather, excessive nitrogen, or drought.
Control: Stop damage as soon as it occurs.
Prevention: Grow in cool weather; control diseases and pests; do not overfertilize. Keep evenly moist.

10. Brown rib is normally caused by a cutworm or caterpillar inside the head, burrowing along ribs. Entire ribs turn an unsightly rotten brown.
Control/prevention: See caterpillar and cutworm control and prevention above.

Other pests that may attack lettuce include:

11. Aphids: page 84
12. Cabbage looper: page 53
13. Cutworms: page 137
14. Flea beetles: page 137
15. Leafhoppers:(whitefly) page 137
16. Slugs and snails: page 84
17. Damping-off or seed rot: page 77

Melons *(Cucumis melo)*

True cantaloupes (charantais) are common in Europe but seldom seen in America. Muskmelons, often referred to as cantaloupes, differ from one another in several ways. Muskmelons have an exterior netting with superficial veins. The edible flesh ranges in color from salmon to various shades of green and has a musky fragrance. When ripe, the fruit pulls from the vine easily. The skin of most true cantaloupe has a rough, scaly texture, with well pronounced, dark vein tracks. The flesh is orange and aromatic. When ripe, the fruit must be cut from the vine. Nichols Garden Nursery, 1190 North Pacific Hwy., Albany, OR 97321 is one seed company that caries many true canteloupe varieties.

Casabas, crenshaws and honeydews are known as winter melons because they are late to ripen and can be stored up to a month. These melons are larger, and oblong, with a waxy skin that can be wrinkled or smooth. And they do not have the robust, musky aroma of cantaloupes. Low disease tolerance and the long season make these melons more difficult to grow.

Watermelons are also included in this group. This long-season melon comes in two basic shapes - round and oblong. Sugar Baby is a small, round short-season favorite. For more background information on melons, see "Cucurbitacae Family" page 72.

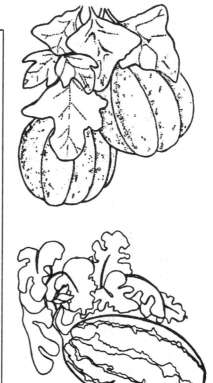

Basic Facts

Germination time: 7-14 days.
Germination temperature: Minimum: 60° (16° C), Optimum: 90° (32° C), Maximum: 105° (41° C).
Approximate seeds per ounce: 1,200.
Yield per vine: 2-12 melons.
Life expectancy of stored seed: 3 years.
Estimated time between sowing and first picking: 11-14 weeks.
Intercrop: Melons sprawl so much that intercropping is difficult.
Effort to cultivate: Somewhat difficult. Needs warm weather. Start seed indoors and grow in a cold frame in cooler climates.
Seed saving: Melons cross-pollinate with other melons. You must segregate breeding melons from other melons. Melons will not cross-pollinate with pumpkins or cucumbers.

Climate

Must have a long, 110-day season with temperatures above 60 at night and 80-110 during the day. Must have full sun, and dry fall weather. Raised beds, and a dark, heat absorbing mulch, applied once the soil has warmed, will increase soil temperature and hasten maturing in cooler climates.

Soil Preparation

Ideal soil is a loose, well-drained sandy loam high in organic matter that holds water well.
The top 2-10 inches of soil hold almost 80% of the roots, but some roots penetrate a depth of 5 feet or more. The surface preparation of the soil is extremely important. Add plenty of well-rotted compost, and manure about two weeks before planting.
Add dolomite lime if the pH range is not within the critical 6.0-6.8 range.

Planting

Plant two or more types of melons that ripen at different intervals. Muskmelons, like determinate tomatoes, characteristically ripen within a short time frame. Canteloupe and watermelon ripen over a longer season.

Set out seedlings, or direct seed, 1/2-inch deep in hills spaced on 4-foot centers two weeks after the last frost. Seedlings in pots may be set out in a hot frame closer to the last frost date in cooler climates.

If set out too early, seedlings will be stunted, and the yield will be cut dramatically.

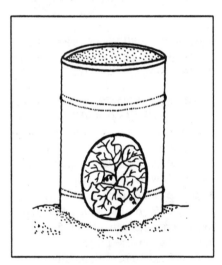

Start seedlings indoors 2-3 weeks before setting them outside in a cold frame to harden-off. Do not let seedlings grow too long in the container (use large pots, not peat pellets), or taproot growth will be checked.

Feed seedlings weekly with a dilute, high-nitrogen complete fertilizer.

Note: Seedlings grown indoors and transplanted to the garden produce about 1/3 more fruit than the same varieties that are direct-seeded. The goal is to replicate the natural tropical conditions, and rapid, unchecked growth.

Raised beds stay about 10° warmer than flat beds when the bed is covered with black plastic or a dark mulch, both of which absorb heat. After the soil warms, it will heat another 5-10° to a depth of 3 inches.

Crop Care

Build a trellis for vines to climb. Make sure the trellis is strong enough to support 10-40 pounds of ripe melons. This saves precious garden space and keeps the fruit off the ground, which discourages insects and rot. A trellis also allows spacing as close as one foot. All but the largest watermelons can be trellised easily.

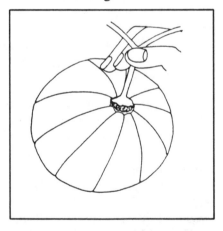

Both plastic row covers and a dark (plastic) mulch are the best ways to ensure strong, sweet melons. In fact, these two techniques increase yields up to 50%.

The first blossoms that set will be male flowers. About a week later female blossoms set and ultimately bear fruit.

Once 6-8 fruit set, remove any new fruit that sets. This will allow the first fruit to ripen sooner. Melons need to grow at least 6 feet of vine to produce healthy, sweet fruit.

Water regularly, especially after fruit sets; remember, the root system is mostly on the surface; feed with a soluble fertilizer every 2-4 weeks. Drought conditions shrink and curtail the harvest.

Muskmelon vines are more fragile than most vines. When training, be gentle, and do not count on them to orient leaves toward the sun when moved.

In cool climates, wait for several melons to set, then remove any new melons that grow. The larger melons will mature before the weather cools.

About a month before the cold weather arrives, pinch off all of the growing shoots and any small melons. This channels all of the plant's energy to the ripening melons.

Harvesting

The aroma of ripe muskmelons is frequently noticed before other signs of peak maturity. The skin of numerous varieties starts to turn yellow but a few types remain green beneath the netting.

To test for peak ripeness of a musk melon, check for cracks in the stem when you lift the melon. Or gently push the stem with your thumb. The melon is ripe if it slips (separates) from the stem. If the melon does not slip from the stem easily, check it again the following day.

Charantais and honeydew melons do not slip from the vine and must be cut. The melon will yellow and the blossom end starts to soften and even split.

Watermelons are ripe that sound hollow when thumped. The rind where it is touching the ground should be yellow rather than white. The tendril closest to the melon will also wither when it is ripe.

Crenshaws and casaba melons are ripe when

The sugars start to dissipate once the fruit is harvested. So eat melons soon after harvesting, or refrigerate quickly to slow the decline of sugar.

In the Kitchen

Fresh: Cut in half and remove seeds with a spoon. Slice and serve succulent flesh. Also makes excellent juice.

Storage: Store in the refrigerator for up to a week with little decline in sweetness. Cover sliced melons with plastic before refrigerating.

Freezing: Melons freeze well if whole slices are dipped in a honey syrup or sprayed with lemon juice.

Varieties

Cantaloupe Varieties

CHARENTAIS is the original French smooth skinned heirloom variety. The sweet, fine tasting flesh ripens even in cool climates. Available (Bu, Ni, Te).

CHACA (67 days) is more popular than it's hybrid cousins **PANCHA** and **FLYER**. it is a very tasty French hybrid Charantais melon. It grows particularly well in short season climates and is tolerant to Fusarium and mildew. Melons weigh 3-3.5 pounds. Available (Ni, Pi).

Muskmelons

BURPEE EARLY CRENSHAW (90 days) yields large oval melons that are pointed at the stem end. The smooth skin turns yellow-green when ripe. Grows well in all climates and freezes well. Available (Bu, Me)

CASABA GOLDEN BEAUTY (110-120 days) is a sweet white fleshed melon that weighs up to 8 pounds. The wrinkly yellow skin in a teardrop form holds the succulent flesh within. Available (Me).

EARLYDEW (80 days) is at home in cool climates. The yellow-green flesh is quite sweet. Vigorous vines set many fruit. Resistant to fusarium. Available (Ni, Te).

HALE'S BEST (80 days) has sweet, bright salmon-colored flesh that is firm and thick. Oval-shaped melon weighs 3-4 pounds. Withstands drought well. Excellent all round melon. Available (Bg, Gs, Ma).

HEARTS OF GOLD (85 days) is the sweetest melon available. Thin firm rind holds super-sweet salmon-colored flesh. Small seed cavity and prolific producer. Available (Gc, Ma)

IRIQUOIS (75 days) reliably yields 5-8 - 2 pound fruits on open-pollinated vines. Sweet flesh, with a larger seed cavity than most. Available (Fa, Fi, Ju, Me, ST, Te).

MINNESOTA MIDGET (60 days) is the earliest of all hybrid muskmelons.

The medium vines bear numerous sweet, small melons. The rich yellow flesh is super sweet clear to the rind. Available (Gc, Ma)

Watermelon Varieties

Watermelon (*Citrullus lanatus*) is a favorite all over North America. A few varieties, such as **SUGAR BABY** and **PETITE SWEET** mature quickly while the rest take over 100 days to mature.

CRIMSON SWEET (80 days) is a high yielding vigorous plant that produces 25-pound watermelons. The flesh is a dark red and it resists anthracnose and fusarium wilt. A good choice for northern gardens. Available (Bu).

MOON AND STARS (100 days) is an heirloom variety with small yellow, starlike markings on a dark rind. Produces 25-40-pound fruits. The flesh is one of the sweetest available. Available (Se, So).

PETITE SWEET (73 days) yields 10-pound round melons. The pale red flesh holds an exceptionally sweet flavor. Available (Fa, Fi).

SUGAR BABY (75 days) produces small, round, 10-pound watermelons. The rind is dark green and the flesh a rich, sweet red. Excellent choice for northern gardens. Available (Bu, Jo, Pa).

TOM WATSON (85-95 days) is a tough plant with abundant growth. The deep red flesh is sweet and tasty. Grows well in most climates. Available (Hu).

Problems

Melons grow over a long season and most varieties thrive in warm weather. Unfortunately, many insects and diseases also favor these conditions.

The main problems afflicting melons are cultural, and when plants are weak, they are more susceptible to insect and disease attack. The trick is to keep the melons growing faster than problems can progress. Nonetheless, all melons are susceptible to powdery mildew, which is especially destructive late in the season in moist, humid climates.

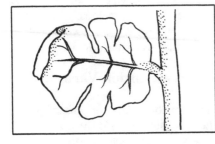

MELONS	SYMPTOM	PROVABLE CAUSES
Seed & Seedlings	failure to germinate rotten at soil line	13, or too cold 13
Leaves	yellowing distorted dark spots yellow leaves, veins green 4 holes powdery, fuzzy fungus	1, 4, 8, 12 1,8 3 9, 11 5
Plants Fruit	stunted sudden wilt small or no harvest	1, 2, 4 2 6, 7

1. Curly top virus is the same virus that causes curly top in beets. Immature leaves are stunted and distorted, while older leaves turn yellow. Stems grow short and thick. Plants seldom produce fruit. The beet leafhopper (Western whitefly) transmits the disease.
Control: Remove and destroy or hot compost affected plants.
Prevention: Avoid planting cantaloupe or muskmelons near beets. Clean up and remove weeds where the disease can live. Control beet leafhopper (whitefly) see page 39.

2. Fusarium wilt is carried by the striped cucumber beetle (page 76). The vines suddenly wilt, and growth grinds to a halt.
Control: Control cucumber beetles with pyrethrum or rotenone. Remove and destroy infected plants.
Prevention: Cover seedlings with spun fiber, cheesecloth or hot caps to exclude cucumber beetles. Grow resistant varieties such as GOLDEN GOPHER or IRIQUOIS.

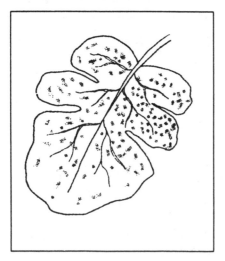

3. Leaf spot fungus can live on decomposing vines or soil for several seasons. A multitude of small dark spots appear on leaves that cause them to wither and die. Fruit does not spot, but grows slower and smaller.
Control: Remove and destroy affected foliage.
Prevention: Clean up garden debris regularly and during the fall. Rotate crops on a three-year plan.

4. Mosaic causes chlorosis, a yellowing of leaves, while the veins remain green. Other symptoms include stunted growth, small yields, mottled leaves, and yellow vine tips. Fruit sunburns easily and forms a threadbare net.
Control: Remove and destroy affected plants.
Prevention: Use seed that is certified disease-free. Remove adjacent weeds. Wash your hands after touching infected plants and before touching healthy plants. Grow resistant varieties such as Honey Ball and Honey Dew.

5. Powdery mildew can be a big problem in humid, wet climates. The powdery fungus grows on the surfaces of leaves and stems. If the disease is not severe, plants will grow and produce over a long season. Severely infected foliage withers and dies. Fruit may not form, or will be small and poorly formed.
Control: Dust lightly with sulfur. Remember, sulfur can easily burn foliage. Many gardeners prefer to ignore the fungus, especially if it occurs late in the season.
Prevention: Plant resistant varieties.

6. Small, or few melons, can be caused by the various diseases and insect attacks listed above. Other causes include a lack of water or nutrients during fruit formation, and hard soil, which restricts root growth. Cool temperatures also retard melon formation.
Control: Always keep well watered and fertilized. Grow in raised beds and use a dark-colored mulch to retain soil heat.

7. Failure to set fruit could be caused by excessive heat, rain, poor seed, poor overall health, or water stress. The best way to circumvent this problem is to grow strong, healthy plants.

Other problems that attack melons include:

8. Aphid: page 76
9. Cucumber beetle: page 76
10. Pickleworm: page 76
11. Potato flea beetle: page 120
12. Spider mite: page 137
13. Damping-off: page 77

Okra *(Abelmoschus esculentus)*

The seed pods of this ancient, warm-weather cultivar add a distinctive flavor to many recipes of the deep South. A main ingredient in gumbo and southern stews, okra has a slimy (mucilaginous) texture that may be difficult to get used to.

Okra is easy to grow, yielding numerous pods over a long season. Warm weather is the key to growing this crop that produces numerous pods soon after setting very ornamental red and yellow flowers. Standard plants grow 4- to 7-feet tall and space-saving dwarf types top out at 2-4 feet.

Basic Facts

Germination time: 7-21 days.
Germination temperature: Minimum: 60° (16° C), Optimum: 90° (32° C), Maximum: 105° (41° C).
Approximate seeds per ounce: 450.
Yield per plant: 50-200 pods.
Life expectancy of stored seed: 1-2 years.
Estimated time between sowing and first picking: 10 weeks.
Intercrop: vining squash and cucumbers.
Effort to cultivate: Easy, given a temperature range between 70-85° (21-29° C).
Seed saving: Cover seed plants to prevent bees from cross-pollinating. Let seeds ripen until pods dry.

Climate

Annual in moderate climates. Must have a minimum of ten weeks of frost-free weather. Needs full sun, and is very susceptible to frost damage.

The ideal temperature range for growth is 70 to 85° (21-29° C). Okra is an excellent crop to grow with protection from cool weather.

Soil Preparation

Any fertile, well-drained soil, with a pH from 6.0-8.0 will support okra. It will not tolerate compacted clay soil.

Prepare soil after the last frost, cultivating much well-rotted manure and compost to a depth of 6-10 inches.

Planting

Direct-seed after the soil temperature has warmed to 60° (16° C). For best results, soak seed overnight to speed germination.

Start seed indoors in cool climates 4-6 weeks before transplanting outdoors.

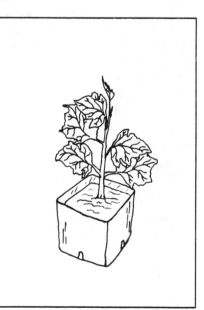

Sow seed 1/2-inch deep on 3-inch centers in rows or raised beds. Keep the soil evenly moist until they sprout.

Thin dwarf varieties to 1-foot centers and standard types to 3-foot centers.

Depending on taste, 3-6 plants per person should be cultivated.

Crop Care

A heavy feeder, okra should be fertilized every two weeks with a high-phosphorus tea, or band manure around plants monthly.

Keep well watered during the entire season, so growth is rapid and succulent.

Pruning may be necessary to contain rampant growth. Prune a few limbs below harvested seed pods.

In cool climates mulch the ground with heat absorbing black plastic; install plastic or spun fiber row covers to add warmth and ensure an abundant harvest.

Harvesting

Within two months of planting, if the weather has been warm, pods will start to form. Start picking pods when they are 2-3 inches long, and soft and succulent. If pods are allowed to enlarge, they become tough and fibrous.

Use scissors or pruners to cut pods from bushes. Harvest every 3-4 days throughout the season for peak production.

Gloves and long sleeves may be necessary to work around okra if you have sensitive skin. The variety CLEMSON SPINELESS produces pods without spines, and are preferred by gardeners with sensitive skin.

Use harvested pods soon after harvest for the best flavor. If pods are allowed to set out on a kitchen counter, they quickly dry out and become tough.

In the Kitchen

Fresh: Okra is rich in fiber and calcium as well as some vitamin A. The seeds are very rich in protein. It is a wonderful ingredient for soups, stews and casseroles. The unique mucilaginous (slimy) texture makes okra an excellent thickener of these dishes. Okra can also be rolled in cornmeal and fried hot and fast, sauteed, or steamed to provide a crisper texture.

When pods grow too large, the seeds can be shelled from the pods and cooked like peas.

Storage: Sprinkle pods lightly with water before storing in the refrigerator. They will keep well for 2-4 days. Okra tends to heat up if stored in an enclosed container.

Freezing: Okra freezes extremely well, with little loss of flavor and food value. Blanch whole pods 3-5 minutes, plunge in cold water, pat dry, freeze in a plastic bag. Or wash and dry pods; slice in 1-inch chunks, and freeze; do not blanch.

Varieties

ANNIE OAKLEY HYBRID (55 days) soon yields lots of pods on 3-4-foot plants. Excellent choice for prolific yield in northern climates, and it has a great flavor. Available (Bu, Fi, Ha, Jo, Pi).

BURGUNDY (60 days) is high yielding and very ornamental. The intense green leaves have vivid red veins with stems that hold delicate golden flowers. Flavorful deep burgundy pods retain color after cooking. Available (Bu, Fi, Jo, Ma, Me, Ni, Pa, Sha).

CLEMSON SPINELESS (56-65 days), an AAS selection, is the type to plant if you have sensitive skin or dislike spines. Plants grow to 5 feet and produce medium-sized, good tasting ribbed pods. Available (Bu, Fi, Ha, Hu, Ju, Ma, Me, Ni, Pa, Pi, So).

DWARF GREEN LONG POD (days) a spineless variety, produces showy, yellow, frilly, hibiscuslike flowers before setting tasty slender pods on 2-3-foot plants. Available (Fa, Fi, Ju, Ma).

EMERALD GREEN VELVET (58 days) yields solid, spineless, round, deep, dark green pods. Plants top out at 3-4 feet and grow well in all climates. Available (Fi).

Problems

Okra falls victim to just a few problems other than cool weather. It grows so fast that pests and problems are generally outpaced.

Other pests and problems that may attack okra include:

1. Corn earworm: page 70
2. Nematodes: page 61, #9 (Eelworms)
3. Root knot: page 40, #5
4. Rot or blight: page 84 (fruit rot)
5. Stink bug: page 137
6. Wilt, Fusarium: page 100

Onions (*Allium cepa*) and Scallions (*A. fistulosum*)

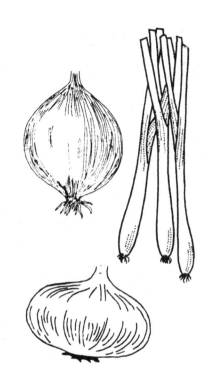

Growing good bulb onions and scallions can be a little tricky. First, you must know the basic differences between the types of onions. *Sweet Spanish* onions, commercially grown in Utah, northern New Mexico and central California, are big, sweet, soft, long-season types. They bulb from July through August. In latitudes above 45° (70° C), bulbing is restricted by decreasing sunlight; bulbs tend to be small and pungent.

Storage onions were developed for northern climates, rapidly producing hard, durable, narrow rings with heavy skins. Early storage types grow well in northern latitudes, while long-season varieties are choice for southern climates.

Overwintered bulb onions can also be long or short season. The large, flat, long-season types grow best in southern California, and east to Texas. Short-season types, developed for temperate climates, are sown in late summer and harvested in June.

Scallions, or bunching onions (*A. fistulosum*), are of three different types. Those derived from Sweet Spanish types are harvested before longer nights of autumn signal bulbs to develop. They are sweet and tender, with a thin skin. They are sown from spring through mid-summer. The long harvest starts about two months after planting. The other two are overwintering types and do not bulb when the nights become longer. So, a single planting can be harvested for months.

Basic Facts

Germination time: 4-21 days.
Germination temperature: Minimum: 35° (2° C), Optimum: 75° (24° C), Maximum: 95° (35° C).
Approximate seeds per ounce: 5,500.
Yield per 10 foot row: 10-20 pounds.
Yield per 4 X 4 foot raised bed: 20-60 pounds.
Life expectancy of stored seed: 1-2 years.
Estimated time between sowing and first picking: 8-9 weeks (summer), 16 weeks (overwintering).
Intercrop: With any plants that do not shade too much.
Effort to cultivate: Somewhat fussy if grown from seed; much easier to grow from sets.
Seed saving: Pollinated by insects, onion varieties should be at least 100 feet apart. Once pollinated, the heads can be covered with a sack that has small air holes. Wait for seed to dry. Remove carefully from pods.

Climate

Annual in all zones. Choose varieties for either short northern seasons, or for long southern climates.

Soil Preparation

Ideal soil for onions is very fertile loam, that drains well. Seeds demand much finer surface soil that does not form a crust.

Prepare the bed up to a month before planting. Incorporate plenty of compost, manure, and a complete organic fertilizer. Rake seed bed smooth so it is fine, and free of all large clods and debris.

Planting

Sets or seed? You can start sets, which are dry bulbs, or seed. Sets have the advantage of fast growth and very high germination rate. But they tend to bolt more readily, are more subject to rot, and store poorly. Seeds offer a much wider variety selection, seldom bolt, and grow into excellent storage bulbs. Seeds germinate slowly, and at a lower rate, than sets. They must be planted early in the season to grow to maturity by fall.

Sweet Spanish seeds should be started indoors except in warm southern regions. Move the thin seedlings outdoors a month after the last frost date. Space seedlings 2-3 inches apart in rows 12-18 inches apart. Space seedlings on 3-inch centers in wide raised beds. Harvest thinnings to make room for adjacent plants.

Onions, especially scallions, are similar to garlic, and radishes, and can be tucked into bare spots in the garden.

Storage onions are sown outdoors soon after the last frost date. Sow seed 1/2-inch deep, 3-4 seeds per inch in rows 18-24 inches apart. In wide, broadcast, seed and thin to 3-inch centers. Sow seed indoors, and transplant the same as Sweet Spanish (above) in short-season climates. Thin to 2-3 inches; eat thinnings as scallions.

Overwintered onions are sown from mid-July through mid-September. They should grow to pencil size prior to the onset of freezing weather. If you plant too early, or fertilize, they may bolt before cold weather curbs their growth! When early spring growth starts, apply an all-purpose fertilizer.

Scallions are sown from the last frost date through July. Sow them the same as Sweet Spanish.

Crop Care

Water regularly. Like garlic and leeks, onions have a small, shallow root system, and need weekly watering. Sweet, mild onions are well-watered. Hot onions receive less water and are a bit smaller.

Thin seedlings when they become large enough to eat as scallions.

Keep weeds pulled or hoed. Onions compete very poorly with other plants.

Fertilize monthly during active growth. Apply the fertilizer close to the bulbs, because the root system does not spread far.

Do not mulch. Onions grow best when the bulb is exposed. The sunshine helps to ripen bulbs.

Harvesting

Harvest scallions as needed. Remove every other one, or harvest scallions that are crowding one another.

Harvest bulbing onions early if they start to go to seed (bolt), or as thinnings to eat as scallions.

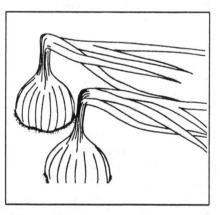

Bulbing onions are harvested after the bulbs are fully developed and the tops dry out. Do not water them after tops start drying and falling over. Once half the tops have dried and fallen over, wait another week before digging.

Uproot the mature bulbs with a spading fork, brush the soil from their roots and set them in the sun to dry. Protect them from rain and dew.

Let the onions dry 2-4 days. Brush the dry soil from the bulbs. Use any bruised or damaged onions first.

In the Kitchen

Fresh: Storage onions bring summer's bounty to life. Scallions and bulb onions are sweet and flavorful when garden-fresh. Cooks love onions - they flavor so many foods so well. Onions are used in a multitude of dishes. Sauteed, they cook to a translucent hue. Their flavor is delectable with anything. Small bulb onions can be boiled whole in stews or soups. Slice large storage varieties to fry, saute, stew, or bread to make into onion rings.

Storage: Once bulbing onions are completely dry, store them in a net onion sack or nylon stocking that provides plenty of air circulation until they are needed. Hang the sack(s) in a cool, dry garage or basement. Tops can also be braided together. The strings of onions are hung in the kitchen. See "Garlic Storage" page 87.

Scallions keep for up to two weeks stored in the refrigerator in a plastic bag.

Drying: Onions dry well. Simply slice into uniform wafers. Lay out on a screen in the sun or place in a food dryer. Store in a glass jar. Keep the lid loose for the first month or two. Check the jar periodically to make sure the onions are dry.

Varieties

Onions can be purchased in the form of seed, sets (immature bulbs grown especially for planting), or actual seedlings. Seed is a little touchy to start, but inexpensive, and offers the largest selection. Sets mature quickly in northern climates and require less skill and soil fertility; but a large percentage of the sets may bolt. You can grow seedlings or buy them at the nursery, which is very handy when you do not want to wait. The most vigorous and disease-resistant types are hybrids.

Sweet Spanish Varieties

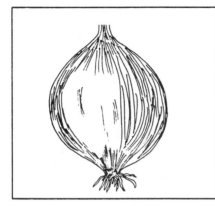

SWEET SPANISH TYPES (140 days) are available with either white and yellow skin. Bulbs are less pungent than storage onions. In Cold climates, start seedlings indoors 2-3 months before transplanting outdoors. Available (Gs, Le, Pi, Sc, Te).

PICKLING TYPES including CRYSTAL WAX (White Bermuda), WHITE BARLETTA, develop small white bulbs, with paper-thin skins. These varieties are outstanding when pickled. They require less fertile soil than other onions. Available (Bu, Fa, Fi, Ma, Me, Pa, She, Te).

Storage Varieties

CARMEN HYBRID (105 days) is rich red in color, and mild in flavor. The long-day hybrid bulbs have improved vigor. Slices taste great on hamburgers or in salads. Available (Pa, St).

EARLY YELLOW GLOBE (100 days) is one of the earliest available. They yield uniform, globular onions to 3 inches across. Available (Bu, Gc, Gs, Le, St).

EBENEZER (110 days) The Japanese introduced this variety in 1900. It is an exceptionally good keeper. The yellow-brown skinned, pungent bulbs grow up to 3 inches across. Available (Le, Ni, Pa, So)

KELSAE SWEET GIANT (*A. giganteum*) (110 days) holds the world record at 7 pounds, 7 ounces! This variety grows well in northern climates. Grows best in rich, sandy soil in full sun. The large bulbs have a remarkably sweet flavor. Available (Bu, Pa, St, Th).

SOUTHPORT RED GLOBE (110 days) yields perfectly round bulbs with purplish skin. The robust white flesh is tastes good for months. Good keeper. Available (Fa, Ju, Me, St).

STUTTGARTER (120 days) grows well from sets. The large, flattened bulbs have a glossy brown skin. Plant them thick and use the thinnings as scallions. Excellent flavor raw or cooked. Available (Ha, Ju).

SWEET SANDWICH (112 days) yields globe-shaped bulbs up to 3.5 inches across with medium brown skin. The light yellow flesh is sweet and mellow. Long-day variety. Available (Bu, Fi, Jo, Ju, Le, Ma, St, Th).

Overwintering Varieties

SWEET WINTER (100-300 days) is exceptionally hardy and grows well even in Northern winters. Temperatures of -20° have not killed this variety. An early crop of flat, yellow bulbs is mild and sweet. Available (Pa, St)

WALLA WALLA SWEET (110-200 days) is a large, mild, jumbo Spanish Sweet variety that should be sown in late August to mid September. The large harvest of pungent, sweet bulbs will be one of the first of the summer. Available (Bu, Cg, Fi, Gs, Jo, Ni, Pi, Te).

Scallion Varieties

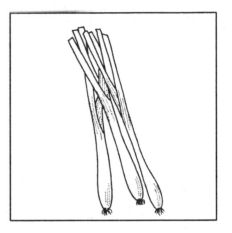

LISBON or White Portugal (60-70 days) Plant in either spring or fall in mild climates. Available (Bg, Fi, Ma, Me, She, St, Te).

RED BEARD (60 days) is a Japanese variety that is red. It is fast germinating, and grows vigorously. Plant in mid summer for a late fall harvest. The longer they are exposed to cold weather, the redder the skin will grow. Available (She, St).

Novelty Varieties

EGYPTIAN types (*A.C. viviparum*) including MORITZ, NORRIS and MCLULIAR'S WHITE TOPSET set a few bulbs in the soil and edible bulbs on the top of the flower stalk. The yield is smaller and it takes up to 6 months for them to mature. Use the leaves of this very cold hardy plant in soups and salads. The bulbs are pungent and go a long way. Available (Cr, So,).

POTATO ONIONS (*A.C. aggregatum*) are also known as multiplier or underground onions. These heirloom varieties include white, yellow and red varieties. The bulb multiplies into 8-12 bulblets, just like shallots. Good flavor and very easy to grow. Available (So).

WELSH perennial (*A. Fistulosum*) is a old heirloom variety of bunching onion. The bulbs can be either bronze-skinned or white. Good sweet flavor. Available (Cg, Sc).

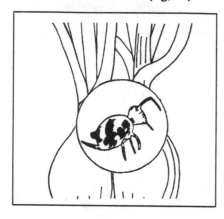

1. Garden springtail, a tiny, dark, flealike insect may attack onion seedlings, leaving holes and teeth tracks in and on the foliage.
Control: Spray with insecticidal soap.
Prevention: Keep onion bed free of weeds.

2. Lesser bulb fly larvae hatch around the bottom of the leaf, and tunnel into the bulb. The worms are 1/2-inch long, dark, dingy yellow in color.
Control: Dig and destroy infested plants.
Prevention: Cover plants with spun-fiber row covers during May and June when adult flies normally lay eggs.

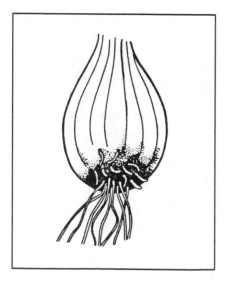

Problems

Onions are remarkably trouble-free as long as they are supplied with adequate water and fertilizer. Wet, humid climates present the best conditions for diseases to take hold, and onions in these areas should be watched closer.

ONIONS	SYMPTOM	PROVABLE CAUSES
Seed & Seedlings	stunted	3
	no germination	crust on soil
Stems	neck rot	7
	thick neck	12
Leaves	leaf tips die back	6, 8 or fertilizer burn
	small holes, tracks	1
	yellowing	3, 4, 6
	wilting	3
	silvery patches	4
	graying, water soaked	5
	rusty spots	15
	black blotches	9
Roots	tunneled	2, 13
	double bulbs	10
	rotting	6, 7, 14
	papery burned spots	11
Plants	wilted, stunted	3, 8

3. Onion maggot is found mainly along coastal zones. The legless, snow-white maggot is 1/3-inch long and feeds on roots, bulbs and leaves at *all* stages of growth. Leaves yellow and wilt. Seedlings often die. Older plants bulbs frequently rot. White varieties are most susceptible to this pest.
Control: Remove affected onions, remove damaged spots before eating.
Prevention: Scatter onions throughout the garden. The maggot needs several sets or seedlings to survive. If unable to find enough food, the maggots starve. Three- to four-year crop rotation.

4. Onion thrips cause the most damage of all onion pests. The adult is minute; the larva is even smaller and can scarcely be seen with the naked eye. They make small, white blotches on leaves that grow together to form silvery patches. Infestations cause stunted growth, bleached leaves that die back, and thick necks.

Damage is worst during hot, dry weather.
Control: Spray with insecticidal soap. Use a nicotine-sulfate spray as a last resort.
Prevention: Do not plant onions near large commercial fields. Remove weeds and debris around the garden to prevent overwintering.

5. Downy mildew, a fungal disease, is easiest to spot first thing in the morning. Recessed, water-soaked spots that are gray-to-yellow appear on leaves. Later, spots turn a fuzzy deep purple.
Control: Remove and hot compost affected plants.
Prevention: Practice a three- or four-year crop rotation. Plant resistant varieties with no bruises or blemishes.

6. Fusarium basal rot first appears as yellow leaf tips that enlarge and die back. Roots rot, and a white fungus grows on bulbs. Onion root maggots promote the disease.

Control: Remove and hot compost affected plants; improve drainage.
Prevention: Good drainage; do not buy onion sets that are shriveled or discolored. Plant resistant varieties.

7. Neck rot (botrytis rot) is nearly impossible to discern until harvest or storage. In storage, bulbs develop soft necks, and the bulb's skin looks water-soaked. Mold frequently grows on and between bulb rings. White onions are the most susceptible.
Control: Remove and hot compost affected bulbs.
Prevention: Keep plants dry. Water the soil, not the bulb or tops. Water in the morning, so that water can evaporate quickly from leaves. Stop watering when bulbs start to ripen.

8. Pink root, a fungal disease, is evident when onions are stunted and tops wither prematurely. Roots turn pink to red, and rot. New, healthy roots fail to form.
Control: Remove and destroy affected plants.
Prevention: Good drainage is essential. Practice a 3-4-year crop rotation, and plant disease-resistant varieties. Buy certified disease-free seed or sets.

9. Smut develops as black blotches, filled with pustules full of fungus spores, on leaves and in bulbs. The disease is most prevalent among white onions. Leaves may contort

into irregular shapes, and infected seedlings typically die from this soil-borne disease.

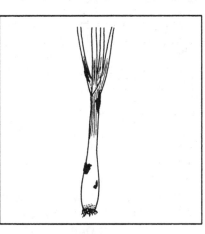

Control: Remove and hot compost or burn affected plants.
Prevention: Practice a 3-4-year crop rotation plan. Buy disease-free sets and seed.

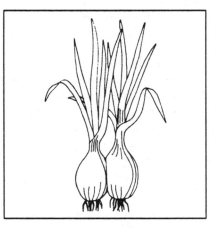

10. Set-division is typical of onion sets. It is caused by planting too early or too late in the year. Drought and nutrient-poor soil can also cause set division. Divided bulbs do not store well.
Control: None
Prevention: Plant at the proper time of year in rich organic soil and keep moisture levels relatively constant.
11. Sunscald occurs when bulbs are harvested on exceptionally hot, sunny days. The outer layers of bulbs, particularly immature white bulbs, become soft and slimy. This condition allows soft rot to destroy the entire bulb.

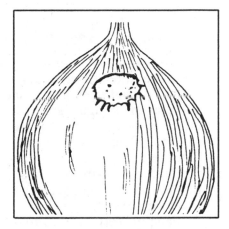

Control: Remove affected outer layers, and protect bulbs from direct sunlight during harvest and curing.
Prevention: Protect bulbs from direct sunlight when harvesting and curing.

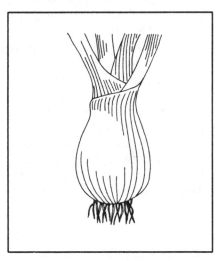

12. Thickened necks keep bulbs from storing properly. This condition is usually caused by too much nitrogen or manure in the soil. It may also be caused by sowing seed too deeply.
Control: Do not store the bulbs; eat onions with thick necks first.
Prevention: Plant in soil where manure has been applied the previous year, and use a low-nitrogen fertilizer.

Other onion pests and problems include:

13. Wireworm: page 61
14. Fusarium rot: page 100
15. Rust: page 25

Parsnip, Rutabaga & Salsify

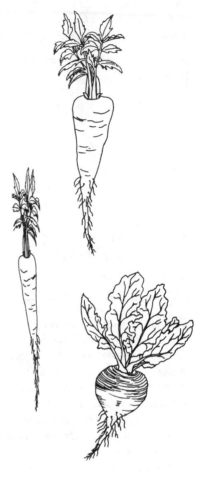

These three root crops are of limited repute and their popularity continues to decline. They all have similar growth habits, even though they are not from the same family. This collection of root crops is very easy to grow, requiring little attention. They are long-season crops that store well for the winter, either in the garden or in a root cellar. They make excellent garden-fresh meals during the winter. Because their growth and care requirements are so alike, we have grouped them together in this book.

Parsnip (*Pastinaca sativa*), a biennial grown as an annual, has a rich, nutty taste that is superb in soups, stews or when steamed and eaten with a pat of butter. The flavor is improved by light frost, and roots store very well in the ground, even in the coldest of climates.

Rutabagas (*Brassica napus*, Napobrassica Group) are also called Canadian or Swedish turnips or swedes. They are prone to a few plant ills common to brassica, especially root maggot attack. However, new disease-resistant varieties have made growing rutabagas nearly trouble-free. A close relative of turnips, rutabagas taste similar, but have yellow flesh and a sweeter flavor. They store well in the ground all winter long if mulched heavily to prevent freezing.

Salsify (*Tragopogon porrifolius*), also known as the "oyster plant", has a delicate flavor similar to oysters. Seldom seen in gardens, salsify looks like a large, white carrot, but is easier to grow. Many salsify aficionados prefer the even more delicate taste of the black rooted *Scorzonera hispanica*, a close cousin of salsify.

Basic Facts

Germination time: 14-40 days.
Germination temperature: Minimum: 35° (2° C), Optimum: 70° (21° C), Maximum: 85° (29° C).
Approximate seeds per ounce: Parsnip - 4,900, Rutabaga - 8,400, Salsify -9,000.
Yield per 10 foot row: 5-50 pounds
Life expectancy of stored seed: 2 years.
Estimated time between sowing and first picking: 13-18 weeks.
Intercrop: Radishes, flowers annual.
Effort to cultivate: Easy.
Seed saving: Easy, just collect and dry. Grow only one variety of brassicas if you plan to save rutabaga seed.

Climate

Annual in all zones. Grows best in climates with 60-70° (16-21° C) temperatures. Small roots grow in hot weather. Plant as a winter crop in hot climates and for a fall/winter harvest in temperate to cold climates. Needs full sun; tolerates some shade in warm climates.

Soil Preparation

Grows best in a nutrient-rich soil that drains well, and is cultivated to a depth of 10-12 inches. Lime soil if the pH is below 6.5. Lower the pH if it is over 7.5.

Prepare soil the previous fall or very early in the spring. To avoid "hairy" roots, refrain from adding manure up to a year before planting. Add manure a year early or for a previous crop.

Include fertilizer that does not contain nitrogen, such as a mix of dolomite and granite dust, when preparing the soil.

For prime root formation, cultivate the bed to a depth of 8-16 inches, removing stones and breaking up large clods. Add compost for several years prior to planting for the best root growth.

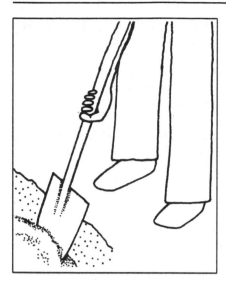

Rake seed bed smooth and remove surface debris before planting.

Planting

Do not plant rutabagas where other brassicas grew the previous two years. Parsnips and salsify are not picky about the previous occupants of their garden bed.

Sow seed 1/2-inch deep directly into beds after last frost. Space seed on 1-inch centers in wide, raised beds, and thin to 12 inches apart when 6 inches tall.

Direct-seed overwintering varieties on 1 1/2-foot centers from July in the north to September in southern states.

Water seeds and seedlings regularly until established.

Cover rutabaga seedlings with a floating row cover to keep flea beetles and cabbage root maggots out. Apply a dusting of diatomaceous earth, sawdust, or a mix of lime and wood ashes to discourage root maggots.

Crop Care

Weed seedlings by hand. Hoe lightly if space allows. Early crops may need protection from birds.

Apply mulch after seedlings are 6 inches tall to check weed growth, cool soil, and retain moisture. Add more mulch as necessary.

Water deeply as needed. Wilting from water stress will stunt root development, and may cause bolting. Mulch helps retain moisture. Fertilize with a top dressing of manure once or twice during the summer.

Do not stimulate tender new growth on overwintering varieties by fertilizing late in the fall. New, succulent growth is more susceptible to frost damage.

Harvesting

Harvest nutrient-packed leaves to eat in salads, or steam with greens.

Store parsnips, rutabagas, and salsify in the soil, mulching the surface with oak leaves or conifer needles to keep soil from freezing. They develop a tough skin, but keep well if not allowed to freeze.

Lift roots grown for storage with a fork by October, after they have matured fully, but before a hard freeze. Take care not to bruise roots. Cut off the tops, leaving an inch of stem.

In the Kitchen

Fresh: Greens (leaves) are sweet, tender, and packed with nutrition. Use the leaf, cutting away the fibrous tough stem. Wash and without shaking off extra moisture, pack loosely into a large kettle. Salt lightly and toss. There should be enough water slinging to leaves for cooking; if in doubt, add 2 tablespoons of water. Cover and bring to a boil. Boil gently, just until wilted - 2-5 minutes. Remove kettle from the heat. Let stand covered 1-2 minutes. Butter and serve. Steam sliced roots 8-12 minutes or boil 6-8 minutes - until tender. Peel skin on larger roots before slicing or dicing if it is tough. Parsnips taste great when sliced thin lengthwise and gently tossed and sauted in butter until lightly carmelized. Use parsnips and rutabagas as potato substitutes.

Storage: Store washed roots in a plastic bag in the refrigerator for up to two weeks.

Lightly brush away the soil before storing; consume or compost damaged roots. Cut the tops off 2 inches above roots, pack in layers of dry peat or cool sand in a box, and store in a cool basement or shed. The temperature should stay between 35-45° (2-7° C) for longest storage. They will keep for up to 6 months.

Freezing: Blanch (boil) greens and sliced roots 2 1/2 minutes or steam 3 minutes, dry, bag, and freeze.

Varieties

Parsnip Varieties

ALL AMERICA (120 days) is judged by many as the best variety available. The tender, white flesh is sweet and fine grained. Grows to a foot long and 2.5 inches across at the shoulder. Good yield. Available (Fi, Ha, Ma, Ni, St).

HARRIS MODEL (120 days) is the other variety that is grown by home gardeners. Available (Ha, Hi, Jo, St).

Rutabaga Varieties

ALL-AMERICA PURPLE TOP (90 days) is a heirloom variety that Americans have been eating for decades. The large purple root is yellow below ground. The flesh is fine textured and very tasty. Available (Fi, Ha, Ju, Ma, Pa).

ALTASWEET (92 days) is a special cross between *LAURETIAN* and *MACOMBER*. The flavor of the deep yellow flesh is mild and one of the best eating rutabaga available. Available (St).

LAURENTAIN (90 days) is the most popular rutabaga grown. The root is uniform in shape and pale brown, smooth, with yellow flesh. Good tasting. Available (Fa, Jo, Ju, Pi, St).

Salsify Varieties

MAMMOTH SANDWICH ISLAND (118 days) matures into long, fleshy, white roots that taste like oysters. The flavor is mild and delicious whether cooked or eaten fresh. Keeps in the garden, even during winter, well. Available (Bg, Bu, Fa, Fi, Ju, Le, Ma, Me, Ni, Pi, Ric, St, Th).

SCORZONERA (120 days) yields long, black-skinned roots. The taste is similar to parsnips and salsify. The leaves and yellow flowers are tasty in salads. Available (Ni, Th).

Problems

Overall, parsnips, rutabagas, and salsify are virtually problem-free. Rutabagas are members of the brassica family and may suffer some damage from root maggots.

Look on pages 60-61 (Carrot Problems) to find solutions to parsnip and salsify problems.

Look on pages 53-56 (Brassica Problems) to find solutions to rutabaga problems.

Pea (*Pisum sativum*)

Plant very early for the best crop of peas. Southern gardeners plant peas in early to midwinter, while northern gardeners plant from February through April. In raised beds, peas can be planted *very early*. If planted too late, peas get heat stress during hot weather; growth is stunted, leaves wilt, blossoms drop, and pod growth terminates. Peas are the season's first vegetable available for harvest that offers the sugary, sweet, succulent taste of the vegetable garden. Ripe, succulent peas also inspire countless gardeners to get out and plant the rest of the garden. Peas also grow late into the fall when planted in mid to late summer.

Peas are a legume, and produce their own nitrogen by capturing it from the air. Nitrogen-fixing nodes, located on the roots, concentrate this nitrogen. Plants need only an initial fertilization. See "Beans" (page 26) for more information on nitrogen-fixing legumes.

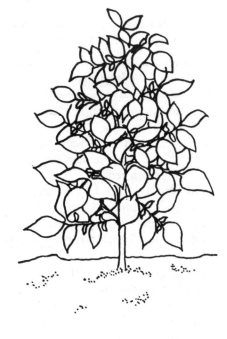

Basic Facts

Germination time: 6-30 days.
Germination temperature: Minimum: 40° (5° C), Optimum: 75° (24° C), Maximum: 85° (29° C).
Approximate seeds per ounce: 70
Yield per 10-foot row: 5-20 pounds
Life expectancy of stored seed: 2-3 years.
Estimated time between sowing and first picking: 10-15 weeks.
Intercrop: Corn. Plant soft annuals and vegetables among peas in late spring. Harvest peas and cultivate established annuals and vegetables.

Effort to cultivate: Easy. Transplanting seedlings grown indoors boosts harvests substantially.
Seed saving: Very easy. Allow open-pollinated varieties to mature fully. Harvest vines and dry in the sun on a tarp. Remove the seed by hand.

Climate

Annual in all zones. Peas love the cool temperatures of winter and spring. They easily survive 20° nights, but growth suffers severely if temperatures top 80° (26° C). They need full sun, and tolerate partial shade in hot weather.

Soil Preparation

Loose, well-drained soil is a must for the strongest crop. Peas host many root diseases. Cold, soggy soil not only promotes these evils, it cuts production by smothering oxygen supplied to the roots. Waterlogged soil also restricts nitrogen uptake.
Add plenty of well-rotted manure and compost when preparing the bed. Add a liberal amount of bone meal as the main fertilizer to the growing bed. Do not use a high nitrogen amendment, which promotes too much green, leafy growth.

Add dolomite lime to correct the pH if the soil is not within the acceptable 6.0-7.0 range.

Raised beds offer the earliest planting opportunity, since they warm sooner and drain better than flat beds.

Planting

Soak seeds in a glass of water overnight to soften and initiate germination before planting. Or place seed between moist paper towels for several days until they sprout. See "Bean Planting", page 29.

If peas have not been grown in your garden within the last few years, inoculate the seeds or soil with the *Rhyzobium* bacteria (page 26) to ensure adequate nitrogen production by root nodes.

For a bumper crop, grow climbing varieties indoors in small pots and transplant them outdoors when they are about 4 inches tall. Sow seed an inch deep in loose, well-drained soil and keep evenly moist. Keep seedlings warm (60-70° (16-21° C)) and in a sunny location until transplanted. Seedlings require warmer temperatures for the first few weeks of growth, but can be moved into 40° (5° C) soil and flourish. This little bit of care could double or even triple yields!

Transplant after hardening-off for 3-4 days. Dig a trench about 3 inches deep in the prepared bed. Set the seedlings next to one another in the trench and backfill. Water in thoroughly.

Sow seeds early, as soon as the ground can be worked in the spring. Sow seed 1 1/2-inch deep, 3-4 seeds per inch, in rows 18 inches apart. Peas do not mind being crowded. Sow seed later in clay soil, which remains cold and wet longer than in a well-drained loam.

Sow fall crops from mid-July through August. They should grow large enough to set pods before the decreasing sunlight of autumn slows growth.

Dwarf bush types (see below) should be sown in succession in two-week intervals for a longer harvest.

Crop Care

Dwarf bush (*determinate*) varieties set all of their pods at once, yield for a short period, about two weeks, then quit. If you plan to freeze peas for the winter, choose a bush type. These types do not need a trellis.

Climbing (*indeterminate*) varieties set blossoms and pods over a longer season. The vines need a trellis, but produce about twice as much as bush types.

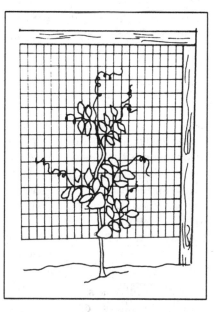

Build a trellis by stringing poultry wire, nylon netting, string or twine from a 3- to 6-foot-tall A-frame constructed of wooden 2 X 4's, bamboo, PVC plastic, or galvanized metal pipe. Rows of peas can be planted on both sides of the bottom of the A-frame. The tendrils of the peas cling to the trellis as they climb.

Water peas until they pop through the soil. After seedlings sprout, little irrigation (about 1/2 inch per week) is necessary until flowering starts. Water weekly through the end of harvest after flowers set.

Mulch soil heavily to keep soil cool, conserve moisture, and stifle weeds.

Weed carefully by hand because fragile pea vines are very easy to sever with a hoe.

Harvesting

Peas, like sweet corn, share the characteristic of sugar turning to starch soon after harvest. For the sweetest eating, serve peas within an hour of harvest.

Snow peas are eaten pod and all. Typically, snow peas are harvested at a length of 2-4 inches, when the seeds are still young and immature. Some varieties, such as Oregon Sugar Pod, become much sweeter if allowed to fatten up. The strings on the seams of the pods that accompany this development can be removed in the garden when harvesting.

Shelling peas are normally harvested when the pods are plump, and turn a pale green. They are most tender before strings form, but develop a much sweeter flavor after strings are allowed to form. Do not let pods over-mature or dry, which causes seeds to become tough.

Dry peas are harvested when the pods begin to split on the vine. Once harvested and shucked, finish drying single layers of seeds by placing them on a cookie sheet in a 120° (48° C) oven. For more information, see "Drying Beans," page 33.

In the Kitchen

Fresh: Both snow peas and shucked peas are a sweet, early treat raw, steamed or stir-fried.

Storage: Fresh peas are similar to sweet corn in that they convert sugar to starch relatively rapidly after harvest. For this reason, they are the sweetest when eaten within an hour of harvest. If peas must be stored, place whole pods in a plastic bag in the refrigerator for up to a week. Shuck and string peas just before cooking.

Dry peas (see "Harvesting" above) are an excellent addition to stews and soups.

Freezing: Simply remove strings on snow peas, or shuck away pods. Rinse, steam blanch 4-5 minutes, or boil 2-4 minutes. Dry before sealing in a freezer container, and pop into the freezer.

Varieties

Bush (determinate) Varieties

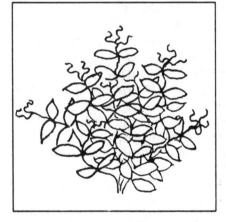

Bush types mature faster and do not need trellising. The majority of pods set at the same time, which is very convenient for freezing or canning. A succession of crops must be planted at 1-2 week intervals for a sustained harvest.

DARK-SKINNED PERFECTION (120 days) is possibly the highest yielding variety available today. They have an excellent flavor, both fresh and frozen. Available (Te).

FROSTY (60-67 days) grows strong, robust bushes with high yields, and is resistant to fusarium wilt. Sweet taste. Available (Fa, Ha, Ma).

LITTLE MARVEL (58-64 days), an open-pollinated, early, heavy-yielding type, produces reliable, 6-inch pods. They are very good either fresh or frozen. Readily available.

Vine (indeterminate) Varieties

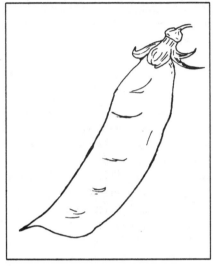

Vine peas are the most flavorful and heaviest yielding. They require a trellis, but yield over a long season. Transplanting seedlings will increase your spring crop substantially, but is not necessary for fall crops.

ALASKA (55 days) is one of the earliest available. It's one of the best choices for short northern climates. Alaska is the standard for dry soup peas, but also tastes good fresh. Available (Bu, Fa, Fi, Jo, Ma, Pi).

ALDERMAN (70-75 days) grows tall vines to produce a long harvest of dark green peas. Peas are excellent for canning and freezing. Available (Bg, Gc, Ha).

OREGON SUGAR POD (100 days) can be eaten as a snow pea, pod and all, shucked and eaten as shelling peas, or left to mature seeds. This variety offers the most versatility available. Enation-resistant. Available (Bu, Ha, Hi, Ju, Le, Te, Th).

SUGAR SNAP (52 days) grows medium-size vines that yield one of the most flavorful peas available. It takes longer to mature than the bush AAS winner Sugar Ann, but the flavor is worth the wait. Readily available.

SUGAR MEL (Super Mel) (70 days) is the among the tallest of snap pea vines. They continue to produce juicy pods when picked regularly. Excellent flavor. Available (Cg, Pi, So)

Problems

There are many diseases and several insects that attack peas. Very little can be done about diseases once they get started, while insects are much easier to control. The keys to preventing diseases are early planting, good drainage, and plenty of sunshine.

Beans and peas have similar enemies. Except for enation and heat stress, all of the solutions to problems can be found on pages 33-36.

Enation virus is common in the Pacific Northwest from the Willamette Valley, South from Puget Sound. Mottled, warty pods form. Flowering and pod-set are curtailed before the vine dies. The disease is carried by green peach aphids.
Control: None, remove and destroy affected vines.
Prevention: Control aphids as soon as they are seen. Plant and harvest early maturing, enation-resistant varieties.

Heat stress sets in when the temperature climbs beyond 80° (26° C). Heat stress is compounded by drought. Plants wilt, flowers and pods drop.
Control: Water heavily, mulch to cool soil. Build a canopy that shades plants and creates a breezeway during midday sun.
Prevention: Plant early or late in the year so that peas ripen during cool weather. Plant in the coolest portion of the garden in warm climates.

Peppers *(Capsicum annuum)*

A member of the tropical and subtropical *Solanum* family (page 78) peppers require ample heat to grow and set fruit. Nighttime temperatures below 50° (10° C) will stunt seedling peppers so badly that they may never recover. A Wall-O-Water(™), cold frame, Remay or hot cap provide young plants cold protection in the spring and early summer. This added warmth allows peppers to develop and bear much heavier. Choose smaller sweet peppers for growing in cool, short-season climates. Just about any pepper will grow in warm climates, including heat-loving bell and all of the hot varieties.

One of the keys to harvesting lots of peppers is to pick them regularly and keep them from suffering heat stress. Since they are a tropical fruit, peppers need a warm, but mild climate for highest yields.

Basic Facts

Germination time: 8-25 days.
Germination temperature: Minimum: 60° (16° C), Optimum: 85° (29° C), Maximum: 95° (35° C).
Approximate seeds per ounce: 4,000.
Yield per plant: 5-15 (large peppers), 20-50 (small peppers).
Life expectancy of stored seed: 2 years
Estimated time between sowing and first picking: 7-10 weeks.
Intercrop: radishes, lettuce, and garlic.
Effort to cultivate: Fairly easy. Must have temperature range between 50-90° (10-32° C) for best production.
Seed saving: Separate different varieties by at least 100 feet to prevent cross-pollination by insects. Seeds are scraped out of fruit and dried slowly.

Climate

Annual in most zones, but can be grown as a perennial in zone 11, where temperatures do not freeze. Seedlings *must have a minimum of 50° (10° C) to grow.* Mature peppers are more tolerant of cooler temperatures (below 50° (10° C)).

The variety Sweet Banana is a standout, producing until first frost.
The ideal temperatures for growth is 70° (21° C) at night and 80° (27° C) during the day. Flowers will drop and fruit develop very slowly if temperatures deviate beyond this ideal range.

> **Temperature is normally the most important factor in growing peppers.**

Soil Preparation

Peppers prefer warm, humusy, well-drained, fertile ground with a pH range of 5.5-6.8 Adding dolomite lime not only adjusts the pH, but adds magnesium, a nutrient often found deficient in peppers.

Planting

Sow seed indoors in flats or small containers. Sow seed 1/4-inch deep, and keep evenly moist until they sprout. Seedlings *must have full sun,* and will grow spindly if starved for light. Raising seedlings indoors or purchasing them from a nursery will give your crop a big jump on the

season in both warm and cool climates.
Direct-seed in warm climates. Sow seed 1/2-inch deep in fine, well prepared soil. In wide, raised beds, broadcast seed, or sow 2-3 seeds per inch in rows spaced at 12-18 inches.

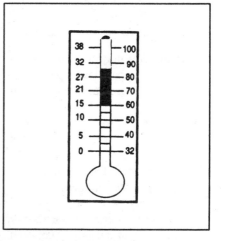

Peppers respond well to transplanting and suffer little or no shock if handled gently, given plenty of water, and shaded for the first few days after transplanting. The soil temperature *must be at least 60° (16° C)* for a smooth transplanting move.
Transplant seedlings under plastic or a Wall-O-Water™ if temperatures are below 50° (10° C). If temperatures fall below 50° (10° C), seedlings may be stunted

for several months. Retain temperature protection until the temperature stays above 60° (16° C), both day and night.

Plant peppers so that they are shaded from the midday sun in climates with temperatures that soar beyond 80° (27° C) regularly. Many peppers produce poorly in hot weather

Crop Care

A black plastic, or dark mulch, will help raise soil temperature 5-10° in cool weather and boost production.

An organic mulch is very useful in warm climates to keep soil cool and retain moisture. Wait until the soil has warmed before mulching.

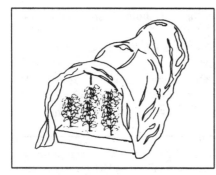

Daily watering may be necessary in hot weather. Peppers lose a good deal of moisture via transpiration through the leaves, which keeps them cool. This water must be replaced regularly. Daily watering leaches nutrients from the soil, and a mild solution of manure tea added to each watering will replenish them.

Fertilize every 2-4 weeks with a complete mix. Peppers are heavy nitrogen, potassium, calcium and magnesium feeders. Feeding is most important just before and during fruit set.

Cut down on the fertilizer nitrogen content in August, to promote fruit development.

Harvesting

For highest production, pick the first few peppers that set when they are about half-size. This will cause more fruit to set. Use scissors or pruners to snip the ripe fruit from the stem.

Numerous bell and hot pepper varieties grow thicker, juicier walls and become sweeter as they ripen, changing color from green, to yellow or red. If possible, leave fruit on the vine to turn color and grow sweeter. But remember, leaving them on the vine stops new peppers from developing.

Near the end of the season, uproot the entire plant of hot, thin-walled varieties such as cayenne and red chile before rains or a sudden cold snap destroy ripening fruit. Hang the plants upside down so the fruit can dry slowly and keep for the winter.

Thick-walled bell and hot varieties should all be harvested as soon as the first frost is predicted, because they cannot stand a light freeze. They are also easily damaged by chilling rains.

In the Kitchen

Fresh: Sweet peppers add a pleasant flavor and color to salads and stir-fry dishes. Simply cut away the crown and remove the seeds. Slice the pepper into strips or dice.

Hot peppers are one of the main ingredients in *salsa*. Along with the other ingredients, hot peppers are diced, pureed in a blender or ground with a stone *metate* (mortar & pestle) to form a rich, hot sauce.

Storage: Peppers will keep in the refrigerator, wrapped in plastic, for up to 3 weeks. When kept in a moist location with good air circulation, peppers will keep for about 2 weeks at 50-60° (10-16° C).

Drying: Both hot and sweet peppers dry very well. To dry sweet peppers, slice fruits into strips and place on a screen in the sun, or in a food drier. Let them dry until they become leathery. Dried fruit rehydrates readily by adding water. Hot peppers can be dried whole, just like sweet pepper slices. They are also very ornamental when strung together with

a needle and thread, and hung in the kitchen to dry.

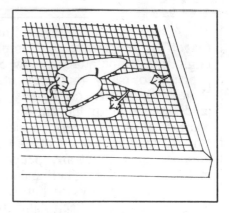

Freezing: Both hot and sweet peppers are easy to freeze. Simply freeze the entire raw fruit or cut into strips, removing seeds and stem, before popping into a freezer bag and freezing; no blanching is necessary.

Varieties

Two seed companies specialize in peppers, each offering over 40 varieties. Tomato Grower's Supply, P.O. Box 2237, Fort Myers, FL, 33902 and Horticultural Enterprises, P.O. Box 810082, Dallas, TX, 75381-0082. Choosing the right variety is very important in both warm and cool climates. It can make the difference between good production, or failure.

Sweet Varieties

CALIFORNIA WONDER (75 days) yields early, large, thick-walled, flavor-packed fruits. A good choice for mild northern regions. Available (Fa, Fi, Ha, Ma, Me, Ni, Pa, St, Sha). Two improved varieties include EARLY CALIFORNIA WONDER, available (Ju), and GOLDEN CALIFORNIA WONDER, available (Gs, Le, Me, Pi, So, Te).

GYPSY (65 days) is a very good producer in cool climates. The yellow, thick-walled fruit are quite sweet. Available (Bu, Fa, Fi, Ha, Hi, Ju, Le, Ma, Ni, Pa, Pi, Te, Th)

KEYSTONE RESISTANT GIANT (79 days) is a "California Wonder" type

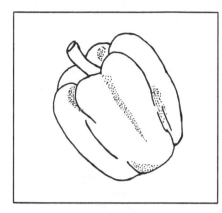

that has large, blocky, fruit 4 inches square. The heavy foliage lessens chance of sunscald. The mosaic resistant plant is well adapted to the Eastern seaboard. Excellent flavor. Available (Fi, So).

STADDONS SELECT (72 days) produces medium-sized, bell-type fruit on tall, heavy-yielding plants. An excellent selection for northern climates with harsh climates. Available (Hi, Pl, St).

SWEET BANANA TYPES (72 days) yield 4-6-inch, slender, yellow peppers that are very sweet and tasty. This variety is outstanding, and one of the best possible choices for northern gardens. Available (Bu, Gs, Ha, Le, Me, Ni, Pa, Pi, Sha, St).

YOLO WONDER (76 days) sets large, weighty fruits with heavy crowns to protect it from sunscald. Mosaic resistant, and strong growth habit. Available (Bg, Ju, Le, Me, St).

Hot Varieties

ANAHEIM TYPES (68 days) are very popular and only moderately hot. The shinny, deep green fruit turns red when fully mature. Large fruit is borne on productive, tall plants. Ample foliage covers fruits to protect from sunscald. Available (Bu, Cg, Gs, Me, Ni, Pa, Pl, She, Tg).

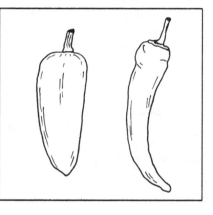

CAYENNE TYPES (70 days) including LONG RED THIN, LONG RED SLIM, ULTRA CAYENNE, HOT PORTUGAL and GOLDEN CAYENNE, which is hotter and bigger, are all excellent fresh or dried when used in hot *salsas*. The fruits are most flavorful after they turn red. Available (Ca, Cg, Fi, Gc, He, Le, Me, Pa, Pi, Pl, Ric, She, St, Tg).

HUNGARIAN YELLOW WAX TYPES (60-65 days) varieties, including HUNGARIAN RAINBOW WAX, produce yellow fruits up to 8 inches long on a bushy plant. They are mildly hot, and a favorite for pickling. Available (Bg, Bu, Fi, Gc, Gs, Ha, Hi, Hu, Jo, Le, Ma, Me, Ni, Pa, Pi, St, Tg).

JALAPENO TYPES (75 days) is a favorite for hot *salsa*. The dark green fruits are occasionally left on the vine to turn red. They are very tasty, extremely hot when fresh, and mellow when pickled or cooked. Readily available.

RED CHILI (80 days) is hot and pungent. This hot red pepper is excellent when dried and used as a seasoning. Good yield and hot! Available (Ma, Sc).

SERRANO (75 days) peppers are thin-walled, red to orange and about 2 inches long. The hot peppers are ideal in chile sauces. This chile is hot both fresh or pickled. Available (Cg, Gs, Sc, So, Tg).

Problems

Peppers are in the tropical *solanum* family, and affected by many of the same problems as tomatoes and eggplants. If you use tobacco, always remember to wash your hands before handling any *solanum* family members. The best way to avoid pepper problems is to keep them growing fast and strong throughout life. The key to strong growth is to maintain the temperature in the 60-80° range. If they become too hot or too cold, growth slows to a halt. When growth is slow, disease and insect attacks are most common and can devastate a season's crop.

PEPPERS	SYMPTOM	PROVABLE CAUSES
Seed & Seedlings	cut off at base	11
	missing	16, 17
	did not germinate	16 or too cold
Plant	stunted	too cold or too hot
Leaves	chewed, holes	2, 10, 13, 14, 15
	dark spots	3
	yellow/green spots	4, 5, 6
	dry spots	7
	curled	6, 9
	sunken greasy spots	5
Fruit	slow development	1, 6
	rotting	1
	tunneled	1, 2
	dark spots	3
	yellow/green spots	4
	sunken greasy spots	5
	bitter	6
	no fruit	8
Flowers	chewed, holes	2
	no flowers	8

1. Pepper maggots invade fruits, causing rapid deterioration. Eggs laid inside the fruit hatch into translucent larvae that start feeding immediately after hatching. See drawing on page 81.
Control: None. Remove and destroy affected fruit.
Prevention: Egg-laying by the yellow adult fly is foiled by dusting fruit with diatomaceous earth or talc from July through August.

2. Pepper weevils, most common in the southern half of America, are dark, shiny 1/8-inch-long beetles with the characteristic long weevil snout that feeds on foliage, buds, and new pods. The white, 1/4-inch-long worm larva consumes buds and tender pods. Flowers and pods are disfigured and may drop.
Control: Apply insecticidal soap or rotenone if heavily infested.
Prevention: Clean up, and till the ground after harvest to prevent overwintering. Rotate crops on a 3-year schedule.

3. Anthracnose shows up on ripening fruit and stems as dark, round, recessed spots of varying diameter. Black dots within the spots contain fungus spores. The disease is spread by water.
Control: Remove and destroy affected plants.
Prevention: Avoid working in a wet garden, and keep water off leaves. Practice crop rotation. Avoid planting anthracnose-prone beans close to peppers.

4. Bacterial spot is common in all but the driest of climates. Small yellowish green spots develop on foliage. As the disease progresses spots darken, leaves yellow and drop.
Control: Remove and destroy affected plants.
Prevention: The bacteria lives in the soil. Rotating crops on a 3-year schedule usually does the trick. Do not plant eggplants, peppers, and

tomatoes in the same ground for at least three years.

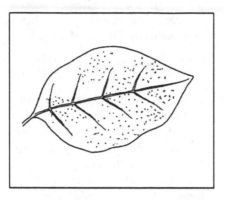

5. Blossom-end rot causes lime-colored, sunken, greasy spots close to the blossom end of the fruit. The spots enlarge as the disease progresses.
Control: Pick affected fruit as soon as the rot is noticed. Cut away rotten portions of the fruit before consuming.
Prevention: Refrain from using high-nitrogen fertilizers; use a mix of soft phosphate and dolomite lime. Keep the soil from drying out or becoming soaked.

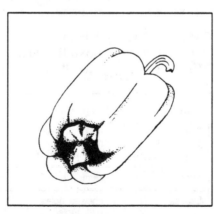

6. Mosaic is caused by several viruses that overwinter on nearby plants. Fruits are stunted; occasionally have a bumpy skin, and a taste bitter develops; few new fruit set. Leaves yellow, and frequently curl.
Control: Aphids spread the disease. Controlling this vector can stop the spread of disease. Remove affected plants and destroy.

Prevention: Avoid planting peppers near alfalfa, clover, cucumbers, tobacco or tomatoes. Spray seedlings a day before transplanting with fresh milk. People that use tobacco should wash their hands before entering the garden. Plant resistant varieties.

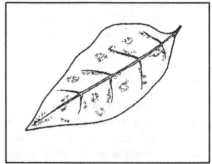

7. Magnesium deficiency is demonstrated by dry spots on leaves, and slow growth.
Control: Water with 2 teaspoons of Epsom salts (magnesium sulfate) per gallon of water.
Prevention: Apply a dusting of fine dolomite lime up to a month before planting.

8. No flowers or fruit are normally the result of temperatures that are too cool, below 60° (16° C) or too hot, above 85° (29° C).
Control/Prevention: To increase heat, use black plastic or aluminum foil mulch; grow under plastic or glass. To lower heat, use organic mulch, water daily, and shade from midday sun.

Other problems peppers might suffer include:

9. Aphid: page 137
10. Colorado potato beetle: page 120
11. Cutworm: page 137
12. Corn earworm: page 70
13. European corn borers: page 71
14. Flea beetle: page 137
15. Tomato hornworm: page 138
16. Damping-off: page 77
17. Slugs and Snails: page 55

Potato (*Solanum tuberosum*)

Potatoes are a major food staple in many parts of the world; in fact the average American eats over 130 pounds annually. Given this information, why do most people think just two or three types of potatoes are available, those sold in supermarkets? There are over 200 different varieties that offer a wide variety of shapes, sizes, colors, textures, and tastes. A very diverse selection can be found by exploring seed catalogs; the most notable is Ronnigers Seed Potatoes, Star Route, Moyie Springs, ID, 83845 that lists some 150 varieties. True, potatoes require ample garden space and can be purchased inexpensively at the supermarket. But unlike commercially grown crops, home-grown tubers are free of sprout-inhibiting chemicals and killing sprays. Once you try garden-fresh varieties, commercial crops will seem like little more than a ball of bland starch.

Sweet Potato (*Ipomoea batatas*) are considered by most gardeners as an exclusive warm-weather Southern cultivar. However, with a little care, sweet potatoes will grow in climates with a minimum of four frost-free months. Careful variety selection, and planting rooted slips (sprouted pieces of older potatoes), when the ground has warmed to 55° (14° C) will overcome most climatic obstacles.

Yams (*Dioscorea*) are often confused with sweet potatoes. Yams are longer, more slender, and a different genus entirely. This tropical vine with edible tuberous roots grows only in zone 11 where the temperatures stay above freezing year round. Finding yam slips is next to impossible in North America.

Basic Facts

Germination time: 7-14 days.
Germination temperature: Minimum: 40°, Optimum: 80°, Maximum: 95°.
Approximate seeds per ounce: 1-6.
Yield per plant: 2-10 pounds.
Life expectancy of stored seed: 1 year.
Estimated time between sowing and first picking: 12-14 weeks.
Intercrop: Beans, radishes, annual flowers.
Effort to cultivate: Easy.
Seed saving: Very easy. Just set aside several potatoes from each variety. Keep the potato "seed" in a cool, dry, dark location. About a month before planting, give the spuds low light to induce sprouting. Plant pieces of the potatoes containing at least two eyes.

Climate

Annual in all zones. Potatoes are easy to grow in most any climate, flourishing in cool northern zones.
Sweet potatoes grow best in long-season tropical zones, but can be cultivated in any climate with 4 frost-free months. Slips require a minimum temperature of 55° (14° C).

Soil Preparation

Good soil preparation is the key to a successful harvest. A light, well-drained, fertile soil is imperative for the tuberous roots to swell to maximum potential.
Amend the garden bed with plenty of nitrogen-rich compost, and manure up to a month before planting. If ample nitrogen is supplied by the amendments, no supplemental fertilization will be necessary. In fact, more nitrogen may promote excessive leaf, and lanky vine growth.
Incorporate a complete fertilizer. A good complete mix includes chicken manure, bone meal, granite dust and greensand.
A pH of 6.0 enhances growth, which is, the opposite of most plant requirements. The problem with an alkaline pH is that scab, a common potato disease, also flourishes at the higher pH.

Planting

Seed potatoes or potato sets (minitubers) may be purchased from seed suppliers. Or potatoes may be saved from the previous year's crop. Growers using seed potatoes often experience much heavier yields of slightly smaller potatoes than when they use potatoes cut for seed.

Supermarket potatoes can also be used as "seed" stock, but many are sprayed with a chemical that inhibits sprouting. Retail nurseries also sell untreated potatoes that are cut up for "seed". When cutting up potatoes for seed, make sure to use a very clean knife. It is a good idea to dip the knife in sterilizing alcohol between cuts to prevent any spread of disease.

A month before planting, cut the potatoes into chunks, each piece having several "eyes" or sprouts. Leave the "seed" in a bright, dry location that stays between 40 and 50º (10º C). Warmer temperatures cause potatoes to dry out, which may retard later development. The pieces will callus and gradually turn green.

Unsprouted potatoes can also be planted, but they take several weeks longer to pop through the soil and should be planted earlier. Unsprouted potatoes also yield about two weeks later.

About 4 weeks before the last frost, dig a trench about 6 inches deep and 12 inches wide, piling the soil from the trench alongside. Space trenches about 12-18 inches apart. Plant 1-3 seeds per foot in a zig-zag pattern along the bottom of the trench and cover the seed with a couple of inches of soil.

As the sprouts emerge, cover them every few days with compost/soil. Continue covering sprouts for about a month until a foot-high mound is formed around the plant.

If a killing frost occurs, the sprouts will die back to the soil line and immediately resprout.

An alternative to digging a trench is to plant seed on the soil's surface, spacing them as for trenches. Continue piling compost around the sprouts to build a mound up to two feet high. Some gardeners plant potatoes under a compost pile, continuing to add more compost as the sprouts mature.

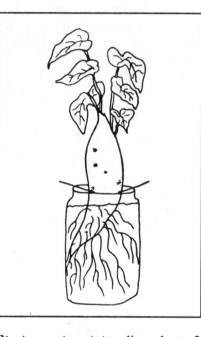

Start sweet potato slips about 3 months before the last frost date. One potato grows about a dozen slips. Submerge about a third of the root end of the potato in a glass of water. Use toothpicks to suspend the potato in the glass. Place the potato in a sunny window. Add water as required. In 1-2 weeks, the first sprouts should appear.

When the vines have grown to 12-18 inches, cut them off in 4-6 inch pieces that have 2 or more leaves each. Place the cuttings in a glass of water to root.

Harden-off the rooted slips outdoors daily as the weather warms. They can also be placed under plastic for added night time protection.

When the soil has warmed to 55º (14º C), plant the slips 3-4 inches deep on 12-18 inch centers in well-drained, raised beds that are amended with plenty of rich compost and manure. Water thoroughly.

Crop Care

Remove weeds by hand or with a hoe. Rapid, early leaf growth will shade weeds, cutting weeding to a minimum. The continual mounding of compost/soil also helps smother weeds.

If growth slows or leaves turn lime green, add a compost, or manure tea.

Water regularly when tubers develop. From 30-70 days after sprouts emerge, tubers begin to develop and flower buds start to form. Use a lot of water during this stage.

Once flowers bloom, water consumption slows dramatically. Applying too much water after blooming causes hollow-hearted-tubers.

Sweet potato vines sprawl and root on the surface of the soil. Pick up the vines once or twice during the season to prevent them from rooting. This ensures that larger tubers will develop.

Harvesting

New potatoes are harvested during and soon after flowers bloom. Carefully dig tubers using a spading fork. Digging new potatoes also serves to thin intensively planted crops.

When the tops begin to die back, tubers are close to maximum size. Start digging fresh potatoes as needed, through summer's end. Use a spading fork to harvest the balance of the crop before fall rains rewet skins.

Bruised, cut, or damaged potatoes should be eaten first. Healthy, blemish-free tubers can be stored in a cool, dry, dark location. See "Storage" below.

Harvest sweet potatoes about the time of the first freeze of autumn.

In the Kitchen

Fresh: Potatoes form the base of hundreds of recipes. They can be boiled, fried, baked or microwaved. Few dishes compare to home-grown succulent "new" potatoes cooked with "baby" carrots or fresh peas.

Storage: Thick-skinned, unblemished potatoes store well for up to 6 months in a dark, cool (40° (5° C)) location. The temperature is important: if warmer than 40° (5° C), they sprout; if cooler, sugar content increases to an inedible state. If kept in a light location, they sprout and turn green, making them inedible. The potatoes should dry for several hours before storing, so external moisture does not initiate rot.

Freezing: Whole potatoes are rarely frozen. Once cut into french fries, slices or riced, they freeze readily. Simply put the blanch the potatoes in boiling water for two minutes and put them in a plastic freezer container and freeze.

Varieties

Some of the best places to find potatoes to use for seed are at local health-food stores, farmers markets, or roadside stands that offer a good selection. Search for stock that tastes the best and make sure to ask if they have been sprayed with an anti-sprouting chemical. One seed company that specializes in potatoes is Ronnigers Seed Potatoes, Star Route, Moyie Springs, Idaho, 83845). They offer over 100 different varieties that are organically grown.

CARIBE was grown in New England for export to the Caribbean Islands. The dark violet skin protects the creamy white flesh. The tender, moist flesh is delicious. **CARIBES**

are heavy bearing, and early to mature. Available (Bec, Ro, She).

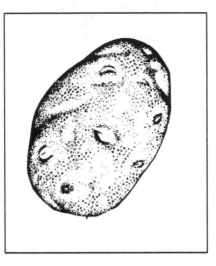

KENNEBEC (115 days), very vigorous growth and enormous yield of large tubers that store well. Grows well in all climates. Good keeper and excellent taste. Available (Bec, Bu, Fa, Fi, Ju, Ma, Ro).

IRISH COBBLER (100 days) is widely adaptable to most climates and yields well. Oblong to round white potatoes have shallow eyes and taste great. Available (Bec, Ro).

NORWEGIAN yields medium-long fingerling tubers with a pinkish skin. The yellow flesh is somewhat sweet and keeps well. Good producer and one of the best fingerlings on the market. Available (Ro)

PONTIAC including **RED PONTIAC** are the choicest tubers for mashed potatoes. Let tubers set in the ground for a week after they mature to make the skin more durable. Available (Bec, Bu, Fa, Fi, Le, Ma, Ro).

PURPLE PERUVIAN develop into exotic deep, dark purple tubers with white internal veins. The flesh lightens slightly when cooked. Great flavor, very hardy and excellent keeper. Available (Bec, Gs, Ro).

RUSSET BURBANK (120 days) is the potato that helped Idaho rise to fame and fortune. Also called the Idaho Netted Gem, the Russet is

grown all over North America. Baked potatoes are generally russets. Available (Bec, Fi, Le, Pa, Ro)

RUSSIAN BANANA is an excellent fingerling with yellow skin and flesh. High yielding, excellent flavor and very disease-resistant. An extremely popular Canadian market potato. Available (Ro).

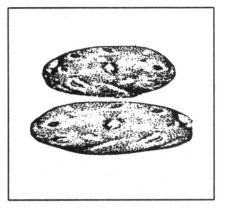

YELLOW FINNS (80-90 days) including **YELLOW FINNISH BINTJE** were developed by the Finnish agricultural researchers. Yellow Finns are some of the most flavorful potatoes available. The tubers set heavily when soil is mounded high. Reducing nitrogen-rich fertilizers will also increase yields. Available (Gs, Ni, Ro, She, Te)

Sweet Potato Varieties

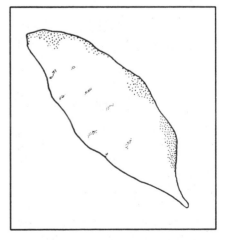

BEAUREGARD (90-100 days) A very productive, red-skinned tuber with rich orange flesh. Resistant to Fusarium wilt but vulnerable to nematodes. Available (Se).

CENTENIAL (90-100 days) This vigorous plant yields an early crop of large tubers on 20-foot-long vines. This long keeper is a good choice for all climates. Available (Bu, Fi, Ge, Ju, Ma, Mar, Me, Mi, Pa).

GEORGIA JET (90 days) is a very early variety that produces a prolific harvest of uniform tubers. The rich, red skin and deep orange-fleshed tubers grow well in all climates. Available (Fi, Ge, Ma, Mar, Me).

JEWEL (Golden Jewel) (120-150 days) is the variety most likely found in supermarkets. A very abundant producer that stores well. Long trailing vines produce copper-colored potatoes with orange flesh. Excellent variety for long seasons. Available (Fi, Ge, Ju, Ma, Me).

Problems

Potatoes are attacked by numerous pests both above and below ground. Commercial farmers use tons of chemicals to combat these pests. Organic gardeners have numerous controls available, all of which are safe, and very effective. Avoid diseases by purchasing and planting certified, disease-free seed stock and grow strong, healthy plants.

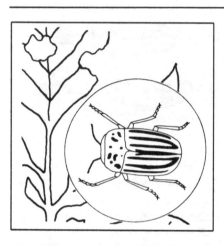

1. Colorado potato beetle, both the adult, which is 3/8-inch long, and yellow, with black stripes, and the red grub larva, defoliate potatoes in all states except California and Nevada.

Control: Hand-pick adults, and squash yellow eggs located on leaf undersides. Homemade sprays, including eucalyptus, cedar, or basil teas, are effective against this pest. Dust moist leaves with wheat bran; beetles eat it, bloat and burst. Pyrethrum or rotenone can be used on infestations.

Prevention: Encourage or introduce toads and ladybugs, which are natural beetle predators. The wasp, *Edovum puttleri*, parasitizes beetle eggs. Nc nematodes prey on hibernating beetles.

POTATOES	SYMPTOM	PROVABLE CAUSES
Seed & Seedlings	missing	2, 23, 26
	short sprouts	5
	wilting, dying	5, 12, 28
	spindly	5, 17, 26
Leaves	chewed, holes	1, 2, 15, 22, 23, 25, 26
	yellow	11, 14, 16
	yellow, burned edges	3, 16
	curling	3, 10, 16, 21
	target-like spots	8
	dark spots	9, 11, 12, 21
Roots	spots	7
	rotting	13, 14, 16, 18, 24, 27
	mushy, rubbery	18
	hollow	19
	tunneled	15, 27
	poor quality	18, 19, 20, 26
Plants	stunted	6, 13, 14
	yellow	11
	wilting	13, 14, 16

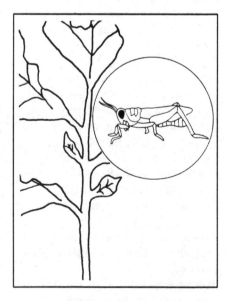

2. Grasshopper adults and nymphs may attack foliage *en masse*.

Infestations are the worst in climates with annual rainfall of 10-30 inches.

Control: Encourage blister beetles, ground beetles, spiders, and bee flies, as well as other natural enemies listed below.

Prevention: Fall and spring tillage disrupts the eggs that are laid near the surface of the soil. Fall cleanup prevents overwintering. Heavy mulch impairs their surfacing. Natural enemies include birds, snakes, toads, spiders, Nc nematodes and mites.

3. Potato leafhopper (bean jassid) causes leaf fringes and tips to appear yellow or burned, curl upward and become brittle. The 1/8-inch, wedge-shaped, winged, green leafhopper adult flits away when disturbed. Nymphs resemble small adults but crawl sideways.

Control: Cover young plants for the first 6-8 weeks of growth with spun fiber to exclude egg-laying adults. Blacklight fluorescent light traps will capture adults, sucking them into a removable receptacle. Apply insecticidal soap

Prevention: Plant resistant varieties. Cover juvenile plants with spun fiber to exclude egg-laying adults.

4. Potato psyllid (tomato psyllid) adults are 1/10-inch long, and grayish. Nymphs are the real problem. The pale green, flat pest injects a fluid that causes short sprouts on tubers, and set after set of new tubers form on the sprouts. Leaves turn yellow to brown as they wither and die.

Control: None. Remove and destroy affected plants. Dust soil with diatomaceous earth.

Prevention: Fall cleanup and dust with diatomaceous earth.

5. Potato tuberworm is a whitish-pink, 1/2-inch long worm with a dark head. It burrows into foliage and tubers, causing new growth to wilt and expire. The pest is worst in the southern half of the U.S.

Control: Cut and destroy affected foliage.

Prevention: The adult moth lays eggs in the eyes of tubers. Do not leave tubers exposed; mound up soil around plant base. Remove weeds.

6. Symphylan (garden centipede or symphilid) adults are milky-white, delicate, 3/8-inch long, with 12 sets of legs; juveniles have fewer legs. These pests feed on roots and tubers, causing stunted growth. The fast-moving creature is rarely seen above ground.

Control: Drench the soil with a garlic tea.

Prevention: Thoroughly rototill the soil. Do not make a compost pile near a symphilid-infested garden.

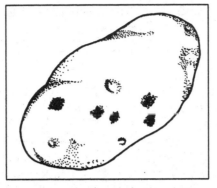

7. Common scab causes light-to-dark spots on tubers that appear coarse or corky. This fungus is worst in soil that is not quite moist enough for ideal tuber development, and has a neutral to alkaline pH.

Control: Destroy all affected plants and tubers.

Prevention: Plant disease-resistant varieties. Crop rotation; wait 3-5 years before planting potatoes in infected soil. Keep infected soil pH below 6.0.

8. Early blight causes small brown spots that look like small targets on foliage. If the disease flourishes, foliage dies and tubers are infected with small, circular blisters that later rot.

Control: Harvest tubers, destroy infected foliage.

Prevention: Plant clean, certified, disease-free seed that does not carry the disease. Grow in well-rotted compost and manure.

9. Late blight attacks foliage and tubers after flowers set. It is worst in the Atlantic and north central states east to the Atlantic. Foliage turns dark-brown to black with a pale green outer margin, which looks like a halo. The fungus spreads very rapidly during warm, moist weather, killing plants in just a few days. The disease travels via wind and water.

Control: None. Remove and destroy all affected foliage.

Prevention: If late blight suddenly strikes, let it kill all of the foliage. Put off digging until two weeks after all the vines are dead. Without a living host-plant, the fungus spores die. If possible, wait until after a hard freeze. Remove and destroy the dead tops. Dig out all of the potatoes. Make sure to wash and dry them before storing in a disinfected location. Do not use seed potatoes grown in infected ground. Rotate potatoes on a 3-year plan.

10. Leaf roll virus can be devastating to the crop. Aphids are the vector of this disease that makes leaves roll upward (cup), becoming hard and crisp. Overall vigor is low and yields are marginal.

Control: None, Remove and destroy plants.

Prevention: Control aphids. Buy certified seed.

11. Mosaic viruses induce motley green-yellow to dark-green growth on distorted leaves, and an overall yellowish appearance. Brown spots sometimes develop on tubers. Most common in warm, humid weather. Infected seed is the main source of the disease.
Control: Remove and destroy diseased plants immediately.
Prevention: Plant only certified disease-free seed or tubers. Plant resistant varieties.

12. Rhizoctonia (black scurf) induces black cankers that destroy new sprouts. The sprouts can also be encircled beneath the growing tip, causing new shoots to grow, which are soon killed by the fungal disease. Advanced symptoms include recessed dead patches on foliage close to the soil. Growth and tuber formation are stunted.
Control: Remove and destroy affected foliage. Cut off affected areas on tubers before eating.
Prevention: Plant only disease-free, certified seed. Rotate crops on a 3-5 year schedule. Plant only in well-drained soil. Plant after weather warms if possible.

13. Ring rot overwinters in infected tubers, but is nearly impossible to detect. Late in the season, foliage wilts and tubers start to deteriorate just below the skin's surface. A yellow puss solution is secreted when the tuber is squeezed.
Control: None. Remove and destroy affected plants.
Prevention: Plant certified disease-free seed. If using your own "seed" stock, dip the knife you use to cut them into pieces in a sterilizing alcohol solution to avoid the rapid spread of the disease.

14. Root knot (nematode gall) causes galls, to grow on roots and tubers. Growth slows, leaves yellow and wilt; tubers are stunted and may rot. Microscopic nematodes cause the galls and are transported by irrigation

water or they hitch a ride on tools, animals or human feet.

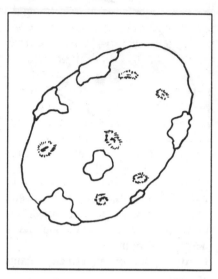

Control: Remove severely affected plants and hot compost in a hot pile.
Prevention: Add plenty of organic matter to the soil. Practice a 3-5-year crop rotation.

15. Sweet potato weevil resembles a large 1/4-inch long ant. This winged insect is a beautiful dark blue and light red. The adult lays eggs near the base of plants. Larvae hatch and tunnel tubers and foliage. Adults riddle foliage with holes.
Control: Remove and destroy affected plants and tubers.
Prevention: Rotate crops. The weevils perish when they are without food for a year. Buy certified seed from resistant varieties.

16. Verticillium wilt is apparent late in the growth cycle when it first causes lower leaves to yellow, turn crispy, and die. Other foliage may curl and appear tip burned before wilting and dying. The top leaves are the last to die.
Control: Remove affected and bordering plants and destroy as soon as they appear to avoid the spread of the disease.
Prevention: Rotate crops on a 4-5-year plan; do not plant where tomatoes, peppers or potatoes have grown for the previous 3 years. Plant

certified disease-free stock. Plant resistant varieties.

17. Spindly shoots are typically caused by keeping the sprouting shoots too warm and dark. If shoots are still spindly when given ample light and cool temperatures, the problem most likely a disease. If sprouts suffered a freeze, they may be spindly.

18. Soft tubers may look normal on the outside, but the inside is mushy and rubbery. This is caused by drought. A lack of water prompts the tuber to send moisture to the leaves.
Prevention: Apply adequate water during drought conditions.

19. Hollow tubers are caused by prolonged moisture following a drought. These tubers are prone to rot during storage.
Prevention: Apply adequate water during dry conditions.

20. Poor quality may not be noticed until potatoes are processed in the kitchen. Typically, a **soapy texture** is caused by harvesting maincrop potatoes too soon. **Overly sweet** flesh is prompted by holding tubers in a cold storage area which is too cold. If the **potatoes turn black** after cooking, the causes are storing them at or above 100° (38° C) or a deficiency of potassium.

Other pests and problems that might attack potatoes include:

21. Aphids: page 137
22. Black blister beetles: page 40
23. Flea beetles: page 137
24. Nematodes: see number 14 above
25. Slugs and snails: page: 55
26. Whitefringed beetles: page 35
27. Wireworm: page 61
28. Black leg: page 55

Radish *(Raphanus sativus)*

Children love to grow radishes. Many varieties are ready to eat within a month and require frequent watering, which is one of children's favorite chores. Even though radishes are a member of the *brassica* family, they are nearly trouble-free when cultured rapidly and grown during cool weather. Grownups enjoy the ease of cultivation, filling in temporary bare areas of the garden or marking rows of slow-maturing crops with fast-growing radishes. There are many long-season radishes such as the giant Japanese (DAIKON) varieties or the black Spanish types. Since radishes are a member of the brassica family, the infamous root maggots have time to launch an attack on longer season radishes. Prevent root maggot attacks by applying diatomaceous earth, wood ash or beneficial Nc nematodes when planting. By planting different types, you can enjoy fresh radishes most of the year.

Basic Facts

Germination time: 3-30 days
Germination temperature: Minimum: 40° (5° C), Optimum: 85° (29° C), Maximum: 95° (35° C).
Approximate seeds per ounce: 2,200
Yield per 10 foot row: 1-20 pounds
Life expectancy of stored seed: 4 years
Estimated time between sowing and first picking: 3-5 weeks (short season) 9-10 weeks (long season)
Intercrop: Tuck short-season radishes in any bare spot in the garden. Harvest before slower maturing crops such as carrots, onions, tomatoes, etc.
Effort to cultivate: Easy, tuck them in where there is space.
Seed saving: Grow only one type of radish when saving seed to prevent cross-pollination. Remove seed from dried stalks. Winter radishes are biennials; follow seed saving as for beets, page 37.

Climate

Annual in all zones. Short-season radishes prefer cool, 60-65° (16-19° C) weather, bolting when temperatures climb beyond 80° (27° C). Summer varieties thrive in warmer weather. Winter varieties size up in the late summer and are harvested throughout the fall into the winter months.

Soil Preparation

Radishes prefer fertile soil that holds moisture but still drains well. Prepare soil to a depth of 6 inches by adding plenty of well-rotted compost and manure a month or longer before sowing seed.
Tuck radish seed in wherever there is a bare spot in the garden for a month or so. Soil preparation is seldom of major concern. However, the better soil is prepared, the lower the maintenance and the higher the yield.

Planting

An early sowing can be made under a cloche or plastic tunnel as soon as the temperature warms to near freezing.
Sow 8-10 seeds per foot at a depth of 1/2 inch in rows spaced 6-12 inches apart. Cover the seeds with light, humusy soil that retains moisture well.

Or broadcast seeds over a raised, wide bed that has been cultivated to an even consistency. Lightly rake the seed into the surface layer of soil before watering.
Sow a succession of seed every week or two from early spring until hot summer weather sets in.
Plant several types of seed that mature at different times in the same plot. The first radishes harvested make room for new swelling roots.
Thin the radishes so they stand 2 inches apart when the first set of true leaves appears. Crowded radishes fail to form bulbs.
Interplanting quick-germinating radishes with slow-geminating crops such as carrots, celery or onions lets the robust radishes "break ground" for the frail seedlings. The radishes are harvested before they shade the later crops.
Sow large winter radishes from mid-July through August, so that they are able to size up before sunlight diminishes and cool weather slows growth.

Crop Care

Radishes require little care except for regular watering. Their root system is shallow and may require daily watering if weather is dry and windy. A lack of water causes roots to become woody and hot.

Protect radishes, especially long-season types, from root maggots with a dusting of diatomaceous earth, wood ash around the base or an application of Nc nematodes. A spun-fiber cover will also exclude adult flies from laying eggs.

Slugs and snails find tender tops and developing roots a real early season treat. Protection may be needed.

Winter radishes may need a heavy layer of mulch to protect them from frost if left in the ground for winter harvest.

Harvesting

Pull spring and summer radishes when their roots swell to the diameter of a dime. Continue harvesting the crop for 1-2 weeks.

Harvest daily. If bulbs start to become woody, too hot or tough, harvest the entire crop. Radishes store well in the refrigerator if too many become ripe at once. Once radishes reach their peak, they cannot remain in the ground over two days without turning pithy.

Japanese varieties are most flavorful when they are about 6 inches long. Let them remain in the ground longer if you plan to use them for cooking.

Winter types are normally left in the ground until needed in the fall or winter. Use a fork to lift roots without breaking or damaging them. Protect roots from freezing temperatures with a heavy mulch of (oak) leaves or straw.

In the Kitchen

Fresh: Radishes are packed with vitamin C and fiber. They are at their best when harvested, rinsed with cold water and eaten raw by themselves or mixed in a salad.

Japanese and winter radishes taste very good steamed, added in a casserole or stir-fried.

Radish greens add a spicy tang to salads or when cooked with other greens. For more information, see "In the Kitchen," above.

Storage: Cut the tops off, leaving a touch of green, and store them in a plastic bag in the refrigerator for up to a week.

Varieties

Spring and Summer Varieties

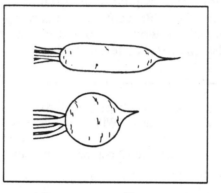

CHERRY BELLE (20-30 days) is a round, red-skinned, popular radish. The white flesh is crunchy and mild tasting. Stays in the ground well without turning pithy. Available (Bg, Bu, Fa, Fi, Gs, Ha, Ju, Le, Ma, Ni, Pi, Si, St, Th).

EASTER EGG (28 days) is one of the best varieties available today. Even when well past normal maturity they taste sweet and succulent. Matures into a large egg-sized root. Available (Bg, Bu, Cg, Fi, Gs, Hi, Jo, Ju, Ma, Ni, Pa, Pi).

FRENCH BREAKFAST TYPES (23 days) yields a cylindrical root with a red top and white tip. The flesh is crisp and mellow when at peak ripeness, but turns woody quickly. Available (Bu, Fa, Fi, Gs, Ju, Le, Ma, Ni, Pa, Pi, St, Te, Th).

SCARLET GLOBE (23-25 days) is a well liked round red radish that matures quickly for early spring harvests. Available (Fi, Le, Ma, Me, St).

VALENTINE (25 days) is an Asian radish with green skin and red and white flesh. They are hot but quite tasty. Great choice for color in salads. Available (St).

WHITE ICICLE (29 days) yields 3-4 inch long, white roots with a nutty-tang. Holds several days in the ground without becoming hot and woody. Available (Bu, Fa, Fi, Hu, Jo, Ju, Ma, Me, Ni, Pi, So, St).

Japanese and Winter Varieties

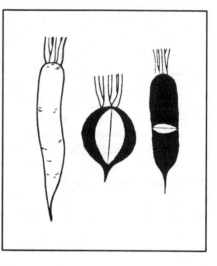

BLACK SPANISH (60 days) develops a large, turniplike, black-skinned root with tangy white flesh. Excellent choice for winter storage. Available (Bg, Fi, Gs, Le, Ni).

DAIKON TYPES (65 days), also called **MOOLI** or **JAPANESE RADISHES**, are juicy, crunchy roots that grow to over a foot in length. The tapered root is chopped and added to soups, stews or stir-fry. A good low calorie snack. The hybrid **APRIL CROSS** is an outstanding variety. It really resists bolting, even if planted early in the spring. Grow as both spring and fall crops. Available (Ni, Pa, She, So, St, Th).

CALIFORNIA WHITE MAMMOTH (60 days) is a fine crisp, white winter radish that grows to 8 inches long and two inches thick. Great mild flavor. Available (Fa, Ma)

Problems

See page 53, "Brassica Problems"

Rhubarb *(Rheum rhubarbarum)*

This perennial crop is an outstanding addition to larger gardens, but tends to take up too much space in smaller plots. The tart, pink to red stalks (leaf stems) are ready to harvest in the early spring, before much of the other garden bounty is ready. *Do not eat the green leaves and roots which are toxic to people.* Rhubarb can be grown in any climate, under just about any conditions. Rhubarb prefers a hard freeze during winter, but this is not necessary for good production. It really benefits from a healthy addition of (chicken) manure very early in the year and once again about midsummer.

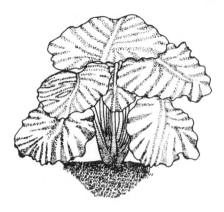

Basic Facts

Sprouting time: (roots) 14-30 days
Germination temperature: Minimum: 30°, Optimum: 65°, Maximum: 90°.
Yield per plant: 10-20 stalks
Estimated time between planting and first picking: 2 years
Intercrop: None, mulch.
Effort to cultivate: Easy. Once planted, very little care is needed.

Climate

Perennial in all zones. Prefers cool weather and a hard freeze in winter but will produce in any climate. In winter climates where temperatures average above 40° (5° C), the crop leafs out in the winter and normally goes dormant during hot summer months.

Soil Preparation

A well-drained loam soil is the most ideal, but rhubarb will grow in most any soil with good drainage.
Dig a trench a foot or two deep and the same width removing perennial weeds. Backfill the trench with well-rotted manure, a shovelful of rock phosphate and two shovels of granite dust. Mix the nutrients together in the trench. Water the mixture in so that it packs down. Finish filling in the trench with 4-6 inches of topsoil.

Planting

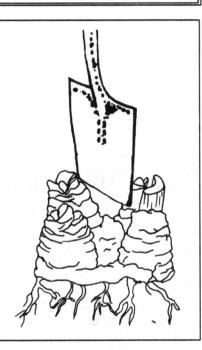

Dormant root crowns (corms) are available at nurseries or from a friend's garden. When they are dug up at a friend's garden, they should be at least three years old. The outer layer of the corm may appear slimy or rotten. This condition is normal and the internal corm is perfectly healthy.
Dig the corms in the late fall or very early in the spring. Separate the corms so that two or more "eyes" or large buds are on each piece, leaving as much of the root as possible. Keep the roots moist, but not waterlogged until they are planted.

Plant the corms 2-3 inches deep and 3 feet apart in the prepared bed. Water-in thoroughly.

Crop Care

Water the roots regularly so they never suffer drought. Production falls substantially if they dry out.
Mulch with grass clippings or compost when the plants are about 6 inches tall. Add more mulch as needed.
Weed around the young plants by hand. Once leaves spread out, weeds are shaded and grow very little.
Fertilize each plant with a shovelful of manure once or twice during the summer.
The top growth will die back with the first good hard freeze. Simply remove the unsightly residue and wait for the following spring when the growth will resume.

Harvesting

The first year of growth is required for the plants to become established. Do not harvest any stalks.
The second year, harvest only a few stalks, about 20%.
Harvest in earnest the third and following years. Twist the stalks from the root and cut the toxic green foliage off with a sharp knife or pruners when they are one to two feet

in length and the leaves are entirely developed. Never harvest more than half of the stalks or production falters in subsequent years. The harvest will continue for 8-10 weeks.

In warm climates, the harvest is taken in the fall and winter, after the hot days of summer that force dormancy.

In the Kitchen

Rhubarb is high in vitamin A and potassium. It's also a fair source of vitamin C.

Fresh rhubarb is tart and tasty, but too bitter to eat raw. It makes an excellent pie filling, sauce base or preserved in jams. The acidic taste is normally sweetened with sugar or other sweet fruit.

Storage: Rhubarb stalks can be stored in the refrigerator for up to three weeks with no loss of quality.

Freezing is a wonderful way to preserve rhubarb for up to a year. Just slice stalks into bite-size pieces, and freeze in a plastic bag. Do not blanch.

Varieties

CANADA RED produces long, thick stalks with a deep, dark red color. They turn to a medium strawberry color when cooked. This variety is much sweeter than most. The best choice for northern climates. Available (Au, Ber, Fi, Ju, Mc).

MACDONALD yields high quality, flavorful brilliant red stalks. the tender skin makes peeling unnecessary. Excellent choice for home gardens. Available (Bu, Co)

VALENTINE produces attractive deep red stalks. The sweet stalks grow to nearly 2 feet in length. The stalks turn pink and taste superb when cooked. Available (Bu, Ju, Ke, Ma, Mi, Sw).

Problems

Few insects or diseases attack rhubarb. The numerous holes chewed by the rhubarb curculio are the only pest that causes serious problems. Regular cultivation and insecticidal soap will stop this pest. Slugs and snails may cause slight damage to leaves but they affect the yield of healthy plants very little. The biggest problem associated with rhubarb is a lack of water. If the roots dry out, production suffers significantly.

Spinach *(Spinacia oleracea)* and Chard *(Beta vulgaris,* Cicla Group)

You can enjoy nutritious spinach leaves for most of the year with the proper variety selection. Unlike the canned spinach that fortified Popeye, garden-fresh spinach is sweet, tender and succulent. There are two basic classifications of spinach: summer and winter, plus the pseudo spinach, New Zealand variety, which is actually a member of the beet family.

Spinach is packed with iron, but the high concentration of oxalic acid renders it a poor choice in large quantities in children's diet.

Chard or Swiss chard, known as beet leaf in England, is also a member of the beet family. It is cultivated for its sweet, tender leaves rather than the root. Chard culture is virtually the same as spinach culture.

Basic Facts

Germination time: 6-25 days
Germination temperature: Minimum: 35° (2° C), Optimum: 70° (21° C), Maximum: 85° (29° C).
Approximate seeds per ounce: 2,200

Yield per 10 foot row: 10-15 pounds
Life expectancy of stored seed: 1-2 years
Estimated time between sowing and first picking: 4-6 weeks
Intercrop with any flower or vegetable.

Effort to cultivate: Easy, but must choose the right variety for your climate.
Seed saving: Easy, but keep away from other spinach plants. Let the spinach run to seed. Let seed dry on plant. Remove seed by shaking flower tops in a paper bag.

Climate

Annual in all zones. This crop grows best in cool 60-80° (16-27° C) weather. Winter varieties will also withstand freezing temperatures. A cold frame offers more protection from freezing temperatures.

Soil Preparation

Rich, fertile soil with good drainage grows the best chard and spinach. As a leaf crop, chard and spinach require abundant nitrogen for the greatest production.
Cultivate in a lot of well-rotted manure and compost one or two months before planting. The soil should be well cultivated at least a foot deep.
Add lime to the soil to bring it into the 6.0 to 6.5 range.

Planting

Soak seeds in water overnight to soften the outer shell and speed germination.
Sow seed directly into garden beds 1/2-inch deep about an inch apart. The seedlings should pop through the soil in about a week. Spinach will germinate in very cold soil and it is not worth starting seedlings indoors.
In the summer, when the soil temperature is above 70° (21° C), the germination rate is cut in half. To enhance warm-weather germination, freeze seeds for 3-4 days before planting. After sowing seed, cover the soil with a plank to keep the soil cool. Remove the plank as soon as the first seed sprouts.
New Zealand spinach needs warm weather to germinate. Plant the seed after soaking overnight or scarifying (page 37) when the soil temperature has increased to 50° (10° C) or more.
Sow seed under a cold frame or plastic tunnel very early in the year or late in the fall. This crop is very hardy and grows well in climates during the entire winter.

Succession plantings should be made every two weeks throughout the growing season. Plant a large winter crop. Harvest outer leaves of plants until spring. New Zealand spinach grows into sprawling vines and succession planting is unnecessary.

Crop Care

Once seedlings start to crowd one another, start thinning by removing entire plants. Do not let plants constrain each other's growth or they tend to bolt sooner.
Weed by hand around tender plants. Mechanical weeding should only scratch the surface of the soil and not disturb tender surface feeder roots.
Mulch to help control weeds, retain cool soil and cut irrigation frequency.
The deep taproot normally finds a good supply of water. But make sure to keep the soil moist. If plants suffer drought, they tend to bolt.
Rapid, unchecked growth produces the sweetest, most tender leaves. If the temperature climbs above 80° (27° C), string a shade cloth (50% or greater) overhead to deflect sunlight and keep the crop cool.
Hot weather may cause plants to bolt, but if picked soon after bolting, you can avoid toughness. New Zealand spinach is an excellent choice for long, hot summer seasons.
Fall, winter and early spring crops need less water and care than summer crops grown during warm weather.
Longer days and shorter nights trigger flowering in spinach. For the best production, plant spinach when the days are short and cool. Harvest before the long summer days trigger premature flowering (bolting).

Harvesting

Under ideal conditions, spinach matures in 6-8 weeks. A plant is fully mature and ready to harvest when at least 6 leaves are over 6 inches long.
Harvest entire plants by snipping the roots off at ground level, which

makes room for smaller plants. Or harvest a few outer leaves and allow the center leaves in the rosette to develop. Cutting only the outside leaves will allow you to pick up to three harvests from each plant as the leaves mature.

In the Kitchen

Fresh spinach stands alone to make a rich and nutritious green salad or it can be an ingredient in a mixed salad. Wash leaves individually to remove gritty soil. Like carrots, spinach is more nutritious when cooked. Steam the washed leaves whole or tear them into smaller pieces. Take care to steam them for just a few minutes or leaves become void of taste and nutrients. For more information, see "In the Kitchen," page 38.
Remove the stems from Swiss chard to cook and serve like asparagus. Steam the greens whole. Steam for less than 5 minutes before checking to see if they are done.
Storage: Spinach will store in a plastic bag in the refrigerator for 2 days with little loss of taste and nutrition. It deteriorates rapidly and is best to eat fresh.
Freezing is possible, however, spinach and chard grow well during cool weather and taste best fresh. Freeze only if necessary.
Canning spinach and chard detracts from the taste substantially. Canning is advised only as a last resort to preserving the crop.
Nutritional value: This leaf crop is packed with vitamins A and B_2. Calcium, iron and protein are also present in large amounts.

Varieties

Spinach Varieties

BLOOMSDALE LONGSTANDING (45 days) is a extraordinary heirloom variety. It will stand in the garden for weeks without running to seed. BLOOMSDALE LONGSTANDING is a very heavy producer and tastes excellent. Available (Bu, Fa, Fi, ha, Hi, Ju, Ma, Me, Ni, Pi, Pl, So, Te).

COLD-RESISTANT SAVOY (45 days) is tolerant to heat, cold and blight. Savoy (crinkled) leaves are quite sweet and tender. Not quite as tolerant to heat as Long Standing Bloomsdale. Available (Gc, Ma, So, St).

INDIAN SUMMER (39 days) is a semi-savoy type that yields heavily. Large, thick crinkled leaves are rich in flavor. Tolerant to mosaic virus and downy mildew. Stands well in the garden after mature. Available (Jo).

NEW ZEALAND SPINACH (55 days)

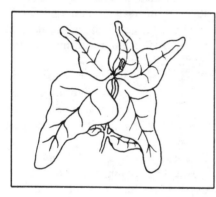

(*Tetragonia tetragonioides*), not a true spinach, is an excellent choice for hot, dry climates. Warm weather (above 50° (10° C)) is needed for germination. In cool climates, sow scarified seed indoors, pinch off the growing tip and set them outdoors when the weather has warmed to 40-50° (5-10° C).

The vines continue to produce until the first hard frost. Harvest leaves from the sprawling vines. The leaf texture is coarse and fuzzy, with a rich flavor. Readily available.

TYEE (42 days) first offered by Johnny's Selected Seeds, it is now the standard of comparison in savoyed spinach for bolt resistance. It grows upright yields clean dark green leaves. Will stand over a week without bolting in hot weather. Tolerant to downy mildew. Available (Jo, Fi, Pi, St, Te)

VIENNA (40 days) is a full savoy type with deep crinkled leaves. Tolerant to downy mildew and blight. Plant for an early spring harvest or a late fall harvest. Yields well. Available (Pa, St).

Swiss Chard Varieties

Known in England as beet top, Swiss chard is actually a variety of beet that is grown for its tasty edible leaves. Chard grows very similar to spinach and withstands warm climates, but warm weather can promote bitterness.

LUCULLUS (60 days) produces large green leaves with broad white stalks prolifically. Steam and serve this tender treat with butter. Excellent flavor. Available (Fa, Fi, Ju, Ma, Me, Pa, Th).

LARGE WHITE BROAD RIBBED (60 days) is the best chard available according to many gardeners. The broad, white, flattened stems are thick and tender. Outstanding tasting greens. Leaves are smooth and easy to clean. Available (Fa, Ha)

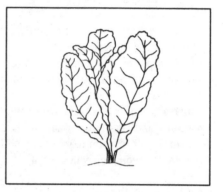

RHUBARB CHARD (Ruby Red) (55-60 days) has deep red stalks and heavily savoyed red leaves. The leaf is very tasty, but the stock somewhat fibrous when mature. Available (Ha, Jo, Ju, Me, Pi, Sha, She, So, Te, Th).

VULCAN (60 days) is very ornamental and edible. Bright red stems and dark green crinkled leaves liven up any garden plot. Excellent flavor, stems are very sweet and rich in vitamin A. Available (Pa).

Problems

When grown in cool weather, spinach and chard are virtually trouble-free. Once temperatures and humidity climb, the leaves are more easily attacked by foliage diseases and insects. New Zealand Spinach is one of the best warm-season types to grow. Growing disease-resistant varieties will prevent most diseases, and vigilant handpicking of insects curtails most damage.

1. Spinach flea beetle is about a quarter of an inch long with a yellow thorax and dark green wing covers. It emerges from a winter nap in the ground to lay eggs at the base of plants. The eggs hatch into dingy white grubs that feed on foliage.
Control: Remove weeds around the garden. Flea beetles avoid shaded areas, so planting a ground cover of radishes or lettuce helps. Spray infestations with a garlic-based mix or use rotenone as a last resort.
Prevention: Practice all of the control measures above.

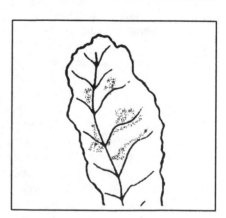

2. Spinach leafminers are one of the most destructive spinach pests. A small fly lays white eggs that hatch small green larvae that burrow into leaves. Leaves blister, growth is distorted and brown blotches develop on stunted plants.

Control: Cut away affected foliage containing leafminer larvae and destroy. Apply insecticidal soap.

Prevention: Cover plants with spun fiber on cheesecloth to exclude egg-laying flies. Cultivate between crops to kill cocoons that live in the soil.

SPINACH	SYMPTOM	PROVABLE CAUSES
Seed & Seedlings	no germination missing	10 or too warm 1, 8
Plants	stunted premature flowering wilting	2, 9 5 3, 9
Leaves	holes, chewed brown patches yellow spots wooly purple fungus curled	1, 8 2 3, 6 3 6
Plants poor drainage	yellowing	1, 2, 3, nitrogen deficiency or

3. Blight or yellows is identified by yellowing and curled leaves on stunted plants. The disease is spread by aphids.

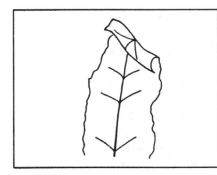

Control: Control aphids by blasting them off leaves with a jet of water; squish between fingers; spray with insecticidal soap or pyrethrum.

Prevention: Encourage or release predators: lacewings, hoverflies and ladybugs. Grow disease-resistant varieties.

4. Downy mildew (chard blue mold) is promoted by damp, cool days, which favor spinach and chard development. Yellow spots with wooly purple growth on leaf undersides soon join together. The soil- and seed-borne fungus grows best when humidity tops 85 percent in a temperature range of 45 to 65° (7-19° C).

Control: Remove and destroy affected plants.

Prevention: Use disease-free seed, plant in well-drained soil, allow "breathing" space between plants, and follow a 3-year crop rotation. Grow disease-resistant varieties.

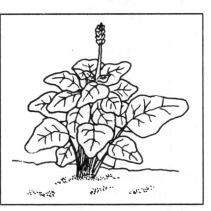

5. Bolting or running to seed is a major problem when the weather warms beyond 80° (27° C). Pick leaves as soon as bolting starts. Once the seed stalks and flowers form, foliage becomes very bitter and tough.

Prevent bolting by growing heat-tolerant types such as Bloomsdale Longstanding, New Zealand spinach or cover the crop with a shade cloth and mulch the ground to lower the temperatures.

Other pests and diseases that attack spinach and chard include:

6. Aphids: page 84
7. Beet webworm: page 39.
8. Slugs & snails: page 84
9. Fusarium rot (wilt): page 100
10. Damping-off: page 77

Squash (*Cucurbita*)

Many of the squash we find in home gardens and seed catalogs were originally cultivated by the American Indians. Today North American seed companies carry on the native breeding stock. Summer squash (*C. pepo* var. *melopepo*) ripens from July through October and has a soft skin. Winter squash (*C. maxima, C. mixta, C. moschata, C. pepo*) is ready in October or November. The hard skin of winter squash make it easy to store without refrigeration for several months. Both summer and winter squash are very easy to grow, but must be protected against the squash vine borer.

If space is limited, grow bush varieties. Sprawling squash vines will take over huge areas of the garden. Trellising small fruiting varieties is easy, but large fruiting varieties need a stout frame to support the weight of the fruit. For more background information about this family, see "Cucurbitaceae Family" page 72.

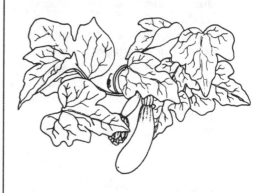

Basic Facts

Germination time: 5-8 days
Germination temperature: Minimum: 60º (16º C), Optimum: 95º (35º C), Maximum: 100º (38º C).
Approximate seeds per ounce: 150-400
Yield per plant: 6-18 fruits on 48" vine
Life expectancy of stored seed: 4 years
Estimated time between sowing and first picking: 12-16 weeks
Intercrop: None, apply mulch.
Effort to cultivate: Easy
Seed saving: Squash cross-pollinate with one another and must be cultivated a mile apart if growing for seed. Squash will not cross with cucumbers or melons, but they will cross with zucchini and gourds. Pollinate female flower by brushing it with male pollen, then cover the female flower with a sack that has air holes. Remove the sack after two weeks.

Climate

Annual in all zones. Needs full sun and moderate temperatures. Cold temperatures slow vine growth, stop flowering and fruit set.

Soil Preparation

Prepare soil in early spring or the previous fall. Incorporate plenty of compost and manure. Add dolomite lime to neutralize the pH (6.0-7.0) and keep squash from "bubbling" and turning pithy on one end. Add a complete organic fertilizer. Soil should hold moisture, but drain well.

A compost pile is also an excellent planting location. Simply mound up fresh, cooking compost into a 3-foot tall pile. Cover the top of the compost pile with 2-3 inches of soil. Plant seed or seedlings in the soil. By the time the roots reach the compost, it will have cooled enough to keep from burning.

Planting

Do not plant where cucumbers, melons or squash grew the previous two years.
Start summer squash indoors. Plant seeds 1/2-inch deep in small containers of fine potting soil. Transplant to mounds or rows after all danger of frost is past.
Space vining squash 3-4 feet apart in rows set 6-12 feet apart. Space mounds of bush varieties 2-4 feet apart.
The soil temperature must be at least 60º (16º C) for gemination and strong growth.
In mounds: Sow four to six seeds 1 1/2 inches deep in mounds or "hills". Drench the mound with water and do not water again until after sprouting, unless absolutely necessary.
Winter squash is direct seeded into the beds. Sow seeds 1 1/2 inches deep, 1 to 2 inches apart. Thin to 6 inches apart when seedlings are 4-6 inches tall.
Build a trellis for vines to climb. This saves precious garden space and keeps the fruit off the ground, which discourages insects and rot. The fruit develops straight and makes them easier to spot when picking. Trellised fruit is protected from sunburn, which causes bitterness.
Replant seeds if the first sowing does not germinate rapidly, or is slowed by spring rains.
Plant 2-4 plants per person.

Crop Care

Keep seedlings moist to avoid wilting, but do not overwater, which promotes damping-off.

Mulch with dark compost or black plastic to heat soil after plants are 6 inches tall, and the soil is well warmed. Continue adding mulch as needed.

Keep soil evenly moist. However deep-watering encourages a long taproot. The crop consumes more water when fruit sets, and regular surface watering is necessary. Fruit is over mostly water and must have an adequate amount to form large fruit.

Water stress will cause deformed fruits, and a smaller crop. Squash are heavy feeders and need lots of water to grow large fruits.

Side-dress with complete low-nitrogen soluble fertilizer as soon as flowers set, and twice a month thereafter until the end of season.

Removing side or lateral shoots will send all the nutrients to remaining fruit, which makes them larger, and mature them faster.

Pinch off the end of vines about 2 weeks before the first frost so all of the fruit that has set will mature.

Harvesting

For maximum production, harvest squash as soon as they become ripe. When left too long on the vine, they become sour and slow other fruit from ripening.

Pick summer squash the day before the blossom opens on the fruit for the most succulent flavor. Winter squash can be harvested as soon as they size up. Keep vines picked so they continue to bear.

Harvest winter squash once they have sized up at the end of the growing season. Continue picking until after the first frost.

Cut the end off each vine about a month before the first frost. Trimming the ends will force all of the energy into maturing the fruit on the vine.

In the Kitchen

Squash is packed with vitamin A. Yellow-skinned squash are the most nutritious. The more yellow the skin, the higher the beta carotene content.

Fresh: Stuff summer squash blossoms and saute fruit in garlic olive oil with blossom attached.

Steam young summer squash and pumpkins for best flavor. Cook when fruit is no larger than a small apple or banana.

Winter squash is easy to bake or add to casseroles. Simply split squash down the middle, remove the seeds, fill the seed cavity with raw sugar, cover with aluminum foil and bake fro 30-45 minutes.

Drying: pumpkin seeds, taste great when dried in the sun or the oven and lightly salted.

Storage: Clean winter squash with ammonia water to abate fungus, dry and store in a cool, dry location. Check fruit periodically for soft spots or rot. Winter squash will last up to 6 months when properly stored.

Varieties

Summer Varieties

SCALLOP OR PATTY PAN TYPES (50-60 days) (custard marrow) including green PETER PAN, SCALLOPINI, and the yellow AAS Winner SUNBURST, are some of the best summer squash on the market. The fruit is bulbed on the stem end and flat with scalloped edges on the bottom. Very productive plants yield sweet, succulent squash. Pick fruit when the flower blooms. Available (Bu, Jo, Pa, St, Te).

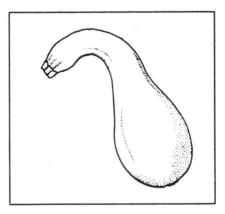

YELLOW CROOKNECK (50-60 days) including BUTTER SWAN, PIC-N-PAC, and SUNDANCE are very high in beta carotene. The flesh of this crookneck is sweet, similar to a zucchini. Pick when very young and succulent for the best flavor. Available (Bg, Bu, Cg, Gc, Gs, Jo, Pa, So, St, Te)

ZUCCHINI (50-60 days) including ARISTOCAT, BLACK BEAUTY, BUTTERBLOSSOM, COCOZELLE, DARK GREEN, GOLD RUSH, GREY and ROUND, are normally various shades of green, but some are yellow or striped. Most varieties produce prolifically on sprawling viney bushes. Pick fruit when no longer than 6 inches for the best flavor. Readily available.

Winter Varieties

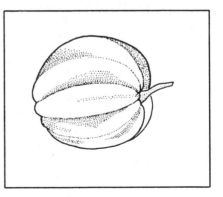

ACORN (*C. pepo*) (90 days) yield 2-pound fruit with ribbed skin. The delicious sweet flesh is great baked. This type tastes best after being stored 3-4 months. EBONY ACORN is one of the best tasting acorn varieties. Available (Bg, Gc, Gs, Jo, Me).

BUTTERNUT (*C. moschata*) (105 days) varieties have the highest beta carotene content. Plenty of sweet flesh and a small seed cavity make this squash a real treat. This late-flowering vine matures 4-5 pound squash soon after they set. It is an excellent winter keeper. Readily available

HUBBARD TYPES (*C. maxima*) (100 days) has a tough, hard, bumpy skin that makes it an excellent storage type. One or two mature fruit that weigh 10-25 pounds are produced by each plant. The flesh is tasty yellow and medium dry. Available (Bu, Gc, Gs, Jo, Le, St, Te).

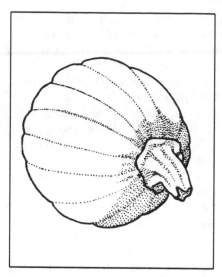

PUMPKINS fall into two major categories - small and large. Small pumpkins grow to 5-7 pounds and mature in 100-110 days. NEW ENGLAND PIE is the standard small pumpkin. Large pumpkins, including ATLANTIC GIANT, BIG MAX and CONNECTICUT FIELD grow to 15-40 pounds and are used

for Halloween Jack O' Lanterns. The large varieties do not make as good of pie filling as do smaller varieties. Available (Bu, Jo, So).

SPAGHETTI (*C. pepo*) (90 days) has pale yellow skin and yellow spaghetti-like flesh. Fruits that weigh 3-5 pounds are packed with delightful flesh. Bake in the oven and top with butter, red or sweet sauce. Available (Bu, Gs, Jo, Ma, So, Te).

Problems

Squash are easy to grow but do suffer from a few frequent pest attacks. Cucumber beetles, squash vine borers and powdery mildew present the most formidable obstacles to overcome for most gardeners. Solutions to problems associated with squash can be found on pages 76 "Cucumber Problems".

Tomato (*Lycopersicon lycopersicum*)

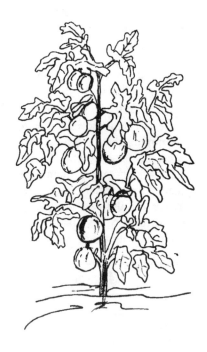

A vegetable garden, whether far to the north or deep in the south, must grow tomatoes to be complete. A special satisfaction comes from picking that first vine-ripened fruit from the vine, slicing it open and enjoying the zesty-sweet taste and refined fleshy texture. Supermarket tomatoes are picked green before developing much flavor; the tough skin that allows it to be handled as a projectile encloses the bland mealy flesh.

Home-grown tomatoes are allowed to ripen on the vine, developing sweet, rich pulp and a tender skin. Variety selection is very important to achieve the best flavor and to get a tomato to produce well in your climate. Of course you can choose from numerous varieties, such as yellow pear, bicolored or beefsteak types, that are impossible to find in the grocery store. Pasta tomatoes are also becoming very popular in home gardens.

As a member of the solanum family (page 78) tomatoes need warm weather to grow and produce fruit; tomato blossoms fall off below 50° (10° C). The variety OREGON SPRING is an absolute cool-season standout. It can be set out on the last average frost date with no damage and produce large flavorful beefsteak fruit before cherry tomatoes are ripe!

Basic Facts

Germination time: 6- 14 days
Germination temperature: Minimum: 50° (10° C), Optimum: 85° (29° C), Maximum: 95° (35° C).
Approximate seeds per ounce: 8,400
Yield per plant: 5-50 pounds
Life expectancy of stored seed: 3-4 years
Estimated time between sowing and first picking: 11-16 weeks
Intercrop: Lettuce, flowers, garlic
Effort to cultivate: Easy; may require a trellis and some pruning.
Seed saving: Let open-pollinated tomatoes self-pollinate. Pick fruit when fully ripe. Set fruit in a jar for 3-5 days to ferment; stir daily. Keep seeds that sink to the bottom of the jar. Dry seeds on a paper towel. Store them in a cool, dry dark location until needed.

Climate

Annual in all zones. Can be grown as a perennial in climates that do not freeze or in a greenhouse. Tomatoes require a temperature range of 50-90° (10-33° C) in order to set flowers and form fruit. Stops flowering and fruiting outside this range.
Plant in a cool location in hot climates and full sun in cool climates. In short-season cold climates, grow in containers that can be moved indoors on cold nights.

Soil Preparation

Heavy feeders, tomatoes need deep, rich, fertile soil. Cultivate the soil to a depth of a foot or more. Prepare the soil the previous fall or up to a month before planting.
Incorporate plenty of compost and manure into the soil. Add dolomite lime, which supplies both calcium and magnesium, two much-used nutrients. Tomatoes use large quantities of calcium when they set fruit.

Planting

Seeds can be started indoors from 6 to 8 weeks before setting the seedlings outdoors. Sow seed in flats or small containers, keep warm and moist until they sprout.
Sow outdoor seed directly into beds. Dig a trench or individual planting holes 1/4-inch deep. Sow 1-2 seeds per inch and cover with very fine soil, compost or peat moss. Keep evenly moist until seedlings sprout.
Do not transplant seedlings without protection early in the year if temperatures are apt to dip below 40° (5° C).
Protect tender seedlings with hot caps, a plastic tunnel or, best of all, Wall-O-Water. Some gardeners use a white 5-gallon plastic bucket with the bottom removed. The lid is secured on the bucket at night and removed in the morning.
Transplant seedlings several inches deeper than they were growing in their seedling container so new roots will sprout along the stem. Pinch off the cotyledon and one or two sets of leaves before transplanting the seedlings deep in the hole.

Another method is to remove all but the last few sets of the leaves from the seedlings and transplant them laying the stem in a shallow 2-inch-deep trench. Just the top few sets of leaves are left on the plants to grow upward. This practice establishes a strong root system.

Crop Care

Most tomato baskets available at garden centers are much too small and restrict growth. The most productive option to baskets is a stake(s) that vines are secured to with a twist-tie or twine.

Pruning to just one or two vines is a very productive cultivation technique used by many gardeners. This allows the sun to shine on fruit and speed ripening. Pruning also permits air to circulate through the bush, helping to prevent fungus and insect infestations.
Water regularly. Tomatoes use much water, especially when developing fruit. If they suffer a drought followed by heavy watering, the fruit will resemble a boxing glove. Encourage deep roots with penetrating watering to make plants more drought tolerant.
Do not water with an overhead sprinkler. When leaves get wet, they suffer temperature stress, opening the door for fungus formation. Water in the mornings either by hand or use a soaker hose that wets only the soil.
Fertilize every 2-4 weeks after plants are about 2-feet tall. Supplemental fertilization should include a complete mix that includes calcium if

dolomite was not added when planting. Be careful about adding too much nitrogen-rich fertilizer after flowers form. Nitrogen stimulates leafy growth at the expense of fruit production.

Thin fruit if it sets too heavily on the vine. After you get an idea of how much the plant can produce, pick off the smaller or remove a few fruit from clusters if they are developing slowly.

Apply mulch after the soil warms. Reapply mulch several times during the growing season as needed. Mulch really holds water well, maintains cool soil and keeps water from splashing up on foliage and fruit.

Harvesting

Use a pruner or a sharp knife to remove fruit from vines. If harvesting by hand, simply twist the fruit from the vine, taking care to leave the vine intact.

Keep ripe fruit picked, daily if necessary, to encourage more fruit to ripen. The lowest clusters of tomatoes will ripen first, progressing up the vine.

Fruit ripens best when exposed to sunlight. However, this exposure must be gradual to prevent the fruit from suffering sunburn. Trimming the foliage away and removing leaves that shade fruit will speed ripening.

Cut the growing tip from each branch about a month before the first expected freeze and remove small fruit that is not likely to ripen.

Once cold weather slows growth to a standstill, the ripening green tomatoes can be harvested. If they are starting to turn red, the fruit will ripen if set in a cool, dry location.

Green tomatoes can still be harvested both early or late in the year. They are very tasty when fried.

In the Kitchen

Fresh: Yellow tomatoes have a lower acid content and are preferred by some people. Beefsteak varieties are exceptionally tasty fresh from the vine. The cherry tomatoes make a nice addition to any salad or simply when eaten in the garden. Large slicers are sweet, flavorful and juicy. Stuffed, made into numerous salads or when eaten vine-ripe from the garden, tomatoes are one of the all-time garden favorites in the world.

Fresh tomato sauce is outstanding! Try making sauce with such varieties as Polish Paste or Roma. Polish Paste yields large, one-pound fruit that are incredibly meaty, perfect for sauce.

Green tomatoes taste great when properly prepared. Pick all the green tomatoes before the last freeze. Fruit showing and red/orange color will ripen on the windowsill. Green fruit should be cooked within a few weeks of harvest. Check your favorite cookbook for recipes.

Storage: Tomatoes can be stored in the refrigerator for up to a week in a plastic bag. However, the fresher they are, the better they taste.

Drying is a good option to keep tomatoes throughout the winter. To dry, slice across axis into thin 1/4-inch rounds and place on a screen in the sun, or in a food drier. Let them

dry until they become leathery. Dried fruit rehydrates readily by adding water. Small tomatoes can be dried whole, just like larger slices.

Canning tomatoes is an excellent way to preserve a large tomato crop. Always grow tomatoes that are very meaty or fleshy when using for canning. Blanch to remove skin before packing. Remember to pack as many tomatoes as possible in canning containers so they fill out the jar completely.

Freezing: To freeze tomatoes, simply blanch for 30 seconds, remove the skin, then pop them into a ziplock plastic bag and place them in the freezer.

Varieties

There are so many different varieties of tomatoes available today, the choices seem infinite! A few seed catalogs specialize in tomatoes, such as the Tomato Grower's Supply, P.O. Box 2237, Fort Myers, Florida, 33902. To add a little structure to the choices, let's categorize tomatoes into two groups: determinate and indeterminate.

A determinate tomato produces flower buds on the end of branches and tends to bear heavily for about a month, then stop. But some varieties, such as Oregon Spring, bear fruit over a long season, only stopping when cold or hot weather sets in. The compact bushes that are common to determinate tomatoes seldom need staking and are an excellent choice for low-maintenance gardens.

Indeterminate tomatoes yield flowers from lateral branches; the tips continue to vine upward. These types produce over a long season, requiring staking, training and in many cases pruning for the best yields.

Cherry Varieties

CHERIO (55-60 days) is very early, producing large cherrylike fruit that is sweet and flavorful. Compact growth on determinate plants growth on determinate plants makes Cherio an excellent container plant. It yields heavily for about 30 days. Available (Ju, Te).

SWEET 100 (70 days) prolifically produces remarkably sweet cherry-sized red fruit. Long clusters of tomatoes cascade from numerous branches. This indeterminate requires staking and quite a bit of pruning to keep the unwieldy growth under control. **SWEET MILLION**, an improved version of the Sweet 100, appears to yield about the same. Available (Bu, Cg, Ha, Ju, Le, Ma, Pa, St, Th).

SWEETIE (65-70 days) ripens before the open pollinated Sweet 100. The small, round, red cherry tomatoes are packed with sweetness. The large indeterminate vines bear large, prolific clusters of fruit. Available (Fa, Fi, Ni, Te).

TINY TIM (55 days) grows to a compact 15 inches producing cherry tomatoes. This determinate plant is an excellent choice for patio containers. Available (Bu, Ju, Pi, So, St).

Early Varieties

EARLY CASCADE (55 days) yields for a long season on indeterminate vines. Plentiful clusters of medium-sized, bright red fruit are just right for snacks, salads, canning or sauce. Available (Ni, Te, Tg).

EARLY GIRL TYPES (52 days) yields bountiful, extra early flavorful fruit. The indeterminate vines produce until the first frost. Available (Te, Tg).

OREGON SPRING (75-80 days) is one of the earliest, most cold-hardy, early and best producing tomato for short seasons and wet climates. It is also an excellent choice for winter gardens in warm southern climates. Set out seedlings when the last frost has just past. Set out a month earlier if using a Wall-O-Water. Available (Gc, Jo, Ni, Te).

SIBERIA (50 days) More Siberian types will be coming available with the opening of Eastern Europe. Available (So, Tg).

Mid Season Varieties

BURPEE'S BIG BOY (78 days) The large, brilliant red fruit regularly weigh in at a pound. This delicious tomato has been an American favorite since 1949. Available (Bu, Da, Fa, Fi, Ju, Pa, Sha, St).

BURPEE'S BIG GIRL (75-80 days) develops large, smooth, crack-resistant fruit. This prolific, heavy-bearing plant produces hefty fruit over a long season. In fact many fruit surpass one pound in weight. Resistant to verticillium and fusarium wilts. Available (Bu, Tg).

CELEBRITY (70 days) is an AAS Winner. This exceedingly flavorful fruit grows on strong determinate vines that bare for over a month. Excellent disease resistance and very productive most climates. Available Readily available.

QUICK PICK (68 days) is an indeterminate hybrid of outstanding quality. The prolific medium-sized fruit offer outstanding flavor and texture. The heavy harvest continues until first frost. Available (Tg).

Late Varieties

BEEFSTEAK TYPES such as **ABRAHAM LINCOLN**, **BEEFMASTER**, **BRANDYWINE**, **DINNER PLATE**, **HEAVYWEIGHT** and **WATERMELON** yield late in the summer, but the wait is repaid a thousand times in flavor. Beefsteak varieties are very difficult to handle mechanically and seldom wind up in grocery stores. They are some of the best eating varieties available. The fruits are large, meaty and with few seeds. Readily available.

OXHEART (79 days) yields huge heirloom heart-shaped pink fruits. The firm, meaty fleshed tomatoes grow on leafy indeterminate vines that protect fruit from sunscald. Available (Fa, Fi, Me, Ni, So).

Pasta Varieties

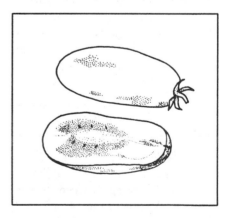

HEINZ 1439 and **HEINZ 2653** mature in 75 days from transplanting into meaty fruits that retain their size well and are perfect for canning. Available (Bu, Fi, Me, Pa, St).

SAN MARZANO (75 days) is an excellent canning, paste or sauce tomato. Large indeterminate vines produce meaty, rectangular, pear-shaped fruit until first frost. Available (She, Tg)

POLISH PASTE (110 days) is one of the best sauce tomatoes available. The large, red, oblong fruits grow to a pound or more, developing very weighty flesh. Each indeterminate plant yields a whopping 40-50 pounds of tomatoes! Requires an early start in cool climates. Available (Te).

ROMA types mature in 75-80 days into a rich red pear-shaped fruits. One of the most popular types is Roma VF. They are very meaty and have few seeds. This determinate type yields over a 4-week period. Available, Bu, Fa, Fi, Ha, Ma, Me, Ni, Pa, St, Tg).

Novelty Varieties

TOMATO TREE (*Cyphomandra betacea*) is often seen advertised in magazines as the Tomato Tree. It is actually a member of a different species entirely. The fruit this perennial plant produces are red and taste somewhat like tomatoes. Available (Hu, Th).

YELLOW LOW-ACID TYPES including **GOLDEN SUNRISE, GOLDEN MANDARIN CROSS, ORANGE QUEEN, GOLDEN QUEEN, GOLDEN BOY** and **YELLOW STUFFER** all contain less acid than red tomatoes. Their flavor is sweet and mild. These are the varieties to choose if your body has a difficult time digesting acidic fruit. Available (Bu, Fi, Jo, Ju, Ni, Tg)

YELLOW PEAR (75 days) yields petite pear-shaped yellow fruit. The clusters of fruit are heavy on fast growing plants that require trellising. The fruit are sweet and delicious straight from the vine. Available (Bu, Ha, Hi, Ma, Ni).

MR. STRIPEY (TIGRELLA) (56 days) yields huge crops of red fruits with yellow-orange stripes. The medium-sized colorful fruits have a rich, tart flavor that enhances salads. Available (Tg).

Problems

When given ample water, fertile, well-drained soil with adequate tilth and good air circulation, tomatoes have few problems. However, heavy rains, hot or cold weather, insect infestations, fungus and tobacco mosaic virus can take a heavy toll on this crop.

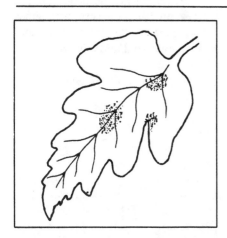

1. Aphids present a small problem to most tomatoes, but can spread several diseases, including tobacco mosaic virus. The green, red, gray or yellow insects attack succulent growing tips, sucking out life-giving juices.

TOMATOES	SYMPTOM	PROVABLE CAUSES
Seed & Seedlings	missing	2, 38
	wilting, dead	12
	yellow, contorted	19
Leaves	yellowing	1, 32, 33, 34, 40
	curling	1, 20, 24, 26, 34
	tiny holes	3
	stippling, small spots	5
	chewed, holes	8, 9
	brown, crispy	10, 22, 25
	greasy spots	10, 13, 17, 22, 27
	dropping	22
	target-like spots	20
Fruit	eaten	8, 9, 37, 39
	dark, recessed spots	11
	greasy spots	13, 17
	end rot	16, 30
	dropping	15, 25, 36
	brown spots	10, 22, 25
	papery spots on skin	28
	deformed	35
	green shoulder	29
Flowers	dropping	15
Plants	wilting	6, 14, 19, 42, 43
	stunted	6, 12, 19, 23, 26, 34, 42, 43
	sudden death	14, 19

Control: Aphids spread the disease and controlling this vector can stop the disease's spread. Remove affected plants and destroy.

Prevention: Avoid planting peppers near alfalfa, clover, cucumbers, tobacco or tomatoes. Spray seedlings a day before transplanting with fresh milk. People that use tobacco should wash their hands before entering the garden. Plant resistant varieties.

2. Cutworms can become a major tomato pest. They are gray to black in color and may be up to 1 1/2 inches in length. They do the most damage in the spring, cutting seedlings off at the soil line. They feed on roots, foliage and fruit.

Control: Sprinkle cornmeal, diatomaceous earth or *Bacillus thuringiensis* around the base of plants. Promptly search under the soil surface around the dead plant for the lingering pest and destroy.

Prevention: Encircle plants with a stiff 3-inch-wide barrier of cardboard or plastic anchored an inch deep in the soil. Birds, firefly larvae, braconid wasps, Nc nematodes, tachinid flies, moles and toads are predators.

3. Flea beetles do the most damage to young plants, riddling the leaves with tiny holes. The tiny 1/16-inch-long beetles bounds like a flea when disturbed.

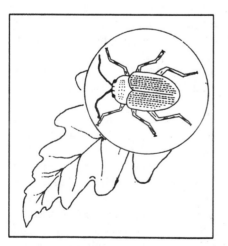

Control: Apply Nc nematodes, spray with a garlic or hot pepper mix, ryana, sabadilla or as a last resort use rotenone.

Prevention: Cultivate the soil frequently to destroy eggs and clear weeds that provide a source of food. Set out small containers full of a half and half mix of lime and wood ash around plants. Or sprinkle small amounts of wood ash around plants several times a week.

4. Spider mites are minute spiders that reside on leaf undersides and suck out life-giving plant fluids. Numerous small light colored spots (stippling) can be seen on the tops of leaves. Tiny spider webs stretch between leaves and branches in advanced stages. Spider mites are occasionally a problem outdoors and quite common in greenhouses, cold frames and indoors.

Control: Blast leaf undersides with a jet of cold water. Release predatory mites. Apply insecticidal soap, pyrethrum or garlic spray on infestations.

Prevention: Allow adequate air circulation.

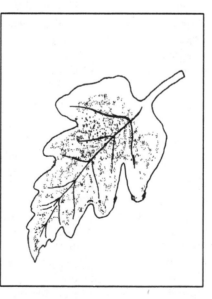

5. Whiteflies, also called beet leafhoppers, create problems with greenhouse, indoor seedlings and purchased plants. Inspect nursery plants closely before purchasing. The pests may persevere outdoors if weather is not too harsh. The tiny, white, mothlike adult flitters from foliage when disturbed. This pest also carries curly top (see page 100 and number 19 below).

Control: Apply insecticidal soap or use yellow sticky traps. Remove and "hot" compost badly affected foliage.

Prevention: Plant resistant varieties. Introduce lacewing larvae or the paracitic wasp *encarsia formosa* that pray on nymphs. Fall cleanup.

6. Stalk borer adults are purple to white worms and grow to a slender 1 1/4 inches long. Young are white with stripes and shorter. The pests burrow into stalks causing stunting, wilting and death.

Control: Look for the entry hole that is surrounded with sawdust. Split the stem open to extract the pest. Bind the stem back together with expandable plastic ties and water heavily for a couple of weeks.

Prevention: Use *Bacillus thuringiensis* and apply rotenone as a last resort.

7. Stink bugs pierce tomato skins to feed on the flesh. The wound causes a white bulge beneath the skin, known as cloudy skin. The flat, 1/2-inch-long bug is green to brown in color and stinks when handled or crushed.

Control: Apply insecticidal soap

Prevention: Remove weedy patches around the garden where they live. Apply a garlic spray to discourage stink bug feeding.

8. Tobacco hornworms are large, showy, bright green caterpillars with white diagonal stripes, red dots and a red "horn" for a tail similar to the tomato hornworm described below. The caterpillar devours foliage and fruit.

Control: Hand-picking the easy-to-spot pests is easiest in small gardens. An application of *Bacillus thuringiensis* will wipe out infestations.

Prevention: Encourage natural predators Trichogramma wasps, *Hyposoter exiguae* wasps and *Polistes exclamans* wasps.

9. Tomato hornworms are one of the most devastating pests east of the Rocky Mountains. The 3-4-inch-long green worm has white diagonal stripes on each side and a black "horn" at the tip of the tail. The adult moth, called the hawk, hummingbird or sphinx moth, has gray wings that spread 4-5 inches. It flies at twilight during early to midsummer, feeding on flower nectar.
Control: Hand-picking is easy and preferable in small gardens. Apply *Bacillus thuringiensis* if an infestation breaks out.
Prevention: Crush single greenish eggs that are laid on leaf undersides. Cultivate soil in the winter to destroy pupae.

10. Tomato russet mites are so small they are almost impossible to spot. The minute mites attack lower leaves first, giving them a greasy appearance. Advanced symptoms include brown, crispy leaves. Arid, hot weather stimulates their life cycle.
Control: Remove affected foliage and clean the rest of the leaves with a jet of water. Use a sulfur-based spray as a last resort.
Prevention: The predatory mites *Phytoseiulus persimilis* and *Metaseiulus occidentalis* are available commercially to combat these mites.

11. Anthracnose appears on ripening fruit as dark, round, recessed spots of varying diameter. The fungus appears so late on the fruit that it is usually not seen until infection is rampant. Black dots within the spots contain fungus spores. The entire fruit soon rots as the disease spreads. The fungus is spread by water and promoted by heavy rains during hot weather.
Control: Remove and destroy affected plants.
Prevention: Avoid working in a wet garden and keep water off leaves. Practice a 3-year or longer crop rotation. Destroy affected foliage and plant in well-drained soil.

12. Bacterial canker is a seed-borne disease that causes stunted growth or wilts and kills seedlings. The margins of leaves on older plants dry, causing them to curl upward. A wide temperature variation between day and night can also cause leaves to curl, but presents no problem. Also see "Leaf roll" below. Often this disease attacks only one side of a plant, but later spreads throughout the foliage. Open cankers (sores) form on the stem in advanced stages. The fruit shows small round white swells that later burst and darken. A whitish halo forms around the swell. Some fruits may begin to rot internally with no signs of damage outside.
Control: Remove and destroy infected plants.

Prevention: Purchase certified disease-free seed. Soak seed suspected of having bacterial canker in 120° (48° C) water for 30 minutes. Do not let the water get hotter than 122° (49° C) or seed will be damaged. Rotate tomatoes on at least a 3-year cycle.

13. Bacterial spot causes dark, slick-looking spots on leaves. Blossoms may drop and greasy-looking spots could form on fruit. The centers of the spots later become sunken. Moist, rainy weather promotes this disease.
Control: Remove and destroy affected foliage.
Prevention: Sow only certified disease-free seed. Do not plant in cool damp areas of the garden or where the disease has occurred before. Water the soil rather than sprinkling the foliage.

14. Bacterial wilt causes rapid wilting and death of an entire plant. The foliage does not yellow or discolor when this disease, that is worst in the South, strikes. To check for the disease, cut the stem in two near the base of the plant. The internal pith is dark, slimy and decaying.
Control: Remove and destroy infected plants at once to stop the disease from spreading.
Prevention: This soil-borne disease is most common in moist soils when temperatures climb above 75° (24° C). Avoid planting eggplants, peppers, potatoes and tomatoes in these areas. Practice a 3-year crop rotation with nontomato family crops.

15. Blossom drop has several causes including drought, temperature stress (below 50° (10° C) or above 95° (35° C)) nutrient imbalance or various diseases. A sudden shift in temperature or water regimen will cause blossoms to drop. Excessive nitrogen as well as a lack of calcium, phosphorus and potassium may cause fewer blossoms to set or to drop. Diseases such as fusarium or verticillium wilts compound blossom drop.

Control/Prevent blossom drop by keeping the crop evenly moist, especially during fruit-set and warm weather. Shade cloth may be necessary when temperatures rise beyond 95º (35º C). Growing heat- or cold-tolerant varieties that have smaller fruit will circumvent much of the problem. Fertilizing with a complete mix containing ample calcium, phosphorus, and potassium will also help prevent the problem.

16. Blossom-end rot causes a sunken discoloring and rotting at the bottom of fruit. The rot is prone to appear after a drought preceded by good growing conditions when the fruit is forming. The rot also occurs after long periods of wet weather that drowns roots and slows moisture uptake.

Control the spread of blossom-end rot by removing the affected fruit.

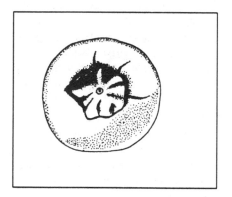

Prevention: Always maintain an even water regimen and do not sprinkle irrigate. Mulch around the perimeter of each plant to conserve water and keep the soil light and fluffy. Cultivate around the plants if necessary, but do not penetrate the soil more than an inch. Add dolomite lime to the soil before planting to ensure an ample supply of calcium and do not apply large amounts of nitrogen after blossoms have set.

17. Botrytis (gray mold) fruit rot becomes a problem during cool, humid weather. Small greasy spots form on fruit that enlarge to cover the fruit, causing it to drop. The characteristic fuzzy gray mold soon covers the spots. Gray mold can also attack foliage and stems.

Control: Remove and destroy affected fruit.

Prevention: If possible, raise the temperature by erecting a plastic cold frame greenhouse over the plants.

18. Split skins are caused by too much moisture during hot weather. The plentiful moisture and high temperatures cause rapid fruit growth, but the skin grows at a slower rate.

Control: Apply water at an even rate to promote slow, controlled growth. Pick the fruit at first sign of cracking.

Prevention: Plant crack-resistant varieties. Apply water at an even rate. Mulch to retain moisture evenly.

19. Curly top, also called western yellow blight, is spread by the beet leafhopper (whitefly). The disease is worst near the Rocky Mountains where a multitude of leafhoppers breed in the sagebrush. The foliage of seedlings, which are the most susceptible, contort, twist and yellow. Plants die as the disease progresses. Most common on plants grown next to (sugar) beets and Russian thistle.

Control: Rid the garden of the beet leafhopper by spraying insecticidal soap. Introduce lacewing larvae. Remove weeds. Fall cleanup.

Prevention: Plant resistant varieties. Introduce lacewing larvae that feed on beet leafhopper nymphs. Remove weeds. Fall cleanup.

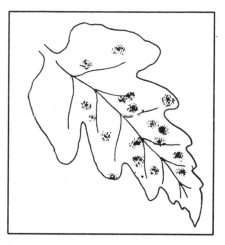

20. Early blight attacks the older bottom leaves first, causing targetlike rings. As the spots run together and expand, leaves brown and die. Cool, humid weather promotes this disease to spread up the plant. When dead foliage suddenly exposes fruit to sunlight, sunscald becomes a problem.

Control: Remove and destroy infected foliage.

Prevention: Fall cleanup will keep the disease from overwintering in plant residues. Hot compost the diseased plants. Practice a 3-year rotation with nontomato family (see "Solanum Family", page 78) crops.

21. Fusarium wilt or yellows is common among tomatoes and sometimes becomes a problem. Leaves begin to yellow and lower leaves wilt. To check for fusarium wilt, slice open a cross section of the stem. The pulpy inside of the stem of infected plants is brown rather than white. Once this disease is established in soil, it may live for years.

Control: Remove and destroy infected plants.

Prevention: Grow on soil that is known to be disease-free. Practice a 3- or 4-year crop rotation, and purchase certified seed.

22. Late blight fungus can cause severe defoliation and fruit rot. First greasy, blotches form on lower leaves. During wet weather, the spots grow rapidly and may have a

powdery, white-frosted appearance. The spots on fruit are dark and rough and can be affected during any stage of development. This disease is spread by diseased tomato-family plants, but can be carried by the wind. Late blight is a problem in the Pacific Northwest and east of the Mississippi.
Control: Spray with copper/sulfur fungicide every 7-10 days. Remove and destroy affected plants.
Prevention: Clean up all debris before the growing season.

23. Leaf mold is normally only a problem when tomatoes are grown under cover. Patches on the lower surfaces of leaves turn a velvety brown to purple color and later die back, stunting development. The disease is spread by contact, air and water.
Control: Keep the relative humidity below 90 percent in plastic tunnels and greenhouses by opening them up to air circulation.
Prevention: Allow good air circulation to maintain low humidity, and plant resistant varieties.

24. Leaf roll can be caused by a wide day and night temperature variation, overwatering, poor drainage, deep cultivation and exceedingly severe pruning. The condition is not especially damaging, but it can lessen yield if too many leaves are removed.
Control/Prevention: Refrain from deep cultivation, which destroys feeder roots, heavy pruning, and grow in well-drained soil.

25. Tobacco mosaic virus disease is difficult to detect. Often infected plants look healthy. Closely inspect young plants for deformed leaves and all plants for the characteristic mosaic pattern of brownish spots on both leaves and fruit. Leaves may also elongate, becoming stringy and sometimes pointed. Infected plants suffer severe wilt during bright days that follow cool temperatures. Mosaic viruses, including cucumber mosaic, are spread by aphids, cucumber beetles and unsanitary garden practices.
Control mosaic viruses by removing and thoroughly hot composting infected plants. Remove plants on both sides of the infected plant, even if they do not show symptoms.
Prevention: Tobacco users should wash their hands thoroughly before entering the garden. After touching an infected plant, be sure to wash your hands before touching a healthy plant. Keep aphid and cucumber beetle populations in check. Periodically spray plants with fresh milk. Practice a 3- to 4-year crop rotation.

26. Psyllid yellows is caused by psyllids, minute milky-colored soil-dwelling creatures that feed on roots. They release a toxic substance that infects plants. Older leaves thicken and roll upward; yellow and purplish veins and fringes may materialize on spindly plants. Little or poor quality fruit develops.
Control: None, remove and destroy plants.
Prevention: Remove weeds, plant garlic close to tomatoes and apply a garlic spray around the base of plants.

27. Septoria blight or leaf spot can be a serious problem east of the Mississippi. Rainy weather and plant crowding promote this disease. Small greasy spots first appear on older leaves. The round spots have a gray core with a dark perimeter. The center of the 1/8th-inch spot darkens as fungal spores develop. Leaves drop as

the disease progresses up the plant, exposing fruit to sunscald.
Control: Remove infected foliage or plants as soon as the disease is diagnosed.
Prevention: Hot compost or bury plant residues at least 8 inches deep. Control weeds, fall cultivation and cleanup. Do not work in the garden when foliage is wet.

28. Sunscald becomes a problem when fruit is suddenly exposed to bright sunlight. The skin of the fruit turns papery and brown in affected areas. Any disease or pruning that suddenly removes leaves and exposes tender fruit promotes sunscald.
Control: None. Remove affected plants and trim off damaged areas before eating.
Prevent sudden exposure of tender fruit to bright sunlight. Refrain from excessive pruning; keep defoliating diseases and insects in check.

29. Green shoulder is caused by too much sunlight striking fruit over extended periods or a lack of potassium (potash).

Control: None. Trim off hard green area before eating.

Prevention: Make sure fruit has enough shade and potash. Feed flowering plants with a low-nitrogen, high-phosphorus and potash fertilizer.

30. Calcium deficiency is manifested by susceptibility to blossom-end rot, abnormally small fruit, slow growth and thickened woody stems. Tomatoes are heavy users of calcium, and deficiencies are relatively uncommon.

Control: Apply hydrated lime diluted in water once weekly until symptoms disappear.

Prevention: Apply fine dolomite lime before planting.

31. Magnesium deficiency is noted by yellowing of lower leaves that gradually moves upward.

Control: Apply Epsom salts diluted in water twice a week until the leaves turn green.

Prevention: Add fine dolomite lime before planting.

32. Nitrogen imbalance: A *deficiency* slows growth and turns leaves a pale green that progresses downward from the top of the plant. Small leaves may have purple veining, and flower buds might drop suddenly.

Excessive nitrogen is noted by extra-broad, soft deep green leaves and little or no flower set.

Control: *Deficiency*: Apply a soluble fertilizer rich in nitrogen, such as fish emulsion or blood meal. Apply fertilizer 1/4 strength as a foliar spray for rapid results.

Excess: Leach (flush) soluble nitrogen by flooding the root zone with water and apply less nitrogen when fertilizing.

33. Phosphorus deficiency causes small leaves, slow growth and occasionally a purple tent on foliage, and fruit-set may be retarded.

Control: Apply a high phosphorus mix that is readily available, such as steamed bone meal.

Prevention: Add an all-purpose fertilizer containing phosphorus when planting.

34. Trace element deficiencies:

Boron: Tip growth curls, yellows and dies; excessively bushy growth.

  Control: Dilute a teaspoon of borax in a gallon of water and apply every other week until the deficiency disappears. *Do not apply a total of over 4 teaspoons.*

Copper deficiency causes checked stem growth and slow overall plant development. Leaves with a bluish hue curl upward and few flowers form.

  Control: Apply a manure tea or liquid seaweed that contains copper.

Iron is deficient when leaves yellow and veins stay green.

  Control: Lower the pH if it is above 6.5 and apply liquid seaweed, which contains iron.

Manganese deficiency causes many of the same symptoms as zinc and copper deficiencies.

Control: Apply a manure tea or liquid seaweed containing manganese.

Zinc is deficient when leaves yellow between veins and spots dot foliage.

  Control: Apply a manure tea or liquid seaweed.

35. Deformed fruit is normally caused when the pulp of the tomato grows faster than the skin. This is caused by drought conditions followed by adequate to excessive moisture.

Control/Prevention: Maintain a regular watering schedule to prevent drought.

36. Failure to set fruit is caused by disease, insect damage, day and night temperature fluctuation, lack of pollination due to wet weather or nutrient imbalances.

Control/Prevention: Remedy the specific cause. See related problems above.

The following pests and diseases might attack tomatoes.

37. Colorado potato beetle: page 120

38. European corn borer: page 71

39. Tomato fruitworm, also known as the corn earworm or bollworm: page 70

40. Cucumber mosaic: page 77

41. Damping-off or soil rot fungus: page 77

42. Root knot nematodes: page 122, number 14

43. Verticillium wilt: page 122

Turnip *(Brassica rapa,* Rapifera Group)

This is probably one of the most underrated vegetables in America. Many varieties mature sweet, flavorful roots quickly and are and resistant to diseases and pests. The trick to harvesting a good turnip is to grow it fast in cool weather. The sugars concentrate in the root during cool weather, making them much sweeter than when grown in hot weather.

Basic Facts

Germination time: 2-5 days
Germination temperature: Minimum: 40º (5º C), Optimum: 85º (29º C), Maximum: 105º (41º C).
Approximate seeds per ounce: 6,000-8,000
Yield per 10-foot row: 30-40 pounds
Life expectancy of stored seed: 4 years
Estimated time between sowing and first picking: 8 weeks
Intercrop: Dwarf nasturtiums and pansies.
Effort to cultivate: Easy
Seed saving: Must be isolated from rutabagas, rape, mustard, radishes and Chinese cabbage to prevent cross-pollination. Plant early in the spring to harvest seeds late in the summer.

Climate

Annual in all zones. Sweeter roots develop if raised in 60º (16º C) weather. Needs full sun but tolerates some shade in warm weather.
Prepare soil the previous fall or early spring adding a complete fertilizer. *Do not add nitrogen-rich compost and manure before planting or "hairy" roots will develop.*
Rake seed bed smooth, removing surface debris.

Planting

Do not plant turnips where other brassicas grew the previous two years. See "Crop Rotation" page 18.
Direct seed 1/2-inch deep. Sow early varieties from March-June. Sow fall crops in August-September. Broadcast seed or dig a shallow trench. Space seed on 3-inch centers in wide, raised beds and thin to 4-6 inches apart when 3-6 inches tall.
Water seeds and seedlings regularly until established. Mulch when seedlings are about 6 inches tall.
Cover seedlings with a floating row cover to keep flea beetles and cabbage root maggots out.

Crop Care

Weed seedlings by hand and hoe lightly if space allows. After they are 6-8 inches tall, apply mulch to check weed growth, cool soil and retain moisture. Add more mulch as necessary.
Fertilize the shallow root system with manure tea or fish emulsion every 2-4 weeks.
Watch for pests and treat problems promptly. Pack soil around base of plant if it is loosened by wind.

Harvesting

Harvest nutrient-packed leaves to eat in salads, or steam with greens.
Harvest fresh roots as soon as they are the size of a walnut. Roots get hot and fibrous if over mature.
Lift roots grown for storage with a fork by October, after they have matured fully, but before a hard freeze. Take care not to bruise roots. Cut off the tops, leaving an inch of stem.

In the Kitchen

Fresh: Greens (leaves) are sweet, tender, and packed with nutrition. Cook the same as greens. See "In the Kitchen," page 38. Steam sliced roots 8-12 minutes or boil 6-8 minutes - until tender. Peel tough skin on larger roots before slicing or dicing.
Storage: Store washed roots in a plastic bag in the refrigerator for up to two weeks.
Store turnips the same as carrots, page 58.
Freezing: Blanch (boil) greens and sliced turnips 2 1/2 minutes or steam 3 minutes, dry, bag, and freeze.

Varieties

GOLDEN BALL (60 days) has very sweet yellow flesh with fine grain. Plant for a fall or spring harvest of 4-inch roots. Available (Ni)

PESTO (30 days) is a small, fast growing flavorful white turnip that is very easy to grow. Available (Ni).

PURPLE-TOP WHITE GLOBE is a very popular variety that yields tasty purple roots above the soil and white roots below the soil line. (55 days) Available (Bu, Jo).

TOKYO CROSS (30 days) is probably the best roots available with a flat globe shape. The roots are smooth, sweet and tender; young tops make excellent greens. Available (Bu, Fa, Fi, Ju, St, Th)

Problems

Turnips are attacked by the same root maggot that assaults other brassicas. Grow turnips quickly so that they mature before the maggots flourish. Solutions to other problems can be found under "Brassica Problems" on page 53.

Xerox this page. Cut out addresses and tape to envelopes.

Abu - Abundant Life Seed Fdn.
P.O. Box 772
1029 Lawrence St.
Port Townsend, WA 98368
Tel. 1-206-385-5660

Au - Aubin Nurseries, Ltd.
Box 1089
Carman, Manitoba R0G 0J0
Tel. 1-204-745-6703

Bea - Bear Creek Nursery
P.O.B. 411, Bear Creek Rd.
Northport, WA 99157

Bec - Becker's Seed Potatoes
R.R. #1
Trout Creek, Ontario P0H 2L0
CANADA

Ber - Bergeson Nursery
Fertile, MN 56540
Tel. 1-218-945-6988

Bu - Burpee, W. Atlee & Co.
300 Park Ave.
Warminster, PA 18974
Tel. 1-215-674-4915

Cat - Carroll Gardens
P.O. Box 310
Westminster, MD 21157
Tel. 1-301-848-5422
Catalog $2.00

Ca - Catnip Acres Herb Farm
67 Christain St.
Oxford, CT 06483
Catalog $2.00

Cg - Cook's Garden
P.O. Box 535
Londonderry, Vt 05148
Tel. 1-802-824-3400

Co - Corn Hill Nursery Ltd.
R.R. 5, Petitcodiac
New Brunswick, E0A 2H0
CANADA
Tel. 1-506-756-3635

Cr - Cricket Hill Herb Farm Ltd.
Glen Street
Rowley, MA 01969
Tel. 1-617-948-2818

Da - Dabney Herbs
Box 22061
Louisville, KY 40222
Tel. 1-502-893-5198
Catalog $2.00

Fa - Farmer Seed & Nursery
818 NW 4th St.
Faribault, MN 55021
Tel. 1-507-334-1623

Fi - Field's, Henry, Seed & Nursery Co.
Shenandoah, IA 51602
Tel. 1-605-665-4491

Gc - Garden City Seeds
1324 Red Crow Road
Victor, MT 59875
Tel. 1-406-961-4837

Ge - George's Plant Farm
Rt. 1, Box 194
Martin, TN 38237

Good Seed Co.
Star Rouute Box 73A
Oroville (Chesaw), WA 98844

Ha - Harris Seeds
961 Lyell Ave.
Rochester, NY 14606
Tel. 1-716-458-2882

He - Heirloom Gardens
P.O. Box 138
Guerneville, CA 95446
Tel. 1-707-869-0967

Hi - High Altitude Gardens
P.O. Box 4238
Ketchum, ID 83340
Tel. 1-208-726-3221

Hu - Hudson, JL Seeds.
P.O. Box 1058
Redwood City, CA 94064
Catalog $1.00

Jo - Johnny's Selected Seeds
Foss Hill Road
Albion, ME 04910
Tel. 1-207-437-9294

Jung, J.W. Seed Co.
Randolph, WI 53957
Tel. 1-414-326-3121

Ke - Kelly Nurseries
P.O. Box 800
Dansville, NY 14437
Tel. 1-800-325-4180

Le - Ledden's Seeds
P.O. Box 7
Sewell, NJ 08080-0007
Tel. 1-609-468-1000

Ma - May, Earl, Seed & Nursery
Shenandoah, IA 51603
Tel. 1-800-831-4193

Mar - Margrave Plant Co.
Gleason, TN 38229

Mc - McKay Nursery Co.
Waterloo, WI 53594
Tel. 1-414-478-2121
Catalog $2.50

Me - Mellinger's Inc.
2310 W South Range Rd.
North Lima, OH 44452
Tel. 1-216-549-9661

Mi - Miller, J.E. Nurseries, Inc.
5060 West Lake Rd.
Canandaigua, NY 14424
Tel. 1-800-828-9630

Ni - Nichols Garden Nursery
1190 North Pacific Hwy.
Albany, OR 97321
Tel. 1-503-928-9280

Pa - Park, Geo. W., Seed Co., Inc.
Cokesbury Road
Greenwood, SC 29647
Tel. 1-803-223-7333

Pl - Plants of the Southwest
1812 Second St.
Santa Fe, NM 87501
Tel. 1-505-983-1548
Catalog $1.50

Ray - Rayner
P.O. Box 1617
Salisbury, MD 21802

Ric - Richters
Goodwood
Ontario, L0C 1A0
CANADA
Tel. 1-416-640-6677

Ri - Riverside Gardens
Rural Route 5
Saskatoon, Sask. S7K 3J8
CANADA
Tel. 1-306-374-0494

Ro - Ronnigers Seed Potatoes
Star Route
Moyie Springs, ID 83845
Catalog $1.00

Se - Seed Savers Exchange
Rural Route 3, Box 239
Decorah, IA 52101
Tel. 319-383-5990

Sha - Shady Acres Nursery
7777 Highway 212
Chaska, MN 55318
Tel. 1-612-466-3391
Catalog $1.00

She - Shepard's Garden Seeds
30 Irene Street
Torrington, CT 06790
Tel. 1-203-482-3638

So - Southern Exposure Seed Exchange
P. O. Box 158
North Garden, VA 22959
Catalog $3

St - Stokes Seeds, Inc.
Box 548
Buffalo, NY 14240
Tel. 1-416-688-4300

Sw - Swedberg Nurseries, Inc.
P.O. Box 418
Battle Lake, MN 56515
Tel. 1-218-864-5526

Th - Thompson & Morgan
P.O. Box 1308
Jackson, NJ 08527
Tel. 1-201-363-2225

Te - Territoral Seed Company
P.O. Box 157
Cottage Grove, OR 97424
Tel. 1-503-942-9547

Tg - Tomato Grower's Supply
P.O. Box 2237
Fort Myers, FL 33902
Tel. 1-813-768-1119

Allium family 85
Apple Cucumber 75
Armenian cucumber 73, 75
Artichoke 22
Arugula 41, 83
Asparagus 23-25
Asparagus bean 29
Aubergine 79-80

Batavian endive 83
Beans, 26
Bean, bush 26-28
Bean, fava 31, 33
Bean, pole 29-28
Bean, problems 33-36
Bean, runner 30-31
Bean, shelling 31-33
Beet, 37-39, problems 39-40
Beds, garden 8-10
Belgian endive 81, 83
Bok Choi 41, 46
Brassica family 41, problems 53-56
Broad fork 9
Broccoli 41-44, problems 53-56
Broccoli raab 44
Brussels sprouts 44-46, problems 53-56
Bunching onion 103-106

Cabbage 41, 46-50, problems 53-56
Cabbage, Chinese 46, 49-50
Calabrese broccoli 43
Cantaloupe 97-99, problems 99-100
Capsicum 113-115, problems 116
Carrot 57-59, problems 53-56
Cauliflower 41, 43, 50-52, problems 53-56
Cayenne pepper 115
Celeriac 62-64, problems 65
Celery 62-64, problems 65
Chard (Swiss) 126-128, problems 128-129
Chilli pepper 115
Compost 11-14
Corn, Sweet 66-69, problems 70-72
Cucubitaceae family 72
Cucumber 73-75, problems 75-78

Daikon radish 123-124
Dolomite lime 8
Double digging 9
Drip irrigation 20-21

Eggplant 79-80, problems 80-81
Egyptian onion 105

Endive 41, 81-84, problems 84
English runner bean 30-31
Escarole 41, 83

Fava bean 31, 33
Fertilizer 14-16, 17-18
Fingerling potatoes 119

Garden beds 8-10
Garlic 85-87, problems 106-107
Gherkin cucumber 74
Green sprouting broccoli 43
Green sprouting cauliflower 52

Indian corn 69
Irrigation 18-21

Kale 87-89, problems 53-56
Kidney bean 33
Kohlrabi 89-90, problems 53-56

Leaf, beet (Swiss chard) 126-128, problems 128-129
Leaky pipe 21
Leek 91-92
Lemon cucumber 75
Lettuce 93-95, problems 95-96
Lima bean 33
Lime 8

Maize 66
Melon 97-99, problems 100
Muskmelon 97-99, problems 99-100

New Zealand spinach 126-128
No-till gardening 9-11

Okra 101-102, problems 102
Onion 103-106, problems 106-107
Onion, bunching 103-106
Onion, Welch 106
Oyster plant 108-110

Parsnip 108-110, problems 53-56
Pea 110-112, problems 39-40
Pepper 113-115, problems 115-116
Pepper, cayenne 115
Pepper, chili 115
Pepper, sweet 115
Pickling onion 105
Popcorn 69
Potato 117-120, problems 120-122
Potato onion 105

Potato, sweet 119-120, problems 120-122
Pumpkin 130-131, problems 75-78
Purple sprouting broccoli 43
Purple sprouting cauliflower 52

Radicchio 81, 83
Radish 123-124, problems 53-56
Radish, Japanese 123-124
Raised beds 8-9
Rhubarb 125-126
Rocket 41, 83
Romanesco broccoli 44
Roquette 41, 83
Runner bean 30-31
Rutabaga 108-110, problems 53-56

Salad onion 103-106
Salsify 108-110, problems 60-62
Savoy cabbage 49
Scallion 103-106
Scarlet runner bean 30-31
Scorzonera 108-110
Seeds 4-5
Seed suppliers 143
Seedlings 5-6
Shallot 103-106
Sheet composting 11
Snap bean 26-28
Snow pea 112
Soil 6-8
Solanum family 78
Spinach 126-128, problems 128-129
Sprout, Brussels 44-46, problems 53-56
Squash 130-132, problems 75-78
String bean 26-28
Sugar pea 112
Swede 108-110
Sweet corn 66-69, problems 70-72
Sweet pepper 113-115
Sweet Potato 119-120, problems 120-122
Swiss chard 126-128, problems 128-129

Tomato 132-136, problems 136-141
Transplanting 4-6
Turnip 142

Watermelon 99
Watering 18-21
Welch onion 105-106